A History of Locomotive Kits Volume 1

Featuring:

K's, Nu-Cast, Wills and South Eastern Finecast

by Robert Forsythe

AMLOR PUBLISHING

BRITISH RAILWAY MODELLING
THE QUALITY MODEL RAILWAY MONTHLY

Published by AMLOR PUBLISHING and Warners Group Publications plc 1999.

Copyright Information:
Foreword copyright ©Tony Wright 1999
All other text copyright © AMLOR PUBLISHING 1999
Photographic copyright is attributed on a per photograph basis throughout the book.

Editor:
Dave Wheatstone.

Printing History:
December 1999 First Edition

A: AMLOR PUBLISHING,
        Box 9, 200 Fulham Road,
        Chelsea,
        London,
        SW10 9PN,
        United Kingdom.

W: www.amlor.co.uk
E: publisher@amlor.co.uk

A: Warners Group Publications plc,
        The Maltings,
        West Street,
        Bourne,
        Lincolnshire PE10 9PH,
        United Kingdom.

W: www.brmodelling.com
E: david.b@warners.co.uk

While every precaution has been taken in the preparation of this book, the publishers assume no responsibility for errors or omissions, or for damages resulting from the use of information contained herein.

A CIP catalogue record for this book is available from the British Library.

ISBN 0-9537720-0-4

Printed by Classic Printers, 3 Crowland Business Centre, Crease Drove, Crowland, Peterborough PE6 0BN.

(front cover) The front cover montage features models of the Stephen Poole originated Neilson 0-4-0ST (bottom right), a K's 14xx (bottom left), a South Eastern Finecast Hush-Hush (above) and a Nu-Cast V2 (top). Amongst box artwork and catalogues is the box for the Wills GER J69. This and the 14xx models are the twin start points to our story in 1957-59
Photo: Tony Wright

(rear cover, top) A montage of the K's Terrier as packaged over the decades from 1957. The prominent brass frames and flat packed wheels instantly date the skinpack kits to the mid-1970s and beyond. The two boxes represent practice towards the beginning (left) and end (right) of K's production. The instructions show the first Hanover Court K's address.
Photo: Tony Wright, courtesy Autocom Collection

(rear cover, middle) Wills SECR Wainwright H class
Photo: Tony Wright, courtesy South Eastern Finecast Collection

(rear cover, bottom) Wills GWR Saint in early BR finish
Photo: Tony Wright, courtesy Ted Kanas

Preface

In 1999, the British model railway hobby could claim to celebrate its centenary. A hundred years before, Bassett-Lowke had issued his first catalogue. Yet for a historically based hobby, interest in its own history has been rather muted. The largest of companies do have their histories recorded, such as Hornby and Trix, yet an account of vast swathes of the hobby has never been provided. A few years back I was directed into one such area. Ever since the 1950s, the hobby has been in large measure reliant on a veritable cottage industry of manufacturers producing kits. Sometimes this has literally been cottage based, whilst other concerns have worked in real factories and have stayed in business over many decades.

Kits, of course, did predate the 1950s but the advent of one kit in 1957 could be said to have changed the hobby. When K's released the GWR 14xx 0-4-2T model a milestone was reached. Use of centrifugal casting in whitemetal allowed considerable flexibility for reasonable cost. Along with other innovators such as Robert Wills, and in 1959 the revolutionary Kitmaster plastic kits, the model railway kit was enabled to have an everyday role in the hobby.

As part of our research, a spreadsheet charting the names of concerns that have offered for sale kits of British outline prototype locomotives had to be prepared. It opened one's eyes to discover some 375 separate names. If something was not done to record this output, an element of our hobby's activity would become unintelligible, the province only of those hanging onto curling magazines and catalogues, with models which often enough carry no details of their provenance.

The hobby, including a number of kit manufacturers and builders, has frequently been indebted to its patrons. Bassett-Lowke himself knew full well the importance of this. Fortunately my own research interests met a remarkable individual, who had himself realised the importance of the kitbuilt heritage and was already making vast strides in securing the models themselves. Over the last three years, we have collaborated in investigating in detail the output of 4mm scale locomotive kits from 20 of the leading names. The result covers only a fragment of the subject's full potential and that is without remembering that these companies often made wagons and coaches or worked in other scales. To the patron of this project and to my wife must go the thanks of one who knows that without both these individuals, there would be no book to read.

In choosing companies we have endeavoured to represent a cross-section of interests. Evidently, the classic names with roots back into the 1950s had to be present. Equally, the advent of commercially effective photo-etching techniques in the 1970s had a vast impact in this field.

Companies with far more recent origins justified consideration.

The first volume covers six of the key names including the two material whitemetal influences from the 1950s. Fortunately, Stephen Knight's history of the plastic-based Kitmaster already exists and that enabled the focus to be on K's and Wills. A fascinating family history of takeovers is present in the hobby as in all walks of life. K's and Wills lead naturally into Nu-Cast and South Eastern Finecast respectively. Nu-Cast incorporated the Cotswold and Stephen Poole and R&J Models ranges. Volume One naturally created itself with four chapters covering six of the twenty key names.

In succeeding volumes - with material presently researched for 15 of these 20 - you can anticipate reading about (in alphabetical but not publication order):

ABS and its constituents, Alan Gibson, Craftsman, Crownline, DJH, Falcon Brass, GEM, Jamieson, Jidenco, Millholme, MTK, Premier Kits, Pro-scale and Q Kits. Their choice enables some further concerns to be incorporated so brands like Model Loco and Maygib will also be covered.

Aware of the value of patronage creates an appropriate point at which to recognise the wider range of thanks that needs to be made. Many of the manufacturers have been extraordinarily helpful. Individuals who need to be particularly associated with their chapters are thanked at the end of each chapter. Certain other individuals have proved a great support in the broader execution of the project. Alan Cliff, Nick Gillman, Fleetwood Shawe, and Tony Wright have either in person or at the end of phone line or computer terminal become greatly valued. In addition, members of the forum Brit_Rail-L on the Internet have contributed to solving obscure prototypical problems.

Mention of Tony Wright allows another point to be made. This is not a kitbuilder's book. If you want to build kits, there are many books available (in stark contrast to the history of the models). These include Tony's own *Building 4mm Loco Kits*. Our volume tries to tell you something of the story behind the creation of these kits and to provide enough information about the prototype and about changes made to a model that the reader might be able to identify a model on a layout.

Catalogue and advert reproductions appear with thanks to:
Autocom Ltd for K's, Cotswold and Nu-Cast;
Robert Wills for Wills;
Rob Hamp for R&J Models.

As ever, an author knows that despite his best

endeavours, errors will creep in. This exercise in model railway history remains a live research subject. If readers feel that they can point out corrections or amplify the story, they are invited to make contact. You may either write to me care of the publisher, enclosing an SAE to enable a reply, or use this E-mail address:- robert@forsythe.demon.co.uk.

In addition, contributions in the form of anecdotal evidence, letters, photographs, catalogues or any other medium will be welcomed for forthcoming volumes. Also, if you have such information which you feel would have benefited this volume, please be in touch - it could be included in a subsequent "round-up" volume or second edition. Again, in all instances, either write to the publishers or E-mail the author.

Magazine terminology justifies some comment. Neither your author nor the hobby itself are perfect examples of consistency. To help clarify things, the following terms in the book are synonymous:

Railway Modeller or the Modeller or RM;
Model Railway Constructor or the Constructor or MRC;
Model Railway News or the MRN (this also covers *Model Railways* and *Your Model Railways* - they are all the same magazine);
Model Railway Journal or MRJ;
British Railway Modelling or BRM.

Robert Forsythe

(below) K's Ivatt 2-6-2T seen on the LNER layout "Fordley Park" built by Wolverhampton MRC.
Photo: Brian Monaghan, courtesy John Parker

Foreword

I'm delighted to have been invited to write this brief foreword to Robert's book. For too long the history of the model railway hobby itself has been overlooked, and, with the passing of many of the pioneers and developers, there is a chance that much factual information will be distorted or lost altogether. It is therefore not before time that volumes such as this are being published.

The fact that this book concentrates on the history of locomotive kits fascinates me greatly. Without doubt, the locomotive is by far the most popular aspect of railway enthusiasm, be it prototype or model. For every book written in general on railways, there are dozens which concentrate solely on the motive power. For every model of a coach, wagon, signalbox, station, tunnel mouth, lineside feature, signal, road vehicle, etc. built, there are often many more just of engines. In fact, some model collections consist of nothing more than railway locomotives. As a correct model representation of true life railway transport, this imbalance is wholly wrong. However, as enthusiasts, we have the freedom to model or collect that which interests us the most.

My own involvement in the hobby, particularly that of building locomotive kits, runs parallel and contemporaneously with the loco kits' development themselves. Though I admit to being only eleven when the first K's kit had appeared, it wasn't long after I'd built all the plastic Kitmaster range. Then I rapidly progressed into the bodging of "margarine" metal locos, hopelessly wrestling with the inadequacies of the product, the constraints of original Araldite, the dire pitfalls involved in getting the chassis to run properly, the parental scolding as more and more mess resulted from the wielding of the gas stove-powered heavy soldering iron, the problems of schoolboy poverty and the ignorance of teenage years. This was tempered only by juvenile belligerence and a desire to actually make the things myself - the real locos I saw on a daily basis. Fortunately (as far as I know), none of those hideous "learning curve" examples now survive, for I would hate them to appear as evidence of my general level of incompetence, though, at the time I was proud of some of them.

Before I finally learnt how to make a proper chassis - and, as intimated, that provided in many early kits was anything but, I exploited the recommended RTR Tri-ang or Hornby Dublo ones, caring little if the wheelbase was correct, the wheel diameters were correct or that the valve gear was correct. Underneath the Araldited whitemetal body, at least the things worked, pulled a train, didn't fall off the track and enabled the railway modellers of the day to expand their loco stud to an extent way beyond that which was available ready-to-run. Though even my uneducated eye could tell that my cre-

ations only had a passing resemblance to the real things, they did capture a bit of the wonderful visual variety on offer in those halcyon days.

Along with the products' improvements and developments, my own abilities also appeared to evolve into something more (I hope) substantial. As a more discerning attitude developed, so did the expectations of the customer and with it, what was on offer. Some were obvious dead ends - cast metal lumps or solid brass slugs for chassis for instance. Other aspects showing me a much desired development included concentric wheels (especially those which didn't disintegrate when being adjusted), better motors, more efficient gearboxes and the use of accurate etchings for chassis and valve gear.

Many kits though, still remained (and remain?) very difficult to build as designed, particularly if using only those parts supplied. For every one completed, running and doing its model equivalent of the prototype, nine remain, either unfinished or undisturbed in their dusty boxes, way beyond the capabilities of their optimistic owners. I categorise loco kits into four main sections, listed in order of merit:-

1. Kit is accurate to prototype and the fit of parts is excellent;

2. Kit is inaccurate to prototype but the fit of parts is excellent;

3. Kit is accurate to prototype but because of vagaries in the production processes, mistakes in the masters and/or the incompatibilities of using mixed media, the fit of parts is poor;

4. Kit isn't right in fidelity to prototype and the bits don't fit.

Fortunately, most of today's kits fit into 1 and the makers of 4 have either gone bust or done better. Category 2 is less likely to be found today (it's the one which includes body kits for fixing on, occasionally unsuitable, RTR chassis). There are still too many fitting into section 3 though.

Today, my involvement in the hobby is on a more professional level. I kit-build locos on commission, build loco kits for magazine reviews and it's been my privilege to photograph examples built from kits by others. At the top end - the Finney/Mitchell spectrum, the results are quite stupendous, though I've never personally tackled such stratospheric products. I dabble more in mainstream OO, exploiting the best of the composite loco kits where etched brass, etched nickel silver, lost wax cast brass and cast whitemetal have all been used, utilising each material's best qualities for suitability of purpose.

In short, we've never had it so good and such is the range and quality of today's loco kits that just about every interest is catered for, no matter how esoteric. How we've arrived at that happy state of affairs is told, in part, in the following pages. For those, like me, who actually make and have made them and are fascinated by the development of the loco kit and its history, this volume will provide endless pleasure. For those who don't build, but acquire models, either through commission or purchase, it should prove equally fascinating, particularly as they come to realise how much of others' blood sweat and tears were used in producing their prized possessions.

For the diligence, painstaking research, detective work and scholarly achievement evident in this volume, I commend it wholly to all who are reading beyond this.

Tony Wright, July 1999

(below) K's ROD 2-8-0 shown on the Wolverhampton MRC's "Stoke Summit" layout
Photo: Tony Wright, courtesy Rob Kinsey

K's

Through a heyday that lasted over 30 years, the simple acronym K's was an indispensable part of the railway modeller's vocabulary. By the one technique of pioneering the centrifugally cast whitemetal locomotive kit, and thence maintaining a leading role in that market with some 100 locomotives modelled, along with many other associated products, the well-run model shop of the 1960s and 1970s simply had to be a K's stockist.

The 1980s witnessed K's decline and eventually the sale of the railway kits by the family. Nonetheless the core series of British loco kits has not been lost. Today the vast majority is still available under the Nu-Cast label, albeit much updated in specification and with absolutely no involvement from the family who originally created the models.

Company History

That family unlocks the K's acronym. The full commercial name of the company was N. & K. C. Keyser Ltd. The "N" was father or "Pop" Keyser, as he was usually known. Of German extraction, he opened a tobacconists which became a model shop in the 1940s at Hanover Court in London's Uxbridge Road. The modelling element seems to date from 1942. The family was totally involved, including Mrs Keyser and their son Ken Keyser. It was Ken's model-making ability and his railway enthusiasm which became the critical ingredient. Ken was making scratchbuilt locos from 1946. When displayed in the shop they sold and the whole enterprise mushroomed. Those scratchbuilt locos that I know of include a Terrier, a GWR County 4-6-0, a Peppercorn Pacific, a rebuilt Scot and an Emett loco. These products deserve far greater appreciation and a full list of K's handbuilt locos would be a great asset. Another group forms the O-gauge stock of the Derby Museum model railway.

Despite the material shortages of the period, business flourished. Fifteen of the contemporary big names like Exley, Leeds and the then infant Peco were stocked in 1949. The scratchbuilding which was mainly Ken's province suggested the manufacture of relevant components, and from late 1952, K's were able to sell their own motor. This had a five-pole armature whose shaft extended from each end, all with the very small dimension of 3/8" width. Here was a very flexible unit for OO modelling; it became the Mark I and by 1954 had been joined by the Mark II.

This point saw rapid movement into manufacturer status. Ken saw a jeweller's centrifugal casting machine and became aware of the possibilities this would create in allowing small-scale production of components in whitemetal. The firm of R. M. Evans who had previously produced some loco kits in 4mm was purchased, although none of these kits ever reappeared in the K's line-up. A range of components including wheels and axleguards followed, and then in 1956 the Easter Model Railway Club Show unveiled complete wagon kits in whitemetal. Robert Wills had however reached this point himself a few months before. K's clearly envisaged big things, there was to be "at least a new kit every month" from that May. Those first two kits were the Coral A and the 20-ton steel sided mineral, both GWR prototypes.

The first locomotive kit

Everything was now in place to move to a locomotive and this was the excitement of the Show a year later. This time K's had beaten Wills and had the honour of releasing the first centrifugally cast complete 4mm UK locomotive kit. These are important definitions, other forms of cast metal kit like Reidpath's diecast offerings had existed earlier. Some may be unaware of the actual process involved - the model has to be designed in drawing form, a modelmaker then produces the patterns or masters, i.e. a set of components in brass. These masters are then placed in the raw rubber mould to form the shape of each component. The mould is vulcanised (heated under pressure) which sets it. The masters are then removed and the final stage is the casting of the components in the mould.

The key point is that K's approach enabled a far greater variety to be achieved far more cheaply than other contemporary methods. The result was a demand that fuelled success and growth for many years. The distinctive point of a K's kit was that it came complete. Wheels, motor and gears so often left to the builder's choice were part of the package. K's kits were therefore a favourite choice for the newcomer to kit building, although in later years this may have become a drawback in marketing to a more sophisticated clientele.

The chosen first prototype was bound to be a sure-fire success in the popular GWR Collett 0-4-2T - that loco will be detailed later in this chapter under its own entry. We now concentrate on outlining the overall development of the OO kit range until its final sale. Amongst K's other products, the OO loco range steadily grew, four in the first year, 15 by the end of 1961. In that year, what had been something of a backroom operation, was moved to a proper factory. 101 Tubbs Road next to Willesden Junction Station became the home of K's for the next 12 years.

When another move was made, the family composition had moved on a generation and the seed that would lead to the end of the locomotive kits had been sowed, even if its germina-

(above) An advert taken from the pages of MRC December 1949 shows the emphasis on service from an era of old fashioned manners!

(right) One of the first adverts, taken from MRC March 1949, shows the handbuilt locos range with an illustration of a GWR County 4-6-0

(below) The K's motor range (MRN October 1954) drawn to actual size in the original advert

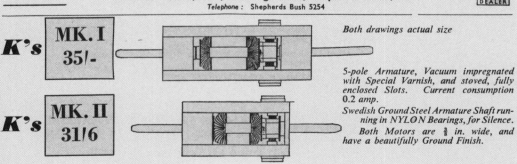

tion was far from apparent. In 1973 the company relocated to a purpose-built factory on the Grimsbury South Industrial Estate at Banbury. Management by then was in the hands of Ken and his own sons Melvyn and Graham. "Pop" Keyser had died in July 1966, greatly mourned throughout the hobby.

Plastic

Both of Ken's sons had taken college qualifications and Graham had a particular interest in plastic injection moulding. The result from 1967 was the appearance of plastic rolling stock kits, and from 1970 as part of the 70 Series revamp of the loco kits, K's own design of phenolic resin centred wheels which replaced the hitherto cast centres. Although the plastic content of K's railway products grew slightly beyond this, it did lead to substantial contracts in other fields during the Banbury era.

By the time of the move to Banbury, the OO loco range numbered thirty-one. Through the mid-1970s, and despite the trying economic times which did lead to some delays, a full house of new models came from Banbury. September 1978 saw the first three in a new Milestones series of historic prototypes, and the range now numbered fifty-four. Only a couple of months later and a sale of K's TT products to ABS may have seemed untoward, but a growing interest in Continental Models that took K's to the Nuremberg Toy Fair in the early 1980s must have seemed promising. The year 1980 itself saw five new U.K. locos produced. This apparently auspicious start to the new decade was not maintained. One published explanation of the decision to sell the loco kits states that the plastic moulding equipment created problems in conjunction with the casting machines. The present commentator wonders to what extent the Continental excursion proved a significant dead-end?

Initially the European move must have appeared successful. In 1980 three Continental releases were announced. By 1982 there were twenty and ultimately the highest continental reference is CL33. Incidentally, although these Continental locos appear as the final phase of K's expansion, the very first, as the Prussian P6 2-6-0 was announced in 1967 (the 1980s' manifestation was virtually a new kit). It was followed around November 1971 by another Mogul, this time the American Green Bay and Western Railroad type. Both were in the 1972 catalogue.

Yet K's were certainly unable to replicate the parallel experience of DJH who have remained a long-term player in this field. Instead, the release of new U.K. outline locos dried up in 1982. The rebuilt Merchant Navy was the one release of 1983 and apparently appeared with very little fanfare. Something was now "up" at K's, but in the not untypical manner of the hobby, factual reports of difficult news are sketchy. K's own adverts in the hobby press disappeared. M&R (a leading dealer) became wholesaler for the range and in 1984 one further new British loco was announced. This was the *Lord Nelson* and despite the lack of K's own adverts, stockists'

adverts indicate that the range was widely available in 1984. The *Lord Nelson* did appear in mid-year. However, the arrangement with M&R was not long lived.

Instead, in June and July of 1985 a new name in the guise of Teign Models Ltd from Teignmouth was placing full-page adverts with the slogan "K's Kits are Back". One new introduction was part of the relaunch, with the GWR *Armstrong* 4-4-0 in the Milestones series. At the same time, much was made of the concept of Body Only options to the range. The whole core range then available was offered as an option for the loco body and, if appropriate, tender and valvegear. These kits were referenced CBLx. 1985 was not the first time Body Only options were promoted; back in January 1966 K's had advertised such an option for all the conventional steam engine kits, and they had been mentioned in the years immediately preceding 1985.

The demise

What is not totally clear is what role the Banbury factory and the Keyser family were now playing; they made the models but had seemingly handed over their marketing. The adverts from Teignmouth continued, and in October 1985 these featured what became the last new British loco under the K's label. This was L51 *Earl Marischal*, the as-built LNER P2. Adverts continued into 1986 from Teign giving the range an exposure it had not had for some time. A year after Teign's involvement commenced, the run of Teign adverts ceased. An advert placed in the October 1987 Modeller from W&H claimed that they had cleared stocks from the distributor and that manufacture by K's had ceased.

In getting the range to its present home, the name Chris Crawley now appears - he was also advertising in 1986. Operating from Goxhill on Humberside, he sold many kit ranges but not K's at this point. In June/July 1987 Chris Crawley Models was absorbed into Brian Emberton's HMC Group and moved to Firsby in Lincolnshire. Around March 1989, K's kits now appeared in Chris Crawley's adverts. The Body Only kits were being cleared from the factory unboxed. Another key step was advertised in January 1990 - by that time HMC had bought a number of model kit ranges including Nu-Cast and K's. The K's railway range was moved lock, stock and barrel to Lincolnshire with the intention that production would restart. Adverts were placed for body products as Nu-Kays, and chassis and valvegear assemblies were available to complete the models (motors were not included, nor generally speaking were wheels). There is a possibility yet to be confirmed that the route actually involved a purchase by Nu-Cast whilst still in Durham. At least one informant states that they saw the K's tooling in the Nu-Cast factory at Blackhall, and that shortly after this the purchase by the HMC Group occurred. We are adamant that if this is so, no production of K's in County Durham took place.

A sad parallel event had been the sudden death of Ken Keyser late in 1989; with that, the heart of the model railway interest at Keyser's had

The Winner of the K's Award

at this year's

Model Railway Hobby Show

Mr. J. Allan,
113, Finney Lane,
Heald Green,
Cheadle, Cheshire

A beautifully assembled kit to which had been added many extra details. The model was nicely painted and lined.
Mr. Allan informs us that the model is a particularly fine performer.

GWR 0-4-2 TANK

The Winner chose as part of his prize another Winner

The K's DEAN GOODS KIT

(above) A fine tradition, shown in MRN November 1958, and one wonders why kit manufacturers don't do this today - build a kit and win another one from the range. Also note the early appearance of the TT-3 range

been extinguished. Meantime some Nu-Cast production was getting under way in Lincolnshire (so advertised in October 1990), including K's material. The quality and quantity of this was so erratic that it has not proved possible to thoroughly detail what was or what was not actually made. An example of what was on offer, and is stated to be new production, is furnished by the "Chris Crawley Models" Modeller advert of March 1991. What detail can be sourced will be narrated in the Nu-Cast chapter. Instead, the next key date is the advert placed in October 1991's *Railway Modeller* classified column. This discrete notice of sale for a "well established whitemetal locomotive kit business" initiated the intervention by Autocom (UK) Ltd of Andover. In April 1993 they announced the purchase of Nu-Cast and K's, their intended amalgamation and upgrading, and their marketing under the Nu-Cast brand. All the K's branding, tooling and stock was purchased by Autocom from the HMC Group.

As the last few years have shown, Autocom has delivered its promises. However, the integrated range is not part of this account. The models now sold are in many respects different from a K's kit. That, plus the Nu-Cast branding, will mean that further consideration of the models will be provided in the Nu-Cast chapter. Meanwhile, some of this company detail, addresses and the like may assist the collector in dating any models or packaging possessed.

Dating models

Another aid to dating is a general appreciation of the major changes in specification that K's implemented across the range. These changes are listed in the following paragraphs.

At an early stage, from April 1959, brass plating of those castings intended to actually represent brass was undertaken.

Another key dating element should be the motor employed. The basic Mark I and Mark II motors were long lived and featured in the K's 70 Series catalogues. They had though undergone their own development. During 1957-8 a Mark III option was also quoted; this does not appear to be long lasting. In the "grey" catalogue c.1962 (see the end of the chapter for a complete catalogue list) only a redesigned Mark I and II were quoted. Dimensions of the motors as quoted in October 1954 have been pictorially reproduced earlier. The redesign appears to date from 1960 and incorporated magnets at both ends of a five-pole unit.

Two major developments followed each other in succession in the late 1970s. From 1977 the new HP2M motor was employed (sometimes confusingly called a Mark III). This looks quite different to any Mark I or II. No conventional magnet was present - metal impregnated nylon performed that function. It was tri-polar and said to be particularly powerful - HP officially standing for Hi-Power. Two years later and this technology was allied to an integral gearbox, the HP2MG. Towards the tail end of production these motors were replaced by a new five-pole and gearbox

version of the HP2M. Lists from 1982 all referred to the previous motor, inferring that the five-pole was introduced during 1983. This motor was offered separately variously as the RM1 or KM1 (see W&H's 1983 catalogue). By the 1985 Teign Models adverts, it was the RN5/14 with a 14mm gearwheel or RM5/7.5 with 7.5mm gearwheel. These are all versions of the same intrinsic design.

Ken Keyser was particularly dedicated to providing an in-house motor as part of the complete package, but there are modellers whose opinion of K's motors is not as high as that of the company's own assessment. The magnet blocks of the classic Mark I-III series were glued into position between two pole pieces. If the motor overheated, the glue could fail and the motor disintegrate.

The final motor is also poorly regarded; it may have been five-pole but it was very small and reportedly prone to burning out. Was it not ambitious to expect that Garratts and P2's would be driven by it? This overall school of thought suggests that K's could have done better through much of their life by using other commercially available motors.

Away from the motor and the major scene change was the 70 Series. These kits were distinctively vacuum packed and included the plastic centred wheels already mentioned, and which initially came assembled. In November 1973 following the move to Banbury, K's advertised that from the 1st October 1973 new "D" wheels were standard in the loco range, and thereupon the wheels ceased to be supplied ready assembled. The wheels were packed flat and sealed, axles likewise. Modellers have told me that the challenge in having to assemble one's own wheels won K's few friends and that the all-metal assembled wheels used in the earlier models were superior. Self-assembly wheels were initially screwed onto axles (so described in the 1978 catalogue), and later they were plug fits onto axles. That change may have coincided with an investment made in all the driving wheels around 1981 (and summarised by Iain Rice in *Model Railways News* March 1982). At that point the entire axle changed to a "D" profile, both BRMSB and ultra-fine flange profiles were provided, and the product was designed to be self-quartering.

From 1972, chemically etched nickel silver valvegear / coupling rod sets had become an added feature. The introduction of nickel silver was also applied to the tyres of the driving wheels, replacing the brass used on earlier 70 Series wheels. Wheel production later utilised plated steel or aluminium. The Garratt of 1976 was reviewed with "wheels....to the latest K's design with turned steel rims on a plastic centre". Other features of the 70 Series were chemically blackened brass frames (up to the mid-1970s) and an injection moulded loco pick up kit. This developed around 1977 into a plastic chassis tender pickup unit which was not highly regarded. Despite this, it was retrospectively fitted across the tender locos.

A resumé of the chassis employed helps date

(above) K's L9 GWR/BR 14xx body on a Nu-Cast
etched chassis. This is the proving model used by Nu-
Cast whilst developing their new etched chassis.

Photo: Tony Wright, courtesy Autocom Collection

(below) K's single deck tram Class E as advertised in
the trade press at the time of the launch

Model Railway News June 1961

models; some could have enjoyed four distinct designs. All initial releases had a totally whitemetal chassis. With the introduction of the Dean Goods, the standard format became side frames in brass sandwiching a cast chassis block for weight (that for the J72 has been seen as a two-piece assembly), which was channelled to fit the frames, all secured by two brass bolts. By March 1959 this chassis was universal.

The next chassis development was the introduction of the brass keyhole chassis detailed for K20 in 1964. This was followed on K26/27 by a split axle chassis which was both unsuccessful and short-lived. The keyhole chassis then reigned until at some point between 1972 and 1978, when it was abandoned and straightforward pressed brass frames were instituted. These two styles are clearly shown in the catalogues for each of those years. The most likely actual date range is around 1976-78 (see Aberdare entry).

A note about packaging may help. Broadly speaking there are three generations. Prior to the 70 Series, orange "coffin" style boxes were used. The 70 Series eventually saw the products mounted on a series of sealed skinpack cards placed in an orange rectangular box. The skinpacks were noted as new at the 1976 Toyfair. During the 1980s the box covers changed to a silver colour and became multi-lingual, reflecting the Continental move. Packaging from Nu-Kays in Lincolnshire was extremely basic: clear unlabelled plastic bags being reported.

Some more references to specification changes applicable to the range will appear in individual loco notes.

Just why did K's fail?

Many different answers are possible. What is indisputable is that from being market leaders through the 1960s, twenty years later and despite a series of innovations, the product was struggling. The massive structural move in the hobby to either etched metal or combined cast and etched kits was not adopted. K's could etch but restricted their use of this technique. The result was that accuracy was not always spot on, and the final K's chassis were very crude affairs compared to their competition. There was no compensation and in the main not much resemblance to the prototypical underframe structure either.

Modellers themselves were different in the 1980s from the 1950s. In the 1950s there was not the choice or the money. You bought a K's kit, you made it work despite any shortcomings, and you were proud of your achievement. Thirty years later the market had more money and more choice. In short it was more sophisticated. Despite changes, a K's kit was not in that bracket.

The new material K's had endorsed was plastic. and for many modellers this did not overcome its cheap and nasty image. This was not helped by the way in which from the mid-1970s kits came with unassembled wheels. Those finely cast and ready assembled wheels of the early K's kits

were actually of better quality. Add to this what in many modellers eyes was actually the inflexibilty of the "complete kit" approach, then add the tough economic climate of the 1980s, the attempts to work abroard and the apparent lack of marketing during the 1980s and some sense of why the sale appeared preferable to continuing may be gleaned.

Below is a per-locomotive account of the range; despite K's own referencing system which appeared in catalogues and on packaging from the advent of the 70 Series, it is necessary to supplement this with our own Kx series. The K's Lx series did not exactly replicate the kits' issue order, nor did it actually cover every release. Prototype information will be severely limited to effect some control on length. Many of K's choices were very well known and only in the case of the more obscure offerings will it be felt necessary to expand on the prototype.

The Range of UK Loco Kits

K01/L9 GWR/BR 14xx 0-4-2T

The trendsetting first model received an extensive welcome in the trade press. Typical was the two-page review in the June 1957 MRN. The kit's comprehensiveness seemed almost shocking; having the motor was one thing, but all that rivet detail and wheels with ready fitted crankpins, it was wonderment! It is interesting that for a first model the relatively challenging 0-4-2T arrangement was taken. The buffers were even sprung. Coupling rods were pressed in nickel silver, nickled turned brass wheels were the standard from the start and through the 1960s, and very fine they were too, being a great plus point of a K's kit prior to 1970. Great Western transfers and cast plates for 1436 were included.

The earliest 14xx models have no handrails, an element which K's generally modelled thoroughly. These finally appear in the "brown" catalogue dated to c.1965. It is likely however that the kit had been amended in the late 1950s. During 1959 its essential partner in the shape of the whitemetal kit for a GWR Autocoach was released - a heavy beast!

K02/ML8 LT E class Electric Tram

Going on the adverts it would appear that an electric tram model was a parallel introduction to the 14xx. The prototype was a four-wheeled single deck vehicle built for the Metropolitan Electric Tramways in 1905 as a class of 60. Apparently offbeat, the London firm perhaps felt that a demand could be stoked up; BEC succeeded in this only a few years later. At K's the model remained unique.

The initial adverts refer to (rubber?) drive bands which may have proved an unsatisfactory form of drive. Through 1958-59, there were a series of adverts from K's listing the entire range and the tram does not feature. Then in June 1961 an illustrated advert for the tram was placed in *Model Railway News*. Its rejuvenation used a

**(above) K's L2 LNWR/LMS/BR Coal tank with matching K's
LNWR coaches, all finished in smart LNWR livery**

Photo: Tony Wright, courtesy Nick Gillman

**(below) K's BL3 97xx bodyline kit on a Dublo R1 chassis with
Romford wheels**

Photo: Tony Wright, courtesy Autocom Collection

simple whitemetal chassis with geared two-wheel drive and a Mark II motor that those other oddities, the Ro-Railbus and J70, utilised. It was still to be seen in the 70 Series catalogues, but without an L series reference. K's advertised a revival for the model in August 1974, but despite this, it had gone by the 1978 K's edition, having been in the W&H 1977 edition. Very late in the day at Banbury a re-release was made in the Milestone series under the ML8 reference. This was without the motor, but intended to use the Milestones separate motorisation package. They were being so advertised by Chris Crawley at Spilsby in November 1988.

K03/L20 LBSCR/SR/BR Terrier 0-6-0T

The second steam engine was bound to be a popular choice, and the diminutive dimensions of the LBSCR Terrier were ideal for the motors K's had available. At present, a degree of supposition is being employed to suggest it was unveiled at the 1957 Model Railway Hobby Show in Central Hall that September; it was certainly available sometime that Autumn. By December, K's adverts were featuring the loco along with newly released four wheeled panelled LBSCR coaches. The loco was released with the Mark III motor.

The Terrier came initially with transfers for lining and LBSCR paint, which remained the standard package through the 1960s. Certainly from the 70 Series the format for the range was no paint and variable practice with transfers. A typical 1960s catalogue states "many of the kits include turned brass handrails knobs, paint and transfers". As the years passed these early releases did date, however major rejuvenation (such as providing essentially more accurate chassis) had to await Autocom. The LBSCR paint might suggest that the model was the unrebuilt A1 and not the later A1X. This is confirmed with features such as the provision of smokebox wing plates and the unextended smokebox of the A1. MRC for April/May 1986 carried a two-part profile of a late production model from Banbury.

K04/L2 LNWR/LMS/BR Coal Tank 0-6-2T

An LNWR Coal Tank arrived for the 1958 Easter MRC Show. The prototype's distinctive H section wheel spokes were reproduced with a special brass turning, and so equally were the sprung LNWR buffers. In later years special 70 Series plastic wheels were moulded, but no amount of chassis upgrading by K's ever overcame the very obvious baldness below the running plate, and the lack of guard irons strike one as a very blatant omission. K's provided cast plates for L&NWR 2357 which was shown in very fine letters, and handrail detailing was provided soon after introduction. Just as the previous release had a matching rake of coaches, so the Coal Tank was to gain a range of three LNWR six-wheeled coaches from K's.

A network of notables from the hobby assisted the Keysers in establishing the range. Well known LNWR scholar Jack Nelson made his mark on the Coal Tank with contributions that included originating the isometric instruction drawings.

K05/L14 GWR/BR Dean Goods i/f 0-6-0

Compared with the first loco which was positively modern in 1957, there had now been three from the Victorian heyday which were still fresh in the minds of the 1950s enthusiast. The reception for the inside framed Dean Goods as the first tender engine was enthusiastic at its launch at the Autumn 1958 Model Railway Hobby Show. It was reviewed in the October 1958 MRN. Unlike the previous offerings, the boiler was split in the vertical and not the horizontal plane. A GWR 3,000 gallon tender was modelled. This was also available separately as a key item to GWR modellers and would be deployed in subsequent GWR K's kits.

A brass chassis was used from the outset and this was implemented across the range in the coming months. Cast numberplates were supplied for 2573. At the outset, paint and Great Western transfers were supplied (through to the advent of the 70 Series). Handrail wire and knobs, lamps, plus a detailed boiler backhead helped add to a high specification for the period.

An insight into how much could change was afforded by the review *Railway Modeller* gave the model in September 1977. This was for a 70 Series kit so some etched components such as rods were fitted. In addition, the boiler by then was a one-piece casting, and the splashers were cast with the running plate. The cast numberplates had survived however.

K06/L6 NER/LNER/BR J72 0-6-0T

The advent in February 1959 of a kit for the simple but classic outlines of the J72 tank had now become almost routine. This loco which remained one of only two pure North Eastern Railway prototypes at K's largely came into being by the efforts of Fleetwood Shawe, a well known modeller and friend of Ken's. Fleetwood, who was very familiar with NER territory, wanted the model and supplied the drawings.

K07/L4 GWR/BR 44xx 2-6-2T

The Autumn 1959 introduction was the first of what became two versions of GWR Small Prairie tanks. This kit was for the ten members built by Churchward and largely associated with West Country branches. The prototypes had 4'1½" driving wheels - smaller than the subsequent build which is covered by kit K31 4575/55xx. K's reproduced these wheels and 1,524 rivets! Prominently advertised in the October and November MRN's, cast numberplates for 4407 were provided. Bear in mind that the model with its extended bunker and smokebox is emphatically a 44xx, not therefore a model of the engine as originally built. A detailed article about the 1980s kit and the prototype by Geoff Gray was published in June 1990's Modeller.

(above) K's L8 LMS Karrier Ro-Rail bus - a rare and forgotten prototype until the K's kit came along
Photo: Tony Wright, courtesy Autocom Collection

(right) Despite actually only possessing four wheels, the enduring K's L7 GER/LNER/BR J70 0-6-0 tram has always been a favourite, doubtless helped by the *Thomas the Tank Engine* phenomenon
Photo: Tony Wright, courtesy Autocom Collection

(below) K's L12 MR/LMS/BR Kirtley o/f 0-6-0 shown in a picturesque setting
Photo: Tony Wright, courtesy Tony Wright

K08/BL2 GNR/LNER/BR J50 0-6-0T

Two years into loco kit manufacture and K's were well established. The field was not entirely theirs; Robert Wills' own range was beginning to develop. His route tended to provide bodies suitable for fitting to proprietary chassis, making the model even simpler for the novice. K's then decided to provide this facility too; in the event no more than three in this Bodyline series materialised. Each appears to have required some dimensional compromises.

The first arrived late in 1959 and provided the GNR J50 Ardsley tank, being reviewed in the January 1960 Constructor. The chassis which the series fitted was the Hornby Dublo, later Wrenn, R1 0-6-0T. That chassis regrettably made a mockery of the J50's wheelbase. In keeping with the idea that this was a beginners kit, components were reduced to a minimum so there was no separate running plate, and K's claimed the kit could be built in 8½ minutes! A driver and fireman were included by way of detail - these appeared in each Bodyline kit and were cast into the cab sides.

The three models in the Bodyline series were available through the 1960s. Shown in the 70 Series catalogues, K's themselves advertised the three as revived in August 1974 (after the Banbury move) but they ceased to feature in K's material from the late 1970s. Kittle Hobby advertised the J50 and the MR tank in K's clearance sales during May 1982. However, the January 1983 Modeller W&H advert listed all three as newly "available again", despite which, further traces in K's official listings have not been noted.

K09/BL1 MR/LMS 3F 0-6-0T

The next seven introductions cover the 1960-61 period. At present, providing precise introduction dates has proved elusive, and our order may be questioned. Despite K's themselves later calling this model BL1, the reviews and adverts would imply that it was the second bodyline kit to appear. Listed in January 1960's Modeller, this was described in 70 Series catalogues as Johnson's 1878 design built for the Midland and the S&DJR systems. This was not the LMS Jinty immortalised by Tri-ang, but the MR class S or U. These were not built in 1878 but were an enlarged version of the older design which were actually made by Vulcan Foundry at the turn of the century. K's 1960s catalogues illustrating the model numbered 1940 form the basis of this identification.

The loco was modelled in an as-built condition with low cab and a round top boiler. Class S carried condensing apparatus which K's did not model. Anyone seeking to finish this model accurately would need to carefully ascertain the exact condition of a prototype at one point in time. From 1919 the engines were rebuilt and took on the Jinty outline.

K10/BL3 GWR/BR 97xx 0-6-0T

The third in the Bodyline series commands interest on two counts. Firstly, K's had pioneered the Bodyline concept in TT scale using this GWR 97xx prototype, and secondly it was to become the one Bodyline prototype to appear in a full kit option. Release would seem to be during the Spring of 1960. The twelve prototypes were unusual quasi side/pannier tank versions of the standard Collett Pannier designed with condensing apparatus to work onto the London Underground. Cast plates for 9701 were provided.

K11/(na) GWR 97xx 0-6-0T

Only two further locos were released by K's in OO during 1960. A full kit option of the 97xx was one of these (MRN for December 1960 has a full range advert wherein this model is twice erroneously called a 94xx). K's instead were putting effort into driving units with which to energise the very popular Kitmaster plastic kits.

The complete 97xx kit was first advertised in the August 1960 MRN, and is in the 1960s' catalogues, but disappears from the 70 Series editions. Significantly, in the W&H editions, whilst present in 1966, it is not in 1967. This will therefore be one of the rarer K's kits.

K12/L8 LMS Karrier Ro-Rail bus

A date for the Ro-Rail bus can be fixed; it was a new release at September 1960's Model Railway Hobby Show. It is hard to conceive of a more unusual choice. Without the K's model, it is possible that the prototype would be virtually unknown today. Who remembers the equivalent goods vehicle used on the West Highland line much more successfully?

This and the next release also mark K's twin dabble in 4mm with "infernal" combustion prototypes (it was a different story with the 1980s Continental series). The Ro-Rail bus was reviewed in the January 1961 Constructor. The prototype had appeared 30 years before and enjoyed an operational life of a matter of months. Karrier made this and the West Highland example which dates from 1934. In fact, the K's kit only had dummy road wheels, and the motor was extremely visible in the passenger saloon.

The kit was available through the 1960s and in the 70 Series catalogues. During the Banbury move it is presumed to have been withdrawn because a revival announcement was made in August 1974, but its spot was vacant again in the 1978 catalogue.

Another re-release advert from K's was made in October 1981, stimulated by adopting an HP2M series motor driving the rear rail wheels. The model made it to the bitter end, even being offered in Body Only form - one supposes this means minus wheels and motor. *Railway Modeller* in September 1983 published a detailed article on the kit by Nelson Twells (an expert on LMS road vehicles) and then in January 1990 published an account by K. P. Robinson of building the Body Only version using a Tenshodo bogie.

K13/L22 GWR/BR Diesel Railcar

Sticking to the tradition of an exciting release for the two major London events in the hobby, the Easter Show in April 1961 marked the next arrival. For the popular GWR branch, this was as key a piece of rolling stock as the 14xx and its autocoach. The GWR had successfully pioneered passenger diesel railcars before the war - in prototype terms, whereas the Ro-Railer and LMS railcars had been a virtual dead-end, the GWR tie up with AEC had produced 38 examples by 1941 and an influence that affected the modernisation plan deliveries. The two models could hardly have been a greater contrast.

There were various GWR railcar outlines and K's opted for number 19, the first of the 1940 build. K's interest in getting Kitmaster kits to work had produced a motor bogie intended for the Deltic and this was cleverly designed to be adjusted to work in the railcar's brake compartment. The K's body which was entirely whitemetal had the roof and sides each cast in two halves. All K's models were sold unglazed, and so this particular kit required the modeller to source the glazing for the saloon windows. The model is in the run of catalogues that we list, until a demise dated to around 1981, but this includes a two year absence from 1972. Its re-appearance in October 1974 was with a revised motor bogie. By 1981, other kits were on the market as was Lima's plastic ready-to-run version.

K14/(na) CR/LMS/BR 0-4-4T

During 1961 two further loco kits became available. Did K's have a nasty experience with this Caledonian 0-4-4T? The prototype should have been popular enough, but this became the only Scottish pre-grouping model, and the only 0-4-4T in the range. Owners report that making the chassis work was a challenge. The model was released at the September Model Railway Hobby Show, and advertised in the trade press in October 1961.

The kit never made it to the 70 Series catalogues and hence the lack of an 'L' number. Apparently the body parts used screw construction in an experiment to ease assembly. The prototype may not be particularly familiar, and in the minimal catalogue information it may not be clear that the description "Standard Passenger Tank" is actually a CR classification for this 1900 McIntosh design. They were also known as the 439 series after the lead engine of 68 examples, and one has been preserved on the Bo'ness & Kinneil Railway.

K15/TL1/L7 GER/LNER/BR J70 0-6-0T tram

The J70 steam tram was still in the oddity league, but in a combination of extreme ease of assembly and great prototypical attraction, this little model must be one of K's all time favourite offerings. The prototypes were the small but well-known GER class largely associated with the Wisbech & Upwell Tramway; immortality came their way via *Toby* in the *Thomas the Tank Engine* books. Certainly available by December

1961, it is possible something was shown at the September Model Railway Hobby Show - can anyone remember seeing any there?

The model was a simple whitemetal box about as complicated as K's' brakevan kits, although fixing couplings was something of a challenge. The chassis was actually four-wheeled, and well into the 70 Series era, indeed probably post the Banbury move and an August 1974 revival, this was entirely whitemetal and drove just one axle. Notwithstanding this, K's always presented the tram as the six-wheeled J70. A four-wheel drive brass chassis was advertised in "New" adverts from K's in January and February 1980. Without the chassis, the kit joined the Body Only club option later that decade.

K16/L17 GWR/BR 57xx 0-6-0PT

The last "conventional" introduction to the range had been the Small Prairie in Autumn 1959. So when some new models came in the second half of 1962, it was back to classic GWR favourites. Collett's ubiquitous large cab Pannier was being advertised from July 1962. The specification did not attempt to ease the modeller's lot, instead both brakegear and a dummy set of inside motion made an appearance, along with the fireman! Plates for 9789 appear to have been provided.

Major changes to the model took place in October 1979. An option to provide the Churchward cab of the 87xx was now supplied along with the HP2MG motor. Either then or slightly earlier, the final brass (no keyhole) chassis saw the brakegear details lost. These changes also added etched numberplates for either 5700 or 8750.

K17/L18 GWR/BR 63xx 2-6-0

The Churchward Mogul was the 1962 Model Railway Hobby Show's innovation. No brakegear and always only available with a Churchward cab, the feature of significance for future kits was a 3,500 gallon tender model for which transfers were supplied in the 1960s. Cast plates for 6332 were always provided.

K18/L21 SR/BR Q1 0-6-0

The Q1 was the most recent prototype K's had offered at its release, being just 20 years old. Back with tradition, this was the Easter Show release, with a Constructor review appearing in July 1963. The loco's outline was deceptively simple yet it actually posed several challenges. Most obvious were the strange BFB wheels which K's diligently provided. The lack of a running plate and very distinctive sandboxes meant that the frame castings had to show some detail, although brakegear was eschewed. These whitemetal frames were fitted outside the brass frames K's had now conventionally adopted. "Southern" transfers and even some black paint featured in the 1960s kits.

This model exists with three generations of its unique wheels. After the cast wheels, initially the

70 Series provided a plastic spoked wheel with a whitemetal BFB overlay. Finally, a plastic moulded centre for the BFB design was generated.

K19/L1 LMS/BR Black 5 4-6-0

The utter ubiquity of the Black 5 prototype meant that whoever first modelled this was bound to win sales. In the event, K's had the field to themselves for a decade. Early in 1963, K's intimated that they were working on the model, adverts stated that components would be on show with the Q1 at the Easter Show. The finished product arrived for the Autumn Hobby Show, and it received considerable attention in the October-December *Model Railways News*. K's had clearly moved to big engine territory. A set of nickel plated valvegear was one challenge. Other details included a fully riveted tender, a hinged fall plate, 19 spoked 6' drivers but no brakegear. It is possible to be quite specific about the K's prototype amongst the huge number of prototype variants - the loco comes from the Armstrong Whitworth build originally numbered 5225-5241. It is unlikely that these were partnered with the riveted tender K's provided, even if most Black Fives were so fitted.

Having gained 70 Series specification during December 1970, the model went onto to become the first fitted with the new chemically etched valvegear. Adverts in November 1971 and December 1972 marked the arrival of its new gear. Otherwise having commandeered the first slot in the catalogue, the model was a K's essential.

K20/L12 MR/LMS/BR Kirtley o/f 0-6-0

Still with the solid tradition of a release timed for each major London show, April 1964 saw the arrival of the first outside framed tender engine, and eleven more would follow. The technique was developed that had been used on the Q1. The model was really inside framed in brass, but cast "overlays", this time outside the drivers, were used to give the detail of the outside framing. The profile of the framing varied on prototype batches, and K's modelled one of forty engines built by Neilson between 1865-69.

Those inside frames were different too. The Kirtley was the first K's model to have "keyhole" brass frames. The wheels were placed in these "keyhole shaped slots into which the axle bushes anchored so doing away with a keeper plate". The result was a more rigid structure and became the norm with K's, and older models were adapted. May 1965's MRN carried a detailed article about the kit.

Some of these engines served with the ROD in Europe during World War One. There is an intriguing reference in 1984 advertising that the kit was available "with Italian modifications". These certainly exist; K's made a number of prototypes for an Italian retailer who also requested the Kirtley in the condition in which the Italians used fifty of them from 1906.

K21/L14a GWR/BR Dean Goods o/f 0-6-0

A logical development of the new technique was to cater for the outside framed variant of the Dean Goods, twenty of which had been built back in 1885. This merely modified the earlier model; both kits stayed firmly in 20th century condition with their Belpaire fireboxes. The model appeared during the Summer of 1964 as an extra in the programme. In latter years no separate mention of the kit was made but it remained available if requested. No suitable numberplates were made.

K22/L5 GCR/ROD/GWR/LMS/LNER/BR 2-8-0

The real focus of work at K's that Summer was on the massive outline of the GCR 2-8-0 heavy freight engine. Did this make it for the Hobby Show? Perhaps not, because the first full-scale advert was placed in December 1964. Like the Black 5, there had been an enormous number; the GCR built 130, and the ROD during World War One ordered another 521. The GWR ended up with 100, the LNER had 403 and the LMS had 50 from the LNWR. Many served abroad in both wars. The model's scope was thus considerable. As supplied, the K's model represented a 1917 ROD build with steam brake only, and no tender water scoop. Despite GWR ownership, no numbers were cast, nor were other Great Westernising parts thrown in.

K23/L11 MR/LMS Spinner o/f 4-2-2

In the previous couple of years Tri-ang had enjoyed great success with its two vintage single wheeler models. K's had now explored outside framing and combining the two themes produced another of the classic 19th century singles. This time it was the Johnson Midland prototype. Release was slated for the Easter Show of 1965. Was this target met? Adverts commenced in the Summer but it was not until December that the MRN reviewed it. The model attracted much attention, in particular a noteworthy three-part account of prototype and model in the MRN from November 1966 by Mills & Jenkinson.

Despite the small motors K's had designed, the new loco was actually a dummy which allowed a detailed backhead - a good idea in such an exposed cab. A K's tender drive unit actually provided the power. The prototypes existed in five sub-classes and enjoyed modifications. K's model presented the first six examples of the 115 sub-class as-built, but simple work with a file could provide the rest of the class. The preserved example comes from the 115 sub-class.

An advert in the July 1979 MRN marked a radical change. An HP2M motor was mounted in the loco in a specially designed brass (and definitely non-keyhole) chassis. The tender castings retained evidence of the motor mountings notwithstanding this. Compared with the previous tender drive, performance went downhill.

(above) K's L5 ROD 2-8-0 but with lower boiler fittings to suit later BR and LNER periods. Built on the original K's chassis with K's gears and MkI motor, and Romford wheels
Photo: Tony Wright, courtesy Tony Wright

(right) K's L19 LSWR Adams Radial built with Romford wheels. Note that this is finished for the member of the trio that spent a number of years with Colonel Stephen's East Kent Railway.
Photo: Tony Wright, courtesy Les Spratt

(below) K's L3 GWR 33xx Bulldog, complete with original wheels and cranks.
Photo: Tony Wright, courtesy Ted Kanas

K24/L19 LSWR/SR/BR Adams Radial 4-4-2T

Releases became compressed in 1965, and the Adam's Radial Tank model was also reviewed in the December trade press, having been advertised from September. Seventy-one prototypes appeared from 1882, and they were obsolete by 1920 apart from a trio retained into the 1960s to operate the Lyme Regis branch, hence allowing one to enter preservation on the Bluebell line. A number of detail changes affected the class and K's model best represented the Adams design, save for added coal rails and a flared Drummond chimney. Only a single slidebar was fitted which meant of the final survivors, the loco was closest to 30583.

One commentator mentions that this loco had whitemetal coupling and connecting rods, which combined with a "notoriously poor four coupled chassis" produced frustration for SR fans. If this is so, and remembering that earlier kits had pressed nickel silver coupling rods, we see a rather early decline in specification.

K25/L3 GWR/BR Bulldog 33xx o/f 4-4-0

Despite the challenges of 1965, another new model was hard on the heels of the previous two, its arrival being intimated in the January 1966 MRN. Actual release of the Bulldog was speedy too with reviews and adverts in the February/March MRNs, and the Constructor reviewed the model that August. Quite a few specification changes were made; the boiler was a one-piece casting which was a major step forward. Cast numberplates were not provided; these and the names were left to the builder's choice, however the transfers and the tin of Humbrol paint survived. The tender was the 3,000 gallon design off the Dean Goods kit. Plastic components made an appearance; these were in the form of wheel inserts for bogie and tender wheels. The aim was to improve appearance by fitting these to the standard Jackson wheels. These were to be used elsewhere in the range until sometime into the 70 Series.

The prototypes were part of a very complex group, and two further closely related GWR outside frame 4-4-0s would come from K's in the 1970s, as well as the smaller Armstrong class in 1985. K's model had a long-cone taper boiler as fitted from 1908, and straight frames as fitted to engines 3341 to 3440. In the Nu-Cast era, a K's derived reference has been issued to NC052 for a GWR Bird class 4-4-0 (3441-3455). These had deeper frames and although K's did not sell this as a separately referenced kit, K's did advertise in the August 1975 Modeller, and the 1978 catalogue, that this prototype could be modelled by purchasing deep frames and a combined top feed and safety valve sold as extras. As kits gained etched plates in the late 1970s/early 1980s, names and numbers for 3375 *Sir Watkin Wynn* were provided.

Kevin Taylor, in a colourful account of a kitbuilt stud in June 1975's Modeller, gave a heartfelt account of the experience that many modellers

will recognise as building a whitemetal kit of the period. Having bemoaned the usual standard of K's cast chimneys and having resorted to buying turned brass replacements, he reached the Bulldog. His verdict: "something of a problem child, this one. The centre of balance of the model turned out to be a few millimetres behind the leading driving axle, which caused problems with stability and current collection". Having improved this with a spring under the leading bogie, poor adhesion followed. Finally the model sounded "like a chainsaw taking down an oak tree".

K26/L15 LMS/BR Fowler 2-6-2T

Production of the Fowler 2-6-2T was announced in April 1966, but it was very late in the year before it materialised. It was still forthcoming in October, with the next two models announced in the same report. It does seem to have made it to the public for Christmas, but a review has not been traced until the Modeller's in June 1967. The one-piece boiler and the plastic wheel inserts were novelties from the preceding kit. The chassis broke entirely new ground - it was of the split axle type with one frame made of fibre, and proved a short-lived blind alley.

Wheel rims were still nickel silver on cast brass centres. This particular model was only the second to require a full set of outside valvegear. These components on the Black 5 had been pressed nickel silver, but on this model, bar the return crank, they were all cast in whitemetal and were thus extremely fragile. Ultimately a change in the 70 Series specification would solve this problem. So, in essence a fine model but not one for the uninitiated.

K27/L10 GWR/BR 1361 0-6-0ST

Announced in October 1966, modellers had to wait until the turn of 1967/68 to obtain the GWR Churchward Docktank, whereupon K's dived down the avenue of offering a 7mm version. The 4mm example had the split axle chassis at the outset, but it is assumed that this did not last long. This chassis utilised peculiar wheels with stub axles slotting into plastic sleeves. There was also a turned brass safety valve which was unique to this loco, and was later replaced with a whitemetal offering.

K28/L16 MR/LMS/BR Johnson 0-6-0

The Johnson 0-6-0 was another of the October 1966 announcements, and the wait for this to actually arrive took until September 1968. In that time K's were heavily occupied with plastic kits. Was the chassis also a cause of delay? It almost certainly re-adopted the brass keyhole chassis approach. A review has escaped my trawl.

K29/L13 GWR/BR Grange 4-6-0

The pace of releases after the Fowler 2-6-2T was palpably much slower and erratic. W&H and other stockists advertised the next release from April 1969, K's themselves from June 1969, and

(above) K's L23 GWR 2-8-0 built as a 38xx and with original K's wheels. The builder of this kit has managed to provide the correct curved front to the running plate that K's did not.

Photo: Tony Wright, courtesy Ted Kanas

(right) K's K32 GWR/BR Dukedog advert taken from *Model Railway News* March 1975

(below) K's L27 GWR 42xx/72xx locomotive; in this instance the 72xx has been built

Photo: Tony Wright, courtesy Ted Kanas

what K's billed as the 21st kit was the GWR Grange 4-6-0, but how was this counted? A review has been elusive. During August, K's advertised that all kits now had the brass keyhole chassis, including the Grange.

Following the Bulldog, the Grange had no numberplates, but during the 1980s etched names and numbers for 6805 *Broughton Grange* and 6857 *Tudor Grange* were added. The 3,500g tender from the 43xx was used from the outset.

K30/L23 GWR/BR 28xx 2-8-0

A brand new British kit to follow the Grange took over two years to materialise. Remember that period saw the major specification changes to the 70 Series being wrought. These were first announced in April 1970 and represent a change in direction from the two split axle chassied models.

After some hype for the new series and the arrival in March 1970 of the Prussian P6, matters were very quiet until late in 1971. The 28xx's arrival appears to have prompted the issue of a revised 70 Series catalogue in which the engine was prominent in the Catalogue Supplement. It appeared in K's adverts from November 1971 through to February 1972. The kit contained alternative splasher and cab parts to allow the original Churchward 28xx and the later Collett 38xx to be built. Even so, only the stepped running plate of the initial design was offered. No numbers seem to have been supplied.

K31/L25 GWR/BR 4575/55xx 2-6-2T

One model was produced in 1972, but it was really a development of the existing 44xx. After that, K's were preoccupied with moving to Banbury, and no new model would appear until 1974. The new GWR Prairie was advertised from April 1972 and reviewed in the Modeller and Constructor during the Autumn.

Churchward's 44xx had 4'1½" driving wheels. The 175 members of the 45xx and 55xx design had larger 4'7½" drivers, and were built by Churchward and Collett respectively. Initial adverts offered the kit as L22 which would allow the straight tanks of those numbered below 4575 to be reproduced, and as L23 which would allow the later sloping tanks. The sloping tank kits certainly appear more common, and by 1976 only one reference (L25) was available for the 4575/55xx groups.

The kit could produce a well-detailed model (allowing for no brakes), but when reviewed challenges in chassis assembly were noted. The kit avoided unsightly joints in the boiler with a one-piece smokebox and first boiler ring casting mating to a combined boiler and tank top casting. Cast numberplates for 5542 were provided.

K32/L26 GWR/BR Earl/Dukedog o/f 4-4-0

When K's did return to the fray with new loco releases, it was 1974, and they continued the task of developing logical extensions of existing

kits. This time it was the Bulldog kit of 1966 which inspired first the Dukedog and then the Duke class 4-4-0s. A 1974 programme was announced that presaged the GNR Atlantic and the GWR 42xx/72xx and Aberdare classes as well.

Bulldog frames were allied to the small boiler of the Duke to produce a class which had only appeared in 1936 despite their antiquated appearance. Their metier was work on the former Cambrian Railways. The kit was released for the Summer or was it? *Model Railway News* in July carried an illustrated release advert. Next March and the Constructor could only report that a prototype had appeared at the Toyfair. The exact date of release is therefore not yet available, but MRN again carried an extensive "New" advert in March 1975 for both this model and K33. K's eventually produced an etched number for 3200 but it is not clear if the short-lived *Earl of Mount Edgcumbe* name was also etched.

K33/L24 GWR/BR 3252 Duke o/f 4-4-0

Despite not featuring in the planned 1974 programme, this model was priced in K's adverts from September. The major development task in the kit was providing the distinctively curved outside frames. Like the Dukedog, it is anticipated that the actual release was sometime in 1975. The prototypes had a small 2,500 gallon tender which K's provided. Some disaster befell this tender model which resulted in it never reaching Autocom, and later K's Dukes had the 3,000 gallon tender model. The kit gained etched plates for 3283 *Comet*.

K34/L27 GWR/BR 42xx/72xx 2-8-0T or 2-8-2T

The GWR 2-8-0T model was part of the 1974 programme, and clear release announcements from that September exist, both from K's adverts, and from the generally reliable W&H adverts. It may have been the only 1974 item to have actually appeared that year. Nonetheless, K's had announced still more kits, and by the year's end the Dukedog, Duke, Aberdare, GNR Atlantic, Ivatt 2-6-2T, LMS Garratt and the GWR Crane Tank were all publicised. Presumably life at K's in the mid-1970s was particularly frenetic, and outside factors like coal strikes may have had a bearing.

The actual kit for this loco enabled four main variants to be built. These were the 2-8-0T or the rebuilt 2-8-2T configuration which enabled the class to get outside the South Wales Valleys, and with a raised or straight running plate over the cylinders. The particularly small bunker for the first 1910 built 4201 was not included. To show the complexity that modelling this class involved, bear in mind that four different bunker designs existed. Modelling engines with/without outside steam pipes was allowed. Despite these variations in the kit, the result is still judged a poor model, and it will not re-appear since Autocom possess the better model originated at much the same time by Cotswold.

K35/L28 GWR/BR Aberdare 26xx o/f 2-6-0

The predecessor to Churchward's 2-8-0T for South Wales freight appeared from the same gentleman only ten years before. It was something of a contrast being a very 19th century styled outside framed Mogul. That K's proposed it as a partner to the large tank in their 1974 programme made sense. Whilst the 2-8-0T appeared in 1974, there was a long wait for the Aberdare. It seems possible that it was released in July 1975; nonetheless *Railway Modeller* did not review the model until December 1976.

The model came with a 3,500 gallon tender which was unfortunate when the 3,000 gallon tender off the Dean Goods would have been a better choice (or even the GCR ROD tender). Otherwise the kit offers the loco in post-1903 condition with a taper rather than parallel boiler.

Until this loco, K's use of one-piece boilers had been limited; the GWR 4-4-0s and the Fowler 2-6-2T had them. It was now announced that one-piece boilers would be the norm and that older models would be amended when patterns were renewed (for example, the ROD certainly received this treatment).

It is clear from the RM review that the vacuum packs had now been adopted, but that change had occurred some years before; however what about the chassis? The critical wording in the review was the "kit is the first we have reviewed since the introduction of the new wheels, new style motor mountings, and above all, the new skin packs [and] the new design chassis". Does this imply packaging changes since the introduction of the 4575 in 1972, or was that overlooked because the famine of *Railway Modeller* reviews otherwise dates back to June 1967 and the Fowler 2-6-2T? What is likely is that the Modeller had before them a kit with the latest design plain pressed brass chassis and self-assembled wheels. Their model, despite "new motor mountings", did not have the HP2M motor since the text itself guardedly announced that as a future development.

K36/L30 LMS Ivatt 2P/BR 84xxx 2-6-2T

Another of the 1974 announcements, this kit was also released for July 1975, an example having been shown at the 1975 Toy Fair. A clue to the delays of the period comes from K's advert of August 1975 in the Modeller. This stated bluntly that both the Ivatt Tank and the GWR Aberdare were available, and they were both fitted with the "new motor". Presumably this suggests the HP2M, but that did not appear until 1977. The Aberdare review of 1976 still saw the motor in the future, and the Ivatt Tank was not actually reviewed until July 1977 in the Constructor, and September 1977 in the Modeller. Numerous options now become possible; K's appear to have intended that the two locos would both have the HP2M. Evidently at least some of the Aberdares (for example that reviewed in the Modeller) did not. It seems probable that all early Aberdares, Ivatt Tanks and Atlantics were

not HP2M fitted. One owner advises that his Ivatt Tank certainly had the previous Mark II motor from new. His model also had a boiler that tapered from smokebox to firebox, a problem the file could not solve. There was an accurate set of etched valvegear from new, but the K's drivers as supplied were a scale 3" over diameter. Smallish improvements could be made, and all are effectively described in an article in the April 1979 Constructor.

The next issue lies in exactly what was modelled. K's called it the "LMS/BR Ivatt 2P 2-6-2T". K's provided parts for both the 1946 LMS design and the BR standard 84000 series of 1953, although the cast chimney in the kit was the later BR version, and the two possible predecessors were not included. The principal differences of the prototypes were a sloped running plate front on the BR design rather than an open one, and different injector and safety valves. Many in both classes were auto-fitted.

K37/L29 GNR/LNER/BR C1 Atlantic 4-4-2

Another of the 1974 hopefuls was the GNR Atlantic. When previewed in 1975 Toy Fair Reports it was intimated that it would probably be tender driven. That October there was a K's advert stating that the model was in production with the new motor. No contemporary release review is yet to hand, but adverts in the following months would seem to confirm that release was that Winter. If so, upon release what motor really did power it, and where was it placed?

K's modelled a loco in its post-1911 state with LNER fittings as the catalogue said. One translates this to mean - in superheated condition and with a choice of safety valve. A detailed portrayal of the kit does exist in a remarkably interesting yet hard to find resource - *Loco Modeller* magazine of November 1983. There were only five of these magazines, being produced by John Paige and dedicated primarily to kit interests.

This source suggests that the actual kits were loco driven but with tender pickup, which arrangement with an HP2MG motor is confirmed by Autocom's example. Under the Jubilee write-up, the tender pickup chassis is noted as new in 1977. Had K's used it earlier on this class, or was this kit altered somewhat in the late 1970s? The engine required special 26mm diameter drivers to be originated.

K38/L32 LMS/BR Beyer Garratt 2-6-0+0-6-2

The LMS Garratt was emphatically K's most ambitious model, and the masters were produced by Vic Green. K's announced the kit in 1974, and release is put down to January 1976. It is just possible that the kit was out before Christmas 1975, as the advertisers in the January Modeller hoped, but K's own hype was left for the February issue. Extensive reviews are in the Constructor and Modeller for October 1977. The mainly etched valvegear was drawn from the now etched set on the Fowler 2-6-2T. Motorisation was intended for the leading chassis unit; powering the second needed the modeller to hack away at the rotary coalbunker (that was not fitted to the first three prototypes). The model overall came to a massive 35cms in length. It is overwhelmingly likely that K38 and K39 were the first kits to appear in the skinpack packaging from new.

A very early Garratt example in the Autocom Collection seems to answer the vexing motor question. We know that the next actual release was the Jubilee and that had the HP2M from new. Autocom's unmade Garratt has the Mark I motor, but most at the time had the HP2M. The Constructor review made clear that the model would accept both motor designs. There is further evidence that, despite adverts to the contrary, locos made prior to 1977 did not carry the newer motor. Puffer's advert in the February 1977 Modeller makes clear that they anticipated all deliveries from the 1st of February to be fitted with the HP2M. In addition, it is possible to identify two different sets of cylinder casting that the model employed, a change dated to around 1980.

Having issued the LMS Garratt, did K's consider producing the LNER example? A tiny piece of evidence from the Puffers May 1977 Modeller advert notes it as "Coming Soon". This never materialised, and no K's reference number is yet known. During the early 1980s DJH plugged the gap.

K39/L31 GWR 322 class o/f 0-6-0

Ironically, the next release sharing the same February 1976 advert was a product of the same works. Despite this, the contrast could hardly have been greater. The GWR Armstrong Goods was somewhat slipped in, not being part of the previews of releases made years before. Recognised numerically as the 322 class, they were designed and built as far back as 1864 by Beyer Peacock in Manchester. There were 30 engines which were heavily rebuilt in the years before their extinction in 1934. Despite a superficial similarity to the outside framed Dean Goods, there were many detail differences; curved framing and top hung springs being obvious. K's model came in final form with the GWR B4 boiler and the 2,500 gallon tender off the Duke. Later models have a 3,000 gallon example (see the Duke).

K40/L34 GWR/BR 850 class 0-6-0PT

K41/L34C Crane Tank attachment for GWR 850 class 0-6-0PT

Back in August 1974, K's own advertising had placed a model as exotic as the Garratt, with whom it shared the billing, into the programme. Only this crane tank with the accompanying 850 class pannier tank in the K's range never came to fruition, and that is a far better record than some of K's competitors! The idea was to model one of the common 19th century GWR 0-6-0 tanks. It would be offered purely as a pannier tank fitted 850 class. That was a Wolverhampton built class

of 170 small wheeled engines which, with the pannier tank K's intended, would represent the majority as working in the 20th century. The same design had been used to build from new three 0-6-4PT crane engines with a steam crane fitted to the rear frame extension, the intention being to cover this with a supplementary kit. The models were in both W&H's 1975 and 1977 catalogues, and the crane tank was afforded a prototypical photograph. How far K's got in generating a model is unknown, but certainly none were sold. K's own L series reference was quickly snaffled by the Jubilee.

K42/L34 LMS/BR Jubilee 4-6-0

K's announced in December 1976 two further forthcoming models - the LBSCR K class Mogul and the LMS Jubilee (a Jubilee for the Silver Jubilee). With this point we pass beyond the extensive plans of 1974-5, and all bar the GWR crane tank and related 850 pannier tank were achieved. We are also safely into the era of the new HP2M motor. The model was released from February 1977, with a review appearing in December 1977's Modeller. The model had a choice of boiler fittings, a set of etched valvegear, and a novelty from K's - there were three sets of etched nameplates, for *Silver Jubilee*, Keyes and *Newfoundland*.

K's provided what is the sole whitemetal kit of this particular type of Stanier tender. This is a 3,500g short wheelbase design which was coupled to short firebox Jubilees in order to suit certain restricted turntables. There were only fifty which were all originally paired with this class. Of the names K's offered, only Keyes was originally paired with the model's prototype.

There were also "chromed" parts (actually etched stainless steel) including numbers for *Silver Jubilee*'s special livery. The review referred to a new tender chassis with electrical pickups. K's advert in the March Constructor made clear that this new tender was new for the four tender locos being planned in early 1977. The chassis made in plastic was widely adopted for the tender locos, both new and old.

It seems possibly that K's plans underwent quite a rethink either side of Christmas 1976. The W&H 1977 catalogue (dated 1.77) retains the GWR crane tank, numbers the Jubilee L35, allocates L36 to the Fowler Docktank, and has no mention of the Stanier Mogul. In reality, the Jubilee became L34, the Docktank took another two years to come and became L39. The Stanier Mogul was actually only a few weeks away.

K43/L33 LBSCR/SR/BR K Class 2-6-0

By the time the LBSCR K was released in March 1977, it had already acquired a partner since the LMS Stanier 2-6-0 was sharing that March's platform. The model had a very extensive review in the *Model Railway News* for September 1977. The class was not common, there being only seventeen built from 1913. With its blocked-in tender coal rails, it is difficult to make this as an LBSCR loco. Otherwise it seems the model was

**(right) K's L30 Ivatt 2-6-2T fin-
ished as an ex-LMS engine**
*Photo: Colin Hey, courtesy Eric
Robinson*

**(below) K's L29 GNR/LNER C1
Atlantic**
*Photo: Dave Wheatstone, courtesy
Dave Wheatstone Collection*

**(bottom) The two GWR pan-
nier crane tanks considered
(at least) for K's patternmaking. The picture shows the
engines standing outside
Swindon Works in September
1927**
*Photo: F.R.Hebron, courtesy RAS
Publishing*

based upon as-built condition. There was an option for the LBSCR or SR style cab and the chimney and dome fittings for each company.

K44/L35 LMS/BR Stanier 2-6-0

The LMS Stanier Mogul model appeared without much fuss in March 1977, but one stockist quotes a 4th week of July delivery. It was illustrated in adverts quite extensively during 1977, but the only review so far traced is in April 1979's *Model Railway News*. The model had etched valvegear, tender pickups, one-piece boiler and HP2M all from new. Both chassis and the valvegear etch were made especially for the model. Another special touch was added cast balance weights on the drivers.

K45/L37 MR/LMS/BR Johnson 1500 series 0-4-0ST

A case of impudence and dignity for the next two releases. K's had never issued a *real* 0-4-0T before - the J70 should have had six wheels! Now came the first of what became three distinctly antiquated and tiny shunters in the range catered around the dimensions of the HP2M. Two of these, being the Johnson 1500 series and the LNER Y8, were announced in July 1977's Constructor. The Johnson was being advertised that October, and reviewed by the Modeller that December.

Since sources give three varying dates of withdrawal for the last member which was 41516 (and which engine K's based their model on) and various other minefields exist such as the MR numbering of these locos, any model may require a considerable degree of research. Essentially, 1500-1517 built from 1883 were nine tons smaller than the later 1518-1527 batch. K's catalogue description gives 1963 for final withdrawal of the class, but this is clearly wrong - most of the class went before 1930, although the brewery branches of Burton retained a hold on the survivors. Number 41516 was withdrawn from Burton on 1st October 1955.

The catalogue likewise implied that the model was in original condition, but this may not be true in respect of the cab - did not the first engines start with a plain spectacle plate? The cab on the modelled version may have seemed a primitive affair, but it was not in original condition. K's detailed etching provided a component for a spectacle plate with a cab roof. The model was in fact quite complex and even sported brakegear.

K46/L36 LNER 1936 build P2 2-8-2

At the same time K's were working away on a Gresley streamlined 2-8-2. This was advertised in May 1977, but with illustrated adverts placed in the January 1978 trade press, I prefer that as the release date. No review is yet to hand. Etched nameplates for all six class members were supplied. The tender current pickup and etched Walschaerts valvegear completed a specification that eschewed brakegear. Despite those

nameplates, only 2003-4 could be directly modelled without further work. The tender supplied did not suit 2001/2. Engine 2005 had a single chimney, whilst the kit has a double. Number 2006 is excluded by virtue of a combustion chamber in the firebox. The original P2 design is referenced under K68/L51.

K47/L38 NER/LNER/BR Y8 0-4-0T

Released with the P2, and also without brakegear, was the second 0-4-0T. This was a tiny design of Worsdell's for the NER, only two of which entered BR stock, the last being York Shed pilot until 1956.

K's had a hectic programme through 1977 and with a display at the London Toy Show in 1978, this pace looked set to continue. There were the brand new Milestones series and on top of the LNER P2 and Y8, the Fowler Docktank, the two versions of Princess Pacific and the *Sir Sam Fay* were added. By March the BR 15xx Pannier and the LNER J3 joined the programme in K's adverts. Many of these seem to have been released without extensive coverage in the trade press. As applicable, further releases have etched valvegear, names and a tender pick up.

K48/L41/BR LMS Turbomotive 4-6-2

K49/L42 LMS/BR Princess 4-6-2

An obvious pairing were the LMS Princess and its derivative, the unnamed Turbomotive. K's sold the latter as an easy route to a big engine for the modeller who feared outside valvegear. 6203 *Princess Margaret Rose* and 6205 *Princess Victoria* were the names with L42. Engine 6205 had some unique components and these K's provided as options (reversing lever and motion brackets for example).

The Turbomotive version allowed for two designs of turbine cover. Along with the *Sir Sam Fay*, these were featured in a K's release advert in July 1978's Modeller. The K's Princess was the subject of a detailed appraisal in August 1993's *Railway Modeller*. That hardly awarded it full marks - if the write up was fair, then by the standards of the 1990s, K's kit was deficient in its wheels, motor, gearbox, lack of brakes, problematic running plate casting and other areas besides. This may help explain the increasing sales challenge during the 1980s.

K50/L40 GCR/LNER B2 Sir Sam Fay 4-6-0

The B2 4-6-0 with its inside cylinders was a relatively straightforward model compared with some on K's agenda at this time. The prototype was popular in its day, although none were inherited by BR. *Sir Sam Fay* and *City of London* along with etchings for GCR numberplates were offered. This kit and the ROD are the only two K's GCR prototypes.

(above) K's L31 GWR outside framed 322 class

Photo: Tony Wright, courtesy Ted Kanas

(below) K's L34 Jubilee, completed with a Comet chassis and Romford wheels. The nameplate *Western Australia* is not one of the examples included in the kit.

Photo: Dave Wheatstone, courtesy Dave Wheatstone Collection

(bottom) K's L36 LNER P2 completed with turned down Romford wheels

Photo: Tony Wright, courtesy Ian Rathbone

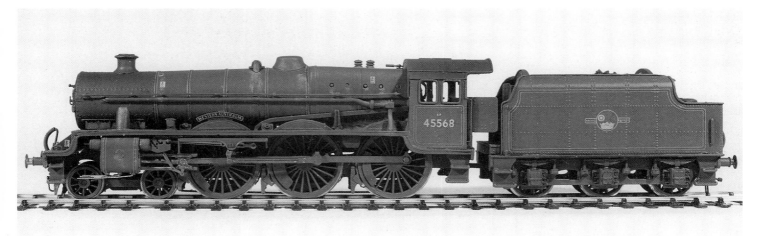

K51/ML1 L&MR Lion o/f 0-4-2

A prototype which virtually every model railway enthusiast has heard of, the *Lion* 0-4-2 of 1838 was the hero of the *Titfield Thunderbolt* film, and so can work beside a K's 14xx. When K's released it with adverts in September 1978, it marked a scene change by K's. A new Milestones series was to be created. Actually, the age difference between some of the Milestones and some of the ordinary kits was not that great.

Perhaps the generic difference was that the Milestones prototypes had been withdrawn many decades previously, whilst K's other Victorian engines were usually portrayed in their final condition within the memory of at least some of those who purchased the kits. Another key difference was that each Milestone was unmotorised, although a separate motorisation kit was marketed. Clearly K's felt these could be showcase models. The Milestones had a different fate to the remainder of the OO kits - in May 1993 *Railway Modeller* reported that they had all been purchased by Keith Butler's The Classic Locomotive Company. Keith also uses the IKB tradename and by early 1997 one model had been re-released (see K58).

K52/ML2 LNWR Problem Class 2-2-2

K's had manufactured single wheelers before, but this was a unique to them, in modelling terms, 2-2-2 - a popular mid-Victorian wheel arrangement. The class were otherwise known as the *Lady of the Lake* class and this Ramsbottom design existed between 1859-1905. Webb made some visual changes with enclosed splashers and with a proper cab in place of a weatherboard. K's modelled both options and provided plates for *Lady of the Lake* and *Pandora*. The LNWR Problem model along with ML1/3 was part of the initial releases of September 1978.

K53/ML3 LSWR Falcon Class 2-4-0

The third of the first tranche of Milestones provided a Beattie design 2-4-0 built back in 1861 for the LSWR, which was extinct by 1898. The rudimentary cab was an etching. Names offered were *Siren* and *Shark*.

K54/L39 LMS/BR Fowler Dock tank 0-6-0T

Although presaged some time previously, it was not until the turn of 1978/79 that the Fowler Dock tank model appeared. It required a unique chassis and set of etched gear. Incidentally, K's made an N gauge kit of this prototype way back in the mid-1960s. With the 4mm release, K's went very quiet, and the Modeller carried nothing about any intended 1979 programme.

K55/L44 GNR/LNER/BR J3 0-6-0

In fact another model appeared with the minimum of fuss in 1979 - a model of a standard GNR Ivatt 0-6-0 goods engine had been on the cards since 1978. A precise release date for this is somewhat elusive, but it was priced at stockists from September 1979. The GNR Atlantic tender was re-used.

K56/L45 TVR/GWR S class 0-4-0ST

The next news from K's was at the turn of 1979-80 when another 0-4-0 tank was added. This time, although sold as a Taff Vale Railway and hence GWR offering, what was modelled was a classic industrial loco of the 19th century. This was due to the real engine simply being a standard Hudswell Clarke product, and thus the modeller, armed with some research, could model other similar engines running on other railways. The kit, labelled as TVR Class S, referred to the one loco of this class bought by the TVR in 1876 and withdrawn in 1926. Etchings came for the cab and plates for TVR 267 or GWR 1342. From pictures, the little model appeared quite complex, but bare beneath the running plate. Hattons marked the kit as new in December's advert, and K's placed their own release adverts in the January and February 1980 trade press.

K57/L43 BR (WR) 15xx 0-6-0PT

The year 1980 saw K's offer a Spring selection of goodies. When Eames advertised that they would be at the Easter Show with five new K's kits, it must have seemed like old times. Actually although we are still six years from the 1986 wind-down, there would only be seven introductions to come after the five which appeared in 1980. The BR 15xx had already been announced back at the start of 1978. K's gave it an illustrated advert in March 1980's Modeller. The etched plates were for the class leader 1500 and also 1506. With them K's modelled the final design of Western Pannier tank.

K58/ML4 Metropolitan/LT 4-4-0T

Activity then returned to the Milestones series with a loco to cater for a range of interests. Models of London's Underground system have been a peculiar story - crude toys were all the rage in the early part of the century, but the usual ready-to-run names have virtually neglected the subject. Kits have been quite a recent vogue, and this K's offering fits into this category by offering the classic Beyer Peacock designed outside cylindered 4-4-0T of 1864. The locos came in various batches and gradual enlargements until there were 66 in 1885. There were alternative cab/chimney/domes/safety valves to create the original design or one as running in their twilight years on the Brill branch.

Electrification at the turn of the century made many redundant, yet some ran into LT days. By this time all-over cabs were fitted, whilst sales had taken the class to the Mersey Railway, the Cambrian, and to various industrial systems. The LNWR had also purchased 16 of the design new in 1871. In 1996 a revised version of this kit was re-released under the IKB label.

(above) K's L42 LMS/BR Princess

Photo: Tony Wright, courtesy Terry Davis

(left) *Railway Modeller* **advert from the July 1978 edition**

(below) The original K's display model of K's L40 GCR/LNER B2 *Sir Sam Fay*

Photo: Peter Wright, courtesy British Railway Modelling

K59/ML5 GWR Dean Single 3031 class o/f 4-2-2

ML4 and ML5 were both advertised by K's in April 1980's Constructor. The second of these was for the Dean Single immortalised by Tri-ang's *Lord of the Isles* model. Etched coal rails and plates for 3046 *Lord of the Isles* and 3047 *Lorna Doone* were provided. The tender was a new model.

K60/L46 LMS/BR Duchess 4-6-2

After a long gap with no news from K's, they placed adverts in October 1981 for three new large LMS Stanier engines. All contained transfers and the two Pacifics had selections of etched nameplates. L46 and L47 would appear to have indeed been released in October, but I have no review tracked down. A choice of a stepped or continuous running plate was allowed. The model had some shortcomings and the modelling public went for the far better Model Loco/DJH offering which was already available. Four nameplates were available for this loco, these being *Duchess of Gloucester*, *Duchess of Atholl*, *City of London* and *City of Nottingham*.

K61/L47 LMS/BR Stanier 8F 2-8-0

Little more can currently be added beyond the notes for K60. The 4,000 gallon tender for this 8F model was taken from the Black Five, and no optional parts were packaged. Both this model and the previous release were competing with the old but nevertheless affectionately regarded Hornby/Wrenn ready-to-run models. Contrasting a K's powered kit with the Ringfield driven alternative might have discouraged some sales.

K62/L48 LMS/BR Streamlined Coronation 4-6-2

This seems to have appeared for Christmas 1981, although another thread of evidence suggests mid-Summer 1982. *British Railway Modelling* in February 1996 illustrated one with the owner's comment "a fair stand-in but not the best!". Back in 1981 when the option was soldering sheet metal with Jamieson or suffering Tri-ang's grotesquely short model, it may have appeared more attractive, but later the DJH model would attract the plaudits. The transfers also provided the chevrons for the LMS livery and an additional stainless steel etching gave the *Coronation* nameplate. Other names were *King George VI*, *Queen Elizabeth*, *City of Bristol* and *Duchess of Rutland*.

An intriguing prospect exists. Did K's actually cast the bodies for the Wrenn Coronations? Wrenn first announced their loco in 1983 as a KIT, the RTR models followed. It actually had a relatively short life centred around 1984-85. Both Wrenn and K's models had a one-piece body casting. K's kit had instructions that also advised how the casting could be fitted to a Wrenn or Dublo chassis. Convinced? Since first floating this idea, sufficient informants have contacted me to convince me that K's did cast the Wrenn body. A full account of the options is

given by Bill Wood in *Model Railway Enthusiast* for March 1999. However, watertight documentary proof is still needed, and it appears the case that the two bodies are not one and the same casting. An additional complication is that the usual practice for Wrenn would be to use mazak, whilst K's would usually cast in whitemetal.

K63/ML6 GWR Broad Gauge Rover class o/f 4-2-2

A model of Gooch's classic *Rover* class broad gauge single wheeler had been announced by April 1980. K's own adverts thereafter became more sporadic, and when K's appeared again with a full-page promotion of the European range, it was April 1981. My record of release suggests ML6 did not reach stockists until around the moment that the *Model Railway News* reviewed the kit in November 1981. It was for 28mm gauge and there was probably one short production run. The names are recorded as *Great Western*, *Great Britain* and *Iron Duke*. Class namesake *Rover* was not included, nor quite correctly, were numberplates. These are locos that were rebuilt (or built) after 1871 and saw out the end of the Broad Gauge. Turnings were used to improve the quality of the chimney and the safety valve.

K64-65/L49-GK49 BR Bulleid Rebuilt Merchant Navy 4-6-2

Without a lot of fuss seemingly, a rebuilt Merchant Navy appeared in August 1983. K's presumably hoped that this model could revive interest, though why was there not extensive advertising and reviews? Some resistance to the plastic geared HP2MG motor had been encountered. In what was the last general change applied to the series, K's now moved to a new five-pole unit with a nylon worm wheel and brass worm. Two versions of the rebuilt Merchant Navy were offered - the regular L49 with plates for *Port Line,* and a new Gold Series reference GK49. The latter provided *Clan Line* with preformed pipework and handrails and a pre-assembled chassis and valvegear. In addition, GK49 had the headboard and trimmings for the *Golden Arrow*. Special BFB wheels were created with nickel-plated steel rims on the plastic centres.

K66/L50 SR/BR Lord Nelson 4-6-0

During 1984 one new release was made. Announced for April 1984, stockists seem to have had the *Lord Nelson* soon thereafter. What press attention the new release obtained seems focussed on the *Model Railway News*, wherein K's own adverts and review material appeared subsequent to that April. Despite this, it was revolutionary - the model had a Rod Neep designed Perseverance etched chassis! There was a foreshortened Bulleid modified bogie tender and names for *Lord Nelson* and *Sir Walter Raleigh*. Few kits were sold and its re-introduction at Autocom is unlikely.

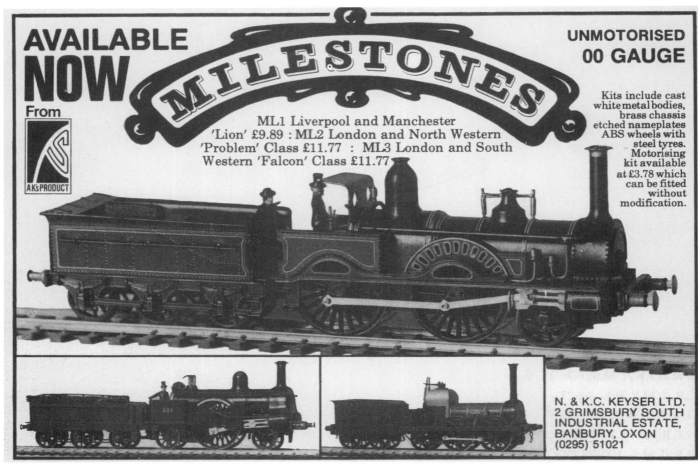

above) K's Milestones range advert taken from *Railway Modeller* September 1978

(below) K's L43 15xx 0-6-0PT built with the original K's wheels

Photo: Tony Wright, courtesy Ted Kanas

Two years after its release, it was the subject of a major write-up by Frank Neatherway in the April 1986 MRN. On the one hand he praised Rod Neep's work, on the other he identified "a major design fault that prevents the loco and chassis being united, a fault which needs surgery to rectify". A fine model could result but only with fun and games on the way. If you have one of these kits to build, you will not regret digging out this MRN reference!

(above) K's Milestones ML6 for the broad gauge *Rover*
Photo: Dave Wheatstone, courtesy Dave Wheatstone Collection

K67/ML7 GWR Armstrong o/f 4-4-0

To mark the attempt by Teign Models to revive interest, another and final Milestone was released, and illustrated in the June 1985 Modeller. Known as the *Armstrong* class, these four 4-4-0s were so-called because their designer Dean named number 7 after his predecessor. They were something of an enlarged 3031 class which allowed K's to replicate parts such as the tender and bogie since the class was modelled in as-built state; later they were increasingly rebuilt. A very attractive prototype but how many models were turned out? Probably they are only a degree more common than their prototypes had been. K's provided names and numbers for all four.

K68/L51 LNER original P2 2-8-2

In a reversal of type, having introduced the 1936 build some years before, core components like the chassis were re-used to offer an as built P2 *Earl Marischal*. Nameplates for all six

P2's allowed theoretically for an impressive line up of K's P2 power on shed. However the only engine to actually resemble L51 was *Earl Marischal* before being rebuilt to the more familiar streamlined shape. This was the second P2 2002 which in 1934 followed 2001 *Cock o' the North*. The latter had poppet valvegear and a different profile to the running plate.

K's model used the tender previously prepared for the streamlined engines when a high-sided non-corridor, instead of streamlined, tender was needed.

Advertised from October 1985 under the Teign banner, and although not evident for a while, this marked the end of the line for K's loco kits. Gresley's massive 2-8-2 designed for the curving Edinburgh-Aberdeen line was quite an engine to conclude with, and far away from the rural Arcadia of the Great Western branch line with its 14xx where it had all started some 28 years before.

SPECIFICATIONS - KEY DATES

Cast Whitemetal Chassis 1957
Pressed Brass Chassis 1958
Brass Plated Castings 1959
Bodyline Kits 1959
Brass Keyhole Chassis 1964
One-piece Boilers 1966
Plastic Centred Wheels 1970
Etched Valvegear 1972
Plain Pressed Brass Chassis 1976
Etched Nameplates 1977
Plastic Tender Chassis and Pickups 1977
HP2M Motor 1977
Milestones 1978
HP2MG Motor 1979
Gold Series 1983
Last Five Pole Motor 1983

(below) K's L51 LNER original P2
Photo: Tony Wright, courtesy Tony Wright

K's Locomotives Table

Text Reference	Actual Reference	Description	New Date	Withdrawal Date	Notes
K01	L9	GWR/BR 14xx 0-4-2T	5/1957	1986	
K02	ML8	LT E class Electric Tram	5/1957	1986	Allocated ML8 later in the kit's life
K03	L20	LBSCR/SR/BR Terrier 0-6-0T	9/1957	1986	
K04	L2	LNWR/LMS/BR Coal Tank 0-6-2T	4/1958	1986	
K05	L14	GWR/BR Dean Goods i/f 0-6-0	9 or 10/1958	1986	
K06	L6	NER/LNER/BR J72 0-6-0T	2/1959	1986	
K07	L4	GWR/BR 44xx 2-6-2T	10/1959	1986	
K08	BL2	GNR/LNER/BR J50 0-6-0T	12/1959	c.1984	Bodyline kit
K09	BL1	MR/LMS 3F 0-6-0T	1/1960	c.1984	Bodyline kit
K10	BL3	GWR/BR 97xx 0-6-0T	by 4/1960	c.1984	Bodyline kit
K11		GWR 97xx 0-6-0T	8/1960	c.1967	
K12	RR1/L8	LMS Karrier Ro-Rail bus	9/1960	1986	L8 was first used by the Prussian P6
K13	L22	GWR/BR Diesel Railcar	4/1961	c.1981	L Number first used for what became L25
K14		CR/LMS/BR 0-4-4T	9/1961	1968/69	
K15	TL1/L7	GER/LNER/BR J70 0-6-0T tram	by 12/1961	1986	L7 was at first used by GB&WRR USA 2-6-0
K16	L17	GWR/BR 57xx 0-6-0PT	7/1962	1986	
K17	L18	GWR/BR 63xx 2-6-0	10/1962	1986	
K18	L21	SR/BR Q1 0-6-0	4/1963	1986	
K19	L1	LMS/BR Black 5 4-6-0	9/1963	1986	
K20	L12	MR/LMS/BR Kirtley o/f 0-6-0	4/1964	1986	
K21	L14a	GWR/BR Dean Goods o/f 0-6-0	5-8/1964	1986	
K22	L5	GCR/ROD/GWR/LNER/LMS/BR 2-8-0	10/1964	1986	
K23	L11	MR/LMS Spinner o/f 4-2-2	4/1965	1986	
K24	L19	LSWR/SR/BR Adams Radial 4-4-2T	9/1965	1986	
K25	L3	GWR/BR Bulldog 33xx o/f 4-4-0	2/1966	1986	
K26	L15	LMS/BR Fowler 2-6-2T	12/1966	1986	
K27	L10	GWR/BR 1361 0-6-0ST	12/1967	1986	
K28	L16	MR/LMS/BR Johnson 0-6-0	9/1968	1986	

Text Reference	Actual Reference	Description	New Date	Withdrawal Date	Notes
K29	L13	GWR/BR Grange 4-6-0	4/1969	1986	
K30	L23	GWR/BR 28xx 2-8-0	11/1971	1986	L number first used for what became L25
K31	L25	GWR/BR 4575/55xx 2-6-2T	4/1972	1986	Released as L22 and L23
K32	L26	GWR/BR Earl/Dukedog o/f 4-4-0	3/1975	1986	
K33	L24	GWR/BR 3252 Duke o/f 4-4-0	3/1975	1986	
K34	L27	GWR/BR 42xx/72xx 2-8-0T or 2-8-2T	c.10/1974	1986	
K35	L28	GWR/BR Aberdare 26xx o/f 2-6-0	7/1975	1986	
K36	L30	LMS Ivatt 2P/BR 84xxx 2-6-2T	7/1975	1986	
K37	L29	GNR/LNER/BR C1 Atlantic 4-4-2	10/1975	1986	
K38	L32	LMS/BR Beyer Garratt 2-6-0+0-6-2	1/1976	1986	
K39	L31	GWR 322 class o/f 0-6-0	2/1976	1986	
K40	L34	GWR/BR 850 class 0-6-0PT	Never Made		Shown in W&H 1975+1977 catalogues
K41	L34C	Crane Tank attachment for GWR 850 class 0-6-0PT	Never Made		Shown in W&H 1975+1977 catalogues
K42	L34	LMS/BR Jubilee 4-6-0	2/1977	1986	
K43	L33	LBSCR/SR/BR K class 2-6-0	3/1977	1986	
K44	L35	LMS/BR Stanier 2-6-0	3/1977	1986	
K45	L37	MR/LMS/BR Johnson 1500 series 0-4-0ST	7/1977	1986	
K46	L36	LNER 1936 build P2 2-8-2	1/1978	1986	
K47	L38	NER/LNER/BR Y8 0-4-0T	1/1978	1986	
K48	L41	LMS/BR Turbomotive 4-6-2	7/1978	1986	
K49	L42	LMS/BR Princess 4-6-2	7/1978	1986	
K50	L40	GCR/LNER B2 Sir Sam Fay 4-6-0	7/1978	1986	
K51	ML1	L&MR Lion o/f 0-4-2	9/1978	1986	
K52	ML2	LNWR Problem Class 2-2-2	9/1978	1986	
K53	ML3	LSWR Falcon Class 2-4-0	9/1978	1986	
K54	L39	LMS/BR Fowler Dock tank 0-6-0T	by 1/1979	1986	
K55	L44	GNR/LNER/BR J3 0-6-0	9/1979	1986	
K56	L45	TVR/GWR S class 0-4-0ST	1/1980	1986	

Text Reference	Actual Reference	Description	New Date	Withdrawal Date	Notes
K57	L43	BR (WR) 15xx 0-6-0PT	3/1980	1986	
K58	ML4	Metropolitan/LT 4-4-0T	4/1980	1986	
K59	ML5	GWR Dean Single 3031 class o/f 4-2-2	4/1980	1986	
K60	L46	LMS/BR Duchess 4-6-2	10/1981	1986	
K61	L47	LMS/BR Stanier 8F 2-8-0	10/1981	1986	
K62	L48	LMS/BR Stanier Streamlined _Coronation_ 4-6-2	10-12/1981	1986	
K63	ML6	GWR Broad Gauge _Rover_ class o/f 4-2-2	11/1981	1986	
K64	L49	BR Bulleid Rebuilt Merchant Navy 4-6-2	8/1983	1986	
K65	GK49	BR Bulleid Rebuilt Merchant Navy 4-6-2	8/1983	1986	
K66	L50	SR/BR _Lord Nelson_ 4-6-0	4/1984	1986	
K67	ML7	GWR _Armstrong_ o/f 4-4-0	6/1985	1986	
K68	L51	LNER original P2 2-8-2	10/1985	1986	

Notes:

1. 1986 is the assumed cessation of Banbury production;

2. The K's numbering system was not adopted until the K's 70 Series catalogue. Its use after that involved a few modifications noted in the table. It still forms the basis of the Nu-Cast listing in 1999.

K's Catalogues Table

Date	Cover	Price	Notes
1962	Light grey and blue	1/-	Claims to be the first
late 1962 / early 1963	Red and white	1/-	63xx added
late 1963	Deep blue and white	1/-	
late 1964	Orange	1/-	Reported in MRN 11.64 ad
late 1965	Brown and cream	1/-	Adams Radial latest kit
circa 6/1967	Yellow and white	1/-	Reported in MRN 7.67 ad
late 1967 or early 1968	Blue and white	1/-	GWR 1361 latest kit
1971	K's 70s Series orange logo	30p	Reported in RM 4.71 ad
1/1972	K's 70s Series orange logo	n/k	Has 4pp supplement bound in
1976	Green A4 landscape	60p	Reported 7.76
1978	As above with 2nd Edition	75p	Advertised by K's 5.78
1982	Black on white	Unpriced	UK outline models folder
1982	Black on white	Unpriced	Continental outline folder

A Note on Catalogues
A good number were produced and I have yet to find one that is unambiguously dated. The range was also thoroughly listed in W&H Catalogues which appeared to use the K's L series numbers. A number of full range list adverts were published. These occur in the *Model Railway News* in the range's earlier years and most helpfully two different in the *Railway Modeller* for June and July 1985.

Further Acknowledgements

Those that deserve particular mention and have not otherwise been quoted include the authors of the range of obituary notices for "Pop" Keyser in the September 1966 trade press, and that written by Donald Mackay for Ken Keyser in *Model Railway Journal* 37 in 1990. Very detailed assistance came from Mike Griffiths at Autocom (UK) Ltd. Help from Messrs Fleetwood Shawe, Nick Gillman and Alan Cliff is also appreciated.

(right) An assortment of K's packaging; the oldest to the bottom, the newest to the top

Photo: Tony Wright, courtesy Nick Gillman

Nu-Cast

Nu-Cast has been a name familiar to railway modellers since 1971, and for most of that time the name has been synonymous with one of the leaders in loco kit manufacture. The genre is essentially that of the cast kit, although etching techniques have not been ignored, especially in the hands of recent owners and in respect to chassis design. In 1999 the name remains very much alive in the capable hands of Mike Griffiths, and Autocom's ownership at Andover. Otherwise the story is essentially that of Bill Stott's Hartlepool enterprise with a confused Lincolnshire interlude between 1988 and 1993.

The story actually originates in a retail shop started by Stott in 1969. It also involves four other one-time independent ranges. R&J will be the most obscure, but all of Cotswold, Stephen Poole and K's were once household names to the railway modeller. K's was such a substantial player over a long period that it has warranted a separate chapter outlining its own history through to its arrival in Lincolnshire. Their kits will only be discussed in any detail from that point forward in this chapter. The other three names are discussed in this chapter and the opportunity to consider them in more depth herein will be taken.

In the mid-1960s Bill Stott was in his late twenties and working as a Salvation Army officer. Following this vocation, he had moved from Brixham to Shotton, County Durham. He was a model railway enthusiast who started doing the rounds of local exhibitions and quickly made friends. From these contacts he began to do a bit of part-time trading. Small ads began to appear; there is one such in the April 1968 Modeller. At around this time, Bill ceased to work for the Salvation Army - time no longer allowed both careers to function. Bill did not lose his allegiance and many years later would resume work for the Salvation Army.

The tale really starts with a 1/16th page display advert in the January 1969 *Railway Modeller*. This launched a concern called Nu-sto Scale Models which was the face for Bill Stott's trading name. The core of what was afoot was the willingness to build any stock from N to Gauge 1, and specifically to seek support for something called the Super 'P' Plan ('P' for pre-grouping). Here lies perhaps the first surprise in the Nu-Cast story - before Nu-Cast there was Nu-sto, and Nu-sto offers us handbuilt batches of Bill Stott's enterprises. There is a parallel here to the formation of the K's range. In this case, the ancestors to the Nu-Cast kits were better advertised and it will be possible to slot them into the account and tables. The initial member was the NER/LNER N10 0-6-2T which featured from that first advert. By April 1969, six pre-grouping prototypes in assorted liveries were being advertised. Prices had been reduced and a welcome

for the new range was claimed.

April 1969 further marked the appearance of what can be called the "shop" element. Hours at which callers were welcomed were given and a considerable range of materials, rolling stock and books made its appearance. Nu-sto was clearly well in business, and in the succeeding months further additions to the handbuilt range were in evidence. Business must quite simply have been booming. In July 1969's advert two more milestones were reached. For the first time, reference to a Q6 model in the handbuilt series was made, a prototype that would become the first landmark in the kit range. Additionally, Bill had outgrown his home, and from the 30th June a shop was opened in Horden.

Thinking of these places at any time over the last 30 years excites something of an intake of breath at the prospect of their fostering of successful model railway manufacture. Peterlee, Blackhall, Horden and Hartlepool all formed the backdrop for operations until 1988 - this was industrial East Durham. Blackhall and Horden had pits, Hartlepool its docks and a steelworks. As time passed, the area went into rapid decline and the idea that moneyed customers could abound might seem strange. Against which in 1969, the area had yet to enter that steep decline, property was never going to be expensive and the engineering base of the area would likely both throw up potential customers and offer access to suitable skills.

One can sense then that Stott was proud and optimistic when he advertised "A New Model Railway Shop in the North East". He must have become inundated with economic activity, and that September advised customers that no more orders for the Super 'P' Plan series could be accepted due to "heavy demand......and a temporary shortage of major parts". Bill had caught up with himself by December and was soliciting further orders in his first half-page advert, and handbuilt buses and lorries made their appearance at that point.

Nonetheless, from now on the Super 'P' Plan series receded into the background. Running a shop set its own agenda and required a further move from the 25th August 1970 into Hartlepool. Having settled in here, the idea that the demand for the sorts of prototypes encompassed by the Super 'P' Plan models could be better met with a series of kits was ripe to be explored.

It seems likely that the handbuilt locos having proved a demand had yet created their own problems of production which investment in a casting machine could circumvent. More product at less cost would encourage an already interested market. Whether any of the NER

0-8-0s actually appeared as Super 'P' Plan models is not yet known, but at the turn of 1971-72 a cast kit for the Q6 was released. This was still done under the Nu-sto label, but at release the sub-brand Nu-Cast appeared. The pace after this was still quite leisurely.

At the end of 1974, only three further locos had appeared, but during 1975 four new kits were released, following which over a decade of hectic activity took place at Hartlepool. A significant factor in the expansion was the realisation that the kit enterprise required to be separated from the retail shop. It seems likely that the key point in that process was reflected in the March 1974 Modeller advert, wherein Nu-Cast Model Engineering appeared as a free standing enterprise now located at Brook Street in Hartlepool. Nu-sto Scale Models carried on as a retail venture at Murray Street for a number of years thereafter. Meanwhile Nu-Cast did not stay at Brook Street very long; after 15 months they had shifted to 189 Park Road, where they settled down.

That growing pace was emphasised in December 1977 with the acquisition of the Stephen Poole 4mm range. The Summer of 1981 marked the take-over of the Cotswold range. With that, far more than just loco kits was on offer. Cotswold brought buses and wagons, and Nu-Cast itself was responsible for more wagons and other road vehicles. The extensive Auto-Replica range of car kits was part of Nu-Cast in 1979. The take-over probably prompted the further move in the Spring of 1982 within Hartlepool. This varied picture to the releases carried on through the 1980s, but as the decade passed undercurrents of difficulty could be discerned. Some of the locos proved a mighty long wait to arrive.

August 1986 marked the last new introductions to the 4mm loco kit range. At that time the company claimed the biggest and best loco kit range available. That was surely debatable even then? Etching had been quite considerably adopted in chassis and valve gear throughout the 1980s, but the market and tastes were changing. By this stage most kits had, in addition to the brass chassis, a Romford wheel and gear pack which accounts for the frequently seen WNC prefix. One can sense the management casting around for new ideas. One of two N gauge prototypes, for the J26, appeared in December 1986. Investment continued to be made, notably in a major move to a plush factory unit at Blackhall, north of Hartlepool in the Summer of 1987. A view of this is that money spent on the business ambience is not always as effective as that spent on the core. Certainly despite the move, new ideas seemed to dry up.

During late 1986 and in 1987, for the first time in many years, there were occasions when there was no Modeller advert. Behind the scenes activity continued; even, as yet unconfirmed, the possibility that the K's range was purchased by Stott and the stock and tools transferred to Blackhall. A contemporary report of that is not known, but what is certain is that 1988 marked a seachange with the arrival of Brian Emberton's HMC group.

Moves South

The landmark in terms of adverts was reached in December 1988 with an advert headed Nu-Cast Model Engineering Ltd (Sales) from Spilsby in Lincolnshire. HMC has previously been discussed under the K's heading. A lot is unclear about the succeeding years until 1993 but in this period stocks were certainly advertised and an amount of new manufacture was undertaken. There were a lot of problems, and it seems that both technical and marketing expertise to make the most of the product was not available. The period surrounding the Lincolnshire move was quite chaotic, and not all the Nu-Cast elements would ultimately move all the way to Autocom. ABS as Adrian Swain, who had already been involved in design work for Nu-Cast, took the ranges of wagons and the Wickham trolley in 1992.

Matters changed in 1993 when Autocom became involved and the whole assemblage once again moved, this time to Andover. Judged by the regular advert in the Modeller and by the reports from owners of the kits, business since then has been far more positive. Both core ranges, the old Nu-Cast and the one-time K's have been thoroughly integrated. A steady programme of upgrading has been carried out and this will be detailed under each individual kit. Much of this has revolved around a new chassis specification, first detailed under loco NU052 in the text. Autocom's specification has been to include all components (generally using Romford wheels) except for motor, gears and paints and transfers. There seems every chance that the respected name of Nu-Cast will be alive in the world of model railways for many years to come. There remains one obvious question: when will a wholly new kit be released? Nothing in that category has appeared since August 1986 and the GWR Halls.

A Note on Stephen Poole

Stephen Poole was advertising from Ongar by February 1970. In April 1970, with some parallels to Nu-sto's own activity, he was soliciting interest in a proposed group of four batch-built locos. Only one of those is confirmed in this form which was for the LNER N2 available by that October. This was translated to kit form soon after and although other batch-built locos existed (such as an N7 which may simply have been assembled Wills kits), 1971 really marked Poole's arrival in the whitemetal kit market. A series of locos followed whose Poole history will be fully detailed under their individual entries. His pre-grouping GER prototypes attracted considerable applause, as did his own range of wheels.

Business increased such that company status came about towards the end of 1972. Poole went on to be a pioneer of a new commercial scale: O/16.5 - this was with the Glyn Valley Tramway *Sir Theodore* loco in 1975. Why Poole then decided to pull out is not known, but 1977 marked the dismantling of the range. The O/16.5 models were sold to Peco and still feature in their Great Little Trains series. The 4mm scale

(above, left) January 1969 *Railway Modeller* Nu-Sto Scale Advert promoting the Super 'P' Plan of handbuilt locos

(above, right) Original Bill Stott *Railway Modeller* April 1968 small ad

(right) An R&J advert taken from *Model Railway Constructor* from May 1971 showing the Jinty and Aspinall 2-4-2T as available

(below) Nu-Cast *Railway Modeller* April 1983 advert showing an interest in Southdown's Queen Mary double deck bus along side railway matters

loco kits went to Nu-Cast, a moment noted in the latter's December 1977 advert. To appreciate Poole's range at its most extensive, the W&H 1977 catalogue provides a good reference to both the scales in which he then worked. There were then six OO locos, with a further two for Sharp Stewart 2-4-0 and 0-6-0 prototypes planned for 1977. These did not materialise either with Poole or Nu-Cast. That W&H catalogue is the source for the SP series references that we quote.

A Note on Cotswold

June 1981 marked the moment when Nu-Cast swallowed whole the "Cotswold" range of what was then Sutherland Model Casters Ltd. For their roots we need to return to May 1968. By then Cotswold Scale Models was active from 4 Walk Mill Lane, Kingswood, Wotton-under-Edge. The provision of finished kitbuilt locos and rolling stock was being advertised for which a first catalogue existed later in 1968. The tail-end of that year is likely to have marked the transition to company status as "Cotswold Model Engineering".

The year of 1969 saw substantial progress made with the provision of the company's own products, and their very first whitemetal kit appeared that year. Appropriately, since the Cotswold range would always offer a substantial list of road vehicles, this was for the 1933 Scammell mechanical horse and trailer. It is thought that the first Cotswold locomotive was released the same year; certainly a handbuilt exclusive for a GWR 28xx was advertised, although absolute confirmation that some examples actually materialised is sought. At the tail end of the year, a range of lost wax brass fittings was released.

During 1970 three bus kits were released and this paved the way for the further progress that was made in 1971. The first bus prototypes were the Bristol LS, Seddon Pennine RU and Harrington Grenadier coach. Early in 1971 Cotswold announced plans for their own first loco kit for a GWR Manor that proved stillborn.

Meanwhile, Cotswold had moved within Wotton-Under-Edge to 3 Orchard Walk, Kingswood, but not for long, as the May 1971 advert announced a move into Bristol to 14 Lilymead Avenue. This maintained a semi-domestic operation. The Orchard Walk address was also used by Westward Scale Models in early 1971; some linkages need unpicking because in the years to come Westward and Cotswold evolved into very different operations.

The move to Bristol prepared the way for a major step that was advertised from September. Cotswold took over the range of R&J Supplies, and so acquired their first loco model kits. R&J had started with an LMS Jinty only the previous year (see the loco narrative for more details). Expansion now started on several fronts embracing the buses, the locos, and general accessories including N gauge.

The first entirely Cotswold originated item of rolling stock was a Hawksworth tender kit in 1972. As work progressed with the locos, the kits were noted for their solid brass milled chassis. These may have lacked the scale detail we now take for granted but they were considerably more effective than the cast type usually the norm in the early 1970s.

A rare and key source for what then happened in the mid-1970s is provided by a company profile in the October 1975 Constructor. At that point, Ron Charlton was the proprietor (as he was from the outset) and by the end of 1973 had identified a pressing need to expand in a cost-effective manner. A combination of a family holiday and the H.I.D.B. grant packages suggested a move to Bonar Bridge in Sutherland. This took place in March 1975 and so was born Sutherland Model Casters, bringing together Cotswold and Western Precision Castings. The contemporary well-known Pirate range of road vehicles joined the brand too. Also involved in the move to Scotland was one Michael Sheppard, a well-known modeller. Staff were taken on and it all looked very rosy.

More and more buses and locomotives followed, the design of many of these was in the hands of Michael Sheppard. A gentleman called Tony Reynald was a patternmaker for some and attracted praise for his body casting work, even in 1993 when the milled brass chassis were decidedly past their sell-by dates. Rob Hamp is credited with the patternmaking of many of the earlier models, in total about half the range. He undertook similar work for M&L, Millholme and Centre Models. Some glossy catalogues were a feature from the Sutherland period. Known examples have been dated to October 1976 and 1978 when 4mm scale railway wagons appeared. Slater's were a Cotswold distributor and the range can be found in their lists.

Whether it was the national recession or whether it was the imaginable difficulties of working in a location so isolated from the rest of the model railway fraternity I do not know, but the move was not the long term success that had been hoped for. In all events, in June 1981 Cotswold and associated ranges were transferred to Nu-Cast and Bill Stott. This brought 26 loco kits into the Nu-Cast range.

The Loco Kits

NU001 Nu-sto Super P Plan NER/LNER/BR N10 0-6-2T

As previously noted, paradoxically, the first entries are not kits at all and do not even bear the Nu-Cast brand. However, any dedicated collector of Nu-Cast is bound to be captured by the idea that the first models in the family tree were handbuilt exclusives in brass and nickel silver, and will want to know what evidence is available. Unfortunately, there is a lot we do not know. Basic quantities for each model are not recorded. Elements of their construction such as wheel standards and motors are unknown, neither is packaging recorded (if any actually existed). Exactly who made the models is a mystery, but it was definitely not Bill Stott himself. There may even be doubt that some exist. The liveries offered were clearly advertised, and it seems likely that the eight prototypes detailed below do form the sum of what was offered.

The very first model was certainly produced and was advertised between January and April 1969. Three finishes were priced - unpainted, NER lined green at £22/9/6, and LNER lined black. BR liveries were never cited as an option on any of these models. The prototypes were a tank version of the J25, and examples were in traffic between 1902-62. The older N8 and N9 prototypes would form the subject of subsequent Nu-Cast kits.

NU002 Nu-sto Super P Plan CR/LMS/BR McIntosh 0-6-0

Second in this group was an 0-6-0 announced in the February 1969 Modeller, and advertised over the next three issues. Its three liveries were cited as unpainted, LMS lined black and CR lined black. I have no doubts that this model existed, but cannot confirm the exact prototype. That is because McIntosh was responsible for four such designs amongst which the 812 or Jumbos were probably the best known. If the black as opposed to CR blue livery was correctly applied, then it is highly likely that the model was either of the 812 or 652 class whose main difference was details of cab design.

NU003 Nu-sto Super P Plan GNR/LNER C1 4-4-2

The glamour of the Atlantic now grasped Stott. Models of this wheel arrangement have never been over-abundant - in the 1920s there were a few ready-to-run O gauge tinplate models, but by 1999 there has not been one 4mm scale ready-to-run model mass-produced. Whilst a number of kits have been released since the 1970s, when Stott offered these handbuilts, there was a real hole in the market to fill. Orders were first solicited for Ivatt's large Atlantic, and the generally similar Marsh LBSCR design, in March and April 1969. Production delays and sheer demand are known to have delayed these models but both certainly appeared, and were again advertised in December 1969. A further batch of the GNR models were advertised in April 1970. At the outset the three liveries quoted for the GNR design were unpainted, LNER lined green and GNR lined green.

NU004 Nu-sto Super P Plan LBSCR/SR/BR H1/H2 4-4-2

Elements of the LBSCR Atlantic's story have been noted above during the GNR version's account. What should be added is that the initial advert just quoted the H2 design. In the second advert the H1 was added so covering both LBSCR prototypes. In the December advert only the H2 was quoted. One can be certain that some models (probably of the H2 exist), the jury on the H1 must presently be out. As far as livery was concerned, the trio was unpainted, SR lined green (which?) and LBSCR umber. In what was probably one of the last adverts by Nu-sto for any of these exclusives, an H2 was seeking a home in November 1972's Modeller.

NU005 Nu-sto Super P Plan GWR De Glehn Large Atlantic 4-4-2

Four months into the programme and the GWR made a first appearance as "Coming Soon". A large De Glehn was to be available in unpainted or GWR lined green finishes. This would have enabled a model of either 103 *President* or 104 *Alliance* to have been bought. In June the model moved into the "Available Now" category, from which we must assume some existed. The model was then advertised throughout the Summer.

NU006 Nu-sto Super P Plan GER/LNER/BR F3 2-4-2T

Some quite contrasting models were offered in this programme. The second and final tank engine in the series took Holden's 1893 design of which 50 were built for the Great Eastern. The model was announced in April and orders were solicited through the Summer, but an advert confirming that the model was made is still sought. The three intended finishes were unpainted, LNER lined black and GER lined blue. Years later a cast kit for the Worsdell designed F4 was produced.

NU007 Nu-sto Super P Plan LNWR/LMS/BR G2 0-8-0

The two final additions to the planned Super 'P' range were announced in May 1969. The LNWR heavy goods engine would have been in unpainted and LMS or LNWR lined black finishes. Like its partner, I am not yet certain any appeared.

NU008 Nu-sto Super P Plan NER/LNER/BR Q5/Q6 0-8-0

The second 0-8-0 prototype would have been popular in Nu-Cast's local patch. Three liveries were proposed - unpainted, LNER lined black, and NER lined green. The initial adverts specified a Q5, but in July the Q6 was added to the proposal. Otherwise there are no other adverts known to me, and no confirmation that any of these LNWR or NER 0-8-0s appeared. The Q5 was Worsdell's predecessor to Raven's Q6, and it would be with a cast kit model of the latter that the headlines would next be made.

NU009/NC101 NER/LNER/BR Q6 0-8-0

By the middle of 1971, the Nu-sto advert was an established part of the Modeller. June had two key lines tucked in amongst all the retail activity. Some Nu-sto castings were already available and an LNER double chimney was being listed after which a bare "Coming Soon" advert announced the Q6 loco kit. Truly the palette was being titillated. In the surrounding pages a concern called Cotswold was doing the same by proposing a Manor kit that would be stillborn, whilst Stephen Poole was on to loco kit number three. No one could have foreseen how these names from three diverse parts of Britain would one day be brought together.

Back with the Q6, release seems to have occurred for the December advert wherein the idea that the next three kits would follow was floated. The name Nu-Cast now appeared but firmly within the Nu-sto fold. Reviews followed in the Modeller and Constructor for May 1972. A typical whitemetal kit of the period was furnished - the package was complete bar wheels and motor. As a first introduction from a new concern in the field, the Constructor welcomed and praised it, which with their impartial and detailed reputation, made for a good start. On the strength of these reviews strong half page illustrated adverts pushed both the Q6 and the Nu-Cast brand that Summer. Nu-Cast Model Engineering had arrived.

Demand for this engine, so typical of the North East and in service until 1967, proved strong and has remained so ever since. The initial model had coupling rods and motion noted as providing "detailed coupling rod knuckle-joints and oilboxes", but what where they made from? By the 1977 catalogue the specification across the kits referred to the motion as "chemically etched in nickel silver". The allocation of the number series NC101 did not take place at the outset but had occurred by late 1973. During the mid-1980s most Nu-Cast engines received brass chassis; a pricelist for July 1986 reveals that that process had been nearly completed for all examples. Two of the locos that had not then been upgraded were the Q6 and the B1 and each were then noted as withdrawn. The Q6 does appear to have been manufactured at Spilsby and was so advertised in March 1991 having by then gained an etched chassis. It was certainly an early candidate for release under Autocom, being advertised from March 1994.

NU010/NC102 LNER/BR B1 4-6-0

Despite the praise, something of a wait followed before the next release, notwithstanding that it was likely to be a popular choice, and so it proved. Edward Thompson's simple two cylinder B1 design of 1942 was quite a contrast to the Gresley LNER ancestry. Thompson was a Darlington man, and in some respects the B1 was more in the lineage of the NER than the GNR. In the conditions of war and post-war austerity, the design was practical and remained not unattractive. Some 410 were built and two are preserved. The locos in the early 1970s would have been widely remembered and filled a clear modelling need. Other models did already exist and more would follow, notably the Replica / Bachmann ready-to-run example after 1988. For 15 years, however, Nu-Cast offered the most accessible 4mm scale route to running the engine.

From as early as December 1971, the Nu-Cast adverts flagged that the B1 was on the agenda. At that time the other intended companions were to be a J27 and the Gresley 2-6-2T. Both appeared but not in such a neat order. However, the B1 was the next release, being given its launch in the January 1973 advert. Reviews followed in the Modeller for May and the Constructor for September. Once again the latter was particularly praiseworthy - it lauded the valve gear without actually revealing whether this early release had etched gear at the outset. To 1990s' eyes the cast chassis looks incredibly crude. But in the 1970s, the reviewer was fundamentally impressed by the kit's design which "will literally drop together". The kit was complete bar motor, wheels and paint. In the Modeller the valve gear was stated to be "nickel silver strip and rail, with cast knuckle joint detail". That probably describes the specification for all the early releases. Chemically etched nickel silver valve gear was specified by January 1976 across the range. Unusually, the Modeller found more to be critical about - specifically not liking the unbushed cast chassis, suggesting that would be a recipe for undue wear. A key element of the model was the generation of a straight-sided LNER group standard 4,200 gallon tender. This was an item which would be used with other models such as the V2.

At differing times Nu-Cast indicated a willingness to supply their kits ready finished and painted. The B1 was so advertised with a batch in December 1973. Incidentally, the NC numbering system started thereabouts with the B1 described as NC102. Subsequently the model became something of a showpiece for the range - an unpainted example having featured in early adverts such as June 1973, and a fully finished one graced later adverts such as April 1979, the example being number 1036.

The first 40 of the class were named after South African antelopes. Atypically, 1036 seemed to break that rule being called *Ralph Assheton*. Only a little later, in December 1979, the example in the advertisements changed to 1145, suggesting some throughput of finished locos at Nu-Cast. A few months later in 1980 the model reached a new height of approbation when Airfix used an example as the mock-up for what was their intended RTR model. Nu-Cast themselves commented on this use in their June 1980 advert. They were probably pleased however when the economic conditions delayed that project for many years.

According to the adverts at the time, the kit was rested around 1982-84, and was welcomed back in late 1984. A December 1984 advert showed 1016 *Inyala* and spoke of a limited quantity only. By this time a combination of popularity and age (resulting in the moulds becoming worn out) are likely to have taken their toll. After a while the model was again made unavailable, resurfacing in November 1987. In what was one of the last initiatives from Hartlepool, Nu-Cast hailed "Welcome, The Return of the *Antelope*". The model was "beautifully cast from a completely brand new set of moulds". That said, the image beside did not hint at any radical changes. The chassis still looked bare, though by now an etched brass chassis was in use. The model was liveried for 1016. No evidence of production in Lincolnshire is known, but at Autocom the engine was featured as early as July 1993. Frank Neatherway profiled the kit's assembly in a two-

(top) Nu-Cast NC101 NER/LNER/BR Q6 0-8-0
Photo: Tony Wright, courtesy of Rob Kinsey

(above) Nu-Cast NC102 LNER/BR B1
Photo: Tony Wright, courtesy Tony Wright

(right) Nu-Cast NC103 NER/LNER/BR G5
0-4-4T shown on the right, with Nu-Cast
NC136 LNER/BR V1/V3
Photo: Tony Wright, courtesy Eivis Layout

parter in the *Model Railway News* commencing in March 1984.

NU011/NC103 NER/LNER/BR G5 0-4-4T

The third release had not been featured in the list initially planned in December 1971 and so jumped the queue. Indeed gestation may have been rapid, first intimation appears in the August 1973 advert, and soon afterwards a release date of 1st November 1973 was quoted. The subject was the standard Worsdell design of NER 0-4-4T with 110 examples spanning the period 1894-1958.

I am not too sure if the scheduled release date was achieved, but reviews followed in the Modeller for September 1974 and the Constructor for December 1974. This was a relatively simple kit, albeit with careful balancing required for the chassis whose bearings remained unbushed whitemetal. All these early kits had two-piece boilers. Alternative fittings were included which enabled the early cased safety valves or the later Ross Pops, and the low or raised bunker to be fitted.

At some point before 1986 a brass chassis was substituted. It is known that there was a new production of the kit at Spilsby around 1991/92, and that from March 1994 it featured in the Autocom advert.

NU012/NC104 LNER/BR V2 2-6-2

Along with the B1, the V2 came to symbolise the best that was in the new range, and has remained an enduring favourite. The Gresley designed prototypes had excited enthusiasm, and like the B1 any ready-to-run model apart from this kit was a long time coming. From March 1974 Nu-Cast's advert announced the model, and release seems to have been that December. That advert announced a "scale chassis and etched valve gear" - the first to do so. Surprisingly, another cast model appeared at almost the same time. Bristol Model's V2 was reviewed in the Modeller in February 1975, Nu-Cast's waited until August. The former company seemed adept at parallel introductions and brought out a B1 early in 1975 too.

In the review of the Nu-Cast V2 model, the etched valve gear fret was an illustrated and prominent feature. Nu-Cast provided the straight sided LNER standard tender as in the B1 kit. Some engines were paired with the flared-sided version; this was available in the Nu-Cast range with the O2/3 model and so such a pairing could be arranged.

In another parallel to the B1, the kit was used by a RTR manufacturer to represent a new model that proved stillborn. In this case it was Lima's V2 around 1980, leaving Nu-Cast with another 11 years free from ready-to-run competition. Shortly before that sea change, Tony Wright assessed the Nu-Cast kit in the Modeller in February 1991. Having made four, he was quite positive in his judgements, though improvement was certainly possible, and he also noted that a

detail of the conjugated valve guides does denote an early prototype. By the time he wrote, the cast chassis had given way to an etched chassis which was a definite plus point. Later that year, the kit was advertised from Spilsby as newly made, whilst at Autocom it first made an appearance in August 1994. Taking note of that development, Wright again looked at the kit in *British Railway Modelling* for November 1994. By that time he had built six and still admired it. A telling picture showed the old cast chassis against a state-of-the-art Branchlines etched chassis - a product designed to replace the Nu-Cast offering at extra cost.

NU013/NC103B NER/LNER/BR N8/N9/N10 0-6-2T

Shortly after the V2 arrived, some deft design work provided a further kit. Back in August 1973 when the G5 was first announced, the typical Worsdell 0-6-2T was also flagged up. When this was released in March 1975, Nu-Cast had created a variant of the G5 kit by removing the chassis elements, adding a pony truck and an assortment of adapting bits. By using a standard Hornby Railways Jinty chassis, any of classes N8/N9/N10 could be modelled. That at least is how Nu-Cast presented it. Things must have been a bit more complicated - the N10 had 6" smaller drivers than the other two classes, and numbers of N9 had extended smokeboxes which the G5 kit would not have provided. After eleven years this kit was replaced by a full kit for N8/N9 (which is referenced NU084).

NU014/NC105 NER/LNER/BR J21 0-6-0

Worsdell of the NER produced a series of 0-6-0 designs which the LNER classified J21 and J24-27. Almost from the outset Nu-Cast had suggested that the J27 would be released at some stage. It was, however, the smallest and oldest of the series that arrived first - the J21. The J26/J27 would be the next release, and the J25 would appear much later, but the J24 was not covered by Nu-Cast at all.

The J21 was originally announced in the November 1974 Modeller advert, and release took place for the following April. A Modeller review was in the September issue, and in a year when four kits were released, it can be remembered that the Stockton and Darlington Railway 150th celebrations probably contributed their own weight to Nu-Cast's growing momentum.

The prototype engines had a complicated life. Most started life as compounds in NER class C. By the time the LNER inherited the 201 members, all were operating as simples in NER class C1. The final example was withdrawn in the early 1960s, and the former BR 65033 is now part of the Beamish collection. The kit was cleverly designed to make the most of these varieties with various alternative parts such as smokeboxes to distinguish between unsuperheated and superheated examples. The kit was apparently produced at Spilsby, and was in the Autocom list by May 1993.

(above) Nu-Cast NC104 LNER/BR V2

Photo: Tony Wright, courtesy Tony Wright

**(below) Nu-Cast NC117 NER/LNER/BR J26/J27 built
as a J27 with pre-1946 LNER number**

Photo: Richard Sawyer, courtesy Railway Modeller

NU015/NC116 NER/LNER/BR J26/J27 0-6-0

Possibly more popular than the J21 was the larger pair of classes J26 and J27, which were closely related to each other. By surviving to the bitter end of North Eastern steam in 1967, fame came their way and the memory is kept alive by the surviving NELPG example. Nu-Cast had promised a kit as far back as December 1971, and finally release with many apologies was achieved with a series of adverts from August 1975. Nu-Cast were in the throes of moving that Autumn - does that account for the much delayed Modeller review which did not appear until December 1977?

The next incident of note was the application of the brass chassis which had occurred by 1986. Although advertised at Spilsby, it is thought that was of old stock. It was present in the first Autocom advert in May 1993. Over the years the kits had to live with many potential motor changes, because Nu-Cast never offered their own motor. The J26 kit was designed around the K's Mk II motor, and that product very soon disappeared - a small amount of bodging to fit the new K's HP2M was therefore recommended by the Modeller. Nu-Cast themselves acted to solve the problem in November 1977 by advertising an adapter to enable the new motor to be fitted into kits designed around the Mk II. By 1986 Nu-Cast were themselves recommending the Anchoridge DS10 or a gearbox-type motor.

NU016/NC111 GNR/LNER/BR K2 2-6-0

In May 1975, one model from that far-off advert of December 1971 was left outstanding. The Gresley 2-6-2T was not mentioned in the May 1975 advert, and would demand another nine years of customer patience. However, this advert did announce seven additions to the Nu-Cast programme. Three of them would never materialise, but the first, for the Gresley designed GNR K2 Mogul of 1913, did by Christmas that year. No review has yet been traced, but in line with now established Nu-Cast practice, choice was built into the release. Two different cabs were provided in order that the as-built 1640 and sisters, or the post-1925 amendment with a side window cab in which guise a number operated in Scotland, could be modelled. Named after Lochs these engines were much associated with the West Highland.

Nu-Cast's own adverts illustrated a variety of engines including GNR 1670, LNER 1732 and BR 61764. The latter two appeared in adverts in February 1986 when it would appear that Nu-Cast had recently re-run the model after a period of unavailability. Subsequently, it has featured at Autocom since June 1993.

NU017/NC151 LSWR/SR/BR Jubilee 0-4-2

The March 1974 Modeller advert first revealed the Adams Jubilee (after the 1887 Jubilee in the year of their origin) to be "coming soon". This might have seemed something of a surprise but bearing in mind Stott's Southern antecedents, logic was apparent. In his mind's eye (revealed by the referencing) this was the first of a Southern series. Development was lengthy, perhaps partly because an 0-4-2 chassis is a classically challenging concept. The adverts heralded a number of false dawns, but September 1976 would seem to be the real release date, and the Modeller reviewed the engine in August 1977. As with the J26, this was a kit designed around the K's Mk II motor which became obsolete almost as the model appeared. The chassis was upgraded to brass by 1986. Around from as early as June 1993 at Autocom, this model has largely had the field to itself in the provision of this typical Southern prototype in 4mm.

NU018/NC117 NER/LNER/BR Y7 0-4-0T

Ultimately the Nu-Cast range would end up with two models of the largely similar ex-NER Y7 and Y8 0-4-0Ts; the Hartlepool spun engines being the Y7 and the slightly larger design of the two. Two of these Y7s are preserved but regrettably there are no Y8s left.

The Y7 model has been a bit shy at Nu-Cast - it appeared with the minimum of preliminary fuss in November 1976, and no review has yet been traced. The kit could be finished with an open backed cab; by BR times some had gained a closed cab but the kit does not allow this.

In February 1987 it was specifically cited as being withdrawn (even though by then it had a brass chassis), but by November 1988 it was in stock at Spilsby - so these withdrawals may not mean too much. First appearance in an Autocom advert was in April 1994.

NU019/NC118 GCR/LNER/BR C13 4-4-2T

There may have been forty of these Great Central 4-4-2T current between 1903 and 1960, but they have not been widely modelled. This gives importance to the Nu-Cast kit which was announced in January 1976, and arrived with the Y7 that November. Like the Y7 no review has yet been traced. There was an announcement that the kit was being withdrawn in August 1985, but indicating how effective that evidence is, the July 1986 pricelist clearly priced it and indicated that it had a brass chassis. The gap MAY actually account for that change. March 1991 saw it being produced from Spilsby, and August 1993 marked its first appearance at Autocom.

NU020/NC112 GNR/LNER/BR 02/2 2-8-0

NU021/NC113 LNER/BR 02/3 2-8-0

The origins of the kit for the second of Gresley's Great Northern 2-8-0 designs can be traced back as far as May 1975 when the Modeller advert first intimated its appearance. About two and a half years later, it appeared with the release advert dated to December 1977. Again no

(above) Nu-Cast NC111 GNR/LNER/BR K2 built with a GNR cab and on a scratchbuilt chassis

Photo: Tony Wright, courtesy Tony Wright

(right) Nu-Cast Hartlepool production NC151 LSWR/SR/BR Jubilee 0-4-2 in major component parts and showing original packaging

Photo: Tony Wright, courtesy Les Spratt

(below) Nu-Cast NC113 LNER/BR O2/3 2-8-0, with scratchbuilt straight-sided standard tender

Photo: Tony Wright, courtesy Tony Wright

review has yet been found. This was actually a momentous time at Nu-Cast because the same advert announced the Stephen Poole take-over, and relatively little attention appears to have been given to the newcomer as a result.

It is highly likely that both the O2/2 and O2/3 were released at the same time, and both were referenced in the 1977 catalogue. The difference between the two models lies in the cab and the tender - clearly shown by Nu-Cast's own advert in the December 1979 Modeller. The original GN design built between 1918-24 was represented by NC112. When more were built after 1932, the standard LNER 4,200 gallon flare sided tender and side windowed cab were substituted to create NC113. On the kit, there was a brass chassis by 1986, and it featured in the Autocom list from May 1993.

NU022/NC251/SP3 GWR/BR 54xx 0-6-0PT

"Back Again" said Nu-Cast's December 1977 advert alongside a picture of 6412, and with that the news that Nu-Cast had acquired Stephen Poole's 4mm range was broken. A note earlier has outlined Poole's history, and as the locos are encountered, their complete history will be narrated. Collett produced three designs of "small pannier" for the Great Western which Poole modelled with one kit. The 64xx and 74xx were almost identical save that the latter were not motor fitted for push-pull working, but both had 4'7½" drivers. The slightly earlier motor fitted 54xx had 5'2" wheels. Poole announced in May 1973 that a body kit for the three classes to go with existing Poole brass frames would soon be available. The body kit seems to have been released that Summer with an advert and review in the September Modeller. Engraved brass plates for 5401 were provided along with nickel silver handrails and copper pipework. Poole's own wheels could also be purchased.

In July 1975 it was announced that the kit had been repackaged as an "orange label" series kit. This brought together the frames and body kit and was part of a process Poole was then undertaking (more detail on the altered specification of this series is given under the E4). As late as September 1976 Poole placed an advert announcing the "re-release" of all the locos bar the E4, which probably really indicates the completion of this "orange label" series. Just over a year later, the kit joined Nu-Cast.

At some point prior to the 1983 W&H catalogue, the NC251 kit was restricted (at least by description) to a 54xx. I guess this was because wheelsets were now provided, and these were only for the larger wheeled engine. Although illustrated in the 1986 Nu-Cast catalogue as a 54xx, the accompanying price list showed it as withdrawn. It was listed in the March 1991 new production at Spilsby advert and in the February 1994 Autocom adverts. The chassis changed in 1976 from brass to part-cast (see E4). During the Hartlepool period, an etched brass chassis appeared. That chassis is still used, but since the moulds which date from Poole incorporate his casting (and this is not unique), that component

is produced and then slung back into the melting pot. By February 1994, Autocom's list had introduced the NC251Z suffix. This is really used to distinguish the wheelsets that are supplied, it being applied to the small wheeled pair of classes.

NU023/NC121/SP2 GNR/LNER/BR N2 0-6-2T

The second loco to feature in Nu-Cast's adverts from the Poole range had been his first introduction, providing a kit for one of those all-time model favourites, the N2 0-6-2T. April 1970 saw Poole advertising in the Modeller seeking interest in a range of handbuilt locos, one of which was to be the N2. October that year saw the advert announcing the N2's availability for £21/14/9. Two months later and a kit was both advertised and reviewed in the Modeller. The Constructor attended to the model with advert and review in their February 1971 issue.

Whether this was always the strategy to Poole's thinking is not known, but it would seem quite possible that having solicited interest earlier in 1970, the volume of orders received made a conventional handbuilt production unrealistic, and instead justified the casting of components which could then either be sold as a kit or made up for clients. Thereafter the range took a direction considerably different to that originally postulated, with a series of finely crafted whitemetal body kits married to sets of milled brass underframes. Initially each half of the loco was sold separately prior to the advent of the "orange label" series.

From the outset of production of the N2, components were supplied allowing the option of fitting condensing gear. I believe only Ross Pops and not Ramsbottom safety valves (as originally built) were provided, although no confirmation of this has been unearthed. Only the shorter of the two chimney options was included. Fine details included engraved works plates, brass buffers, and nickel silver handrail wire. For those not wishing to build the chassis, with minor modifications the classic Dublo/Wrenn N2 chassis could be used. The quality of Poole's body rather eclipsed the older Dublo/Wrenn product which could barely satisfy a precision modeller.

The kit proceeded to have a complicated life with Poole. Late in 1971, a new batch were produced with rather more in the way of fittings included - such as copper pipework, alternative cab spectacle plates, and lubricators to suit all versions. One advert claimed that the revisions extended to a complete re-tooling. Was that really the case and if so why? Built-up versions continued to be supplied into 1972, and then in November 1973's *Model Railway News* advert Poole announced the production of the "final release of this kit" as a "limited production batch". Well, how often have we heard that before? Certainly that batch appeared and was advertised into the Summer of 1974 in that vein. Whether the packaging carried any "limited release" cachet is unknown.

Of course the kit did re-appear - in the Summer

of 1976. A review took place in the September Modeller. Unlike other "orange label" series kits, there was now no chassis whatsoever. Instead, the model had been altered to accommodate either the Tri-ang Jinty or the Wrenn R1/N2 mechanisms, yet Poole did not provide the required pony truck. Nu-Cast obtained the kit in that state and announced its availability in February 1978, and from that point onwards it seems to have led quite a quiet life. Nu-Cast did note in 1980 its use by Airfix in the preparations for their own N2. The kit was certainly on sale in 1983, although in the 1986 catalogue the July pricelist showed it as withdrawn. There is no Spilsby trace (not even in the usually comprehensive lists around November 1988) but from February 1994 Autocom featured it as a body kit.

NU024/NC110 GCR/LNER/BR A5 4-6-2T

No surprise that 1978 turned into a busy year for Nu-Cast, and the month after the N2 the Modeller advert featured two more models. One of the releases, derived from Nu-Cast's own efforts, being amongst those listed for production back in May 1975 - it was for the 1911 Robinson designed A5 tank. As Nu-Cast would point out, the appeal of the prototype lay in its large engine feel, along with the lack of any complicated outside motion, and over the years they cropped up in many quarters of the LNER. The A5 prototypes existed in two groups; the LNER built 13 in 1925-26 for service on the former NER, which had different boiler fittings to the GCR build. In addition, the first GCR engines . did not have a side window cab.

The model was released with an advert in the March 1978 Modeller. Although no review is to hand, we do know that alternative parts for both the LNER and GCR builds were supplied. These allow both cabs, domes, safety valves and chimneys. Current right through to 1986, and with a brass chassis by then, nothing is known of it at Spilsby save that it was stocked by Crawley in November 1988, and by June 1993 Autocom had released it.

NU025/NC124/SP4 GER Y14/LNER/BR J15 0-6-0

The second of the March 1978 models was one of the pair of Poole creations that really drew attention to his work. These were the GER E4 Intermediate 2-4-0 and the GER Y14/LNER J15 0-6-0. Poole had flagged his intention to model the Y14/J15 back in 1971, and it seems that the kit was on sale in August 1972, with it being reviewed in the Constructor and Modeller that November. Both were impressed with the components which followed the Poole pattern of a body kit and separate brass frame kit. The alternatives provided were considerable, and included three different chimneys, and a set of those prominent GER numberplates.

Such were the possibilities that the related J14 can also be built. This is not often referred to, indeed the prototype is not nearly so well known. It is strange that the older Worsdell

design J15 lasted from 1883-1962 with an example still about today, whilst Holden's newer J14 only managed an existence between 1893-1925. The Autumn of 1976 saw the kit making the transition to the "orange label" series.

Having re-appeared at Nu-Cast by March 1978, the kit seems to have led a straightforward life through to June 1986. At that point, having been unavailable for a while, it was re-released having been "re-tooled to incorporate a number of improvements" including reversion to a brass chassis. The J15 was produced at Spilsby, being so advertised in September 1991. In Autocom's hands it made its re-appearance from August 1993.

NU026/NC152 SR/BR Remembrance N15x 4-6-0

One more month passed and Nu-Cast was releasing an in-house design for a Southern prototype. The plan for the N15x can be traced back to December 1976. The origins of its prototype lie with the famous Brighton Baltic tanks, these appearing from 1914. The last of the post-war batch was number 333 which was turned out in 1922, and as the final engine to be built by the old LBSCR, the management decided to dedicate it as their war memorial engine - a procedure also adopted by the LNWR and GCR. Hence engine 333 became known as *Remembrance*, and the name survived the 1935 transmutation from a Baltic to a 4-6-0. The rebuilding of the seven engines occurred following the electrification of the Brighton line, and they were rebuilt into something with the usefulness of the parallel N15 *King Arthur,* and existed in this state until withdrawal in 1957.

Nu-Cast's publicity always focused on the *Remembrance* link, so making their model unusually specific. The kit release took place without a review yet traced, but with considerable promotion and a reminder that "chemically etched valve gear, full cab and tender interior detail" were supplied. Still current in 1986 having gained a brass chassis, it was stocked at Spilsby in 1988, but it is unlikely to have been produced again until it re-appeared from Autocom in June 1993.

NU027/NC204 CR/LMS/BR Pickersgill 4-4-0

North of the border pre-grouping prototypes did appear from Nu-Cast, but not in abundance, and with only one Caley example which was this Pickersgill 4-4-0. The kit was totally of Nu-Cast origin, and was released for September 1978. Again no review is known, but the illustrations of the model that Autumn in the adverts showed a fine beast. The prototypes wandered widely around Scotland between 1916 and 1962, but did not gain the following of the McIntosh 4-4-0, which probably explains the scarcity of such models.

The kit was current with a brass chassis in 1986, replacing an initial whitemetal offering. Thereafter it seems to have been neglected, and it is unlikely that anything much was done with the kit at Spilsby, but it was stocked in November 1988. It was not listed at Autocom in their 1994 or 1996 lists, but matters changed from August 1997 when Autocom produced and advertised a small batch. These had sold out by the Winter, but production of another batch is not ruled out, demand depending.

NU028/NC123/SP6 GER/LNER/BR Y5 0-4-0ST

Released beside the Caley engine was another from Poole. Definitely a charmer and with Scottish origins, here was the Neilson built 0-4-0 ogee tank design which the GER purchased from 1874, the last of which as an LNER Y5 just scraped into BR hands in 1948. It was advertised in its Poole mode from August 1974 and reviewed in the Modeller in January 1975.

Poole provided alternatives for several versions so that the GER and LNER conditions were supplemented with a typical industrial finish. With full cab details, etched GER plates, and etched motion, this was a fine kit for its time. The chassis was not in the original Poole norm, being cast whitemetal with brass bushes, but can be seen as paving the way for the "orange label" series specification.

Subsequently, it was available though the reference points of 1979, 1983 and 1986, having gained a full brass chassis by the latter point. March 1991 saw its apparent production at Spilsby, and by June 1993 it was available from Autocom.

NU029/NC115 NER/LNER/BR B16/2 & B16/3 4-6-0

The public gestation of the B16 model seems to have lasted between December 1976 and February 1979. This large 1919-designed NER 4-6-0 had existed in several forms. Two out of the three major variants could be modelled from the Nu-Cast kit which covered twenty-four engines out of the seventy-seven. These B16/2 and B16/3 sub-classes reflected rebuilds by Gresley in 1937 and Thompson in 1944 respectively, and whose visually prominent features were new cylinders and higher running plates. The difference in the two sub-classes was right and left hand drive respectively, which choice the kit allows. There was no Nu-Cast model of the original B16 design although DJH versions of both B16 and B16/2/3 were more or less contemporary.

Apart from the release adverts in February and March 1979, the kit seems to have led a quiet life. There was a brass chassis by 1986, and it was advertised during the Spilsby venture. Otherwise nothing has been traced prior to appearance with Autocom from August 1993.

NU030/NC125/SP5 GER/LNER/BR E4 2-4-0

It seems that more or less contemporary to the B16 release came the re-release of the ex-Poole GER Intermediate loco. This was a classic

Victorian design whose ultimate following came as the last 2-4-0 tender locos working on British Railways. Places like Cambridge and the Mildenhall branch had been their stronghold, and at final withdrawal 62785 joined the National Collection. Along with his J15, the pair excited great attention in Poole's plans. The twin body and chassis kit was scheduled for release at Easter 1972, and the Modeller reviewed it in July. In the Poole style, parts for alternatives were provided along with detailing like pipework.

Quantities made of kits naturally interest us, and equally they often remain a guarded commercial secret. Poole placed illustrated adverts for the E4 that Summer which helpfully revealed that the first run of the E4 was for 500 kits. By 1977, it had become part of the "orange label" series before its translation two years later to Nu-Cast, and thereafter the model continued to be available. In the early part of 1984, the *Model Railway News* carried a major two-parter on the model by Allan Sibley. Looking at that and the 1977 W&H catalogue poses several issues.

The original kit came with brass chassis frames. In the MRN review, Sibley is engaged in building a Poole kit with a cast chassis block which he despairs of. The explanation is supplied by the specification given in the 1977 W&H catalogue - this talks of the "orange label" series including "cast sideframes, brass frame spacers, axlebox inserts and etched motion parts". From this it is concluded that the "orange label" series as a whole was more than the re-packaging of body and chassis elements together. However, some would instead judge it to be technological regression.

If that is how Nu-Cast inherited the kit, then by 1986 they had wrought more changes. The catalogue that year specifically spoke of the kit having been re-tooled, and this appears to have included a new brass chassis. Did this cure the problems that builders reported with the earlier chassis? 2-4-0s can suffer from unequal weight distribution, and some modellers found considerable alterations were required for effective haulage.

The 1986 model had quite a radical new option for the prototype. From 1935 onwards, several E4s departed for the extremely hilly Stainmore route of the erstwhile NER. To cope with the geography, these were fitted with a single side window variant of the typical NER design cab, and by 1986 that cab was in the kit. Nothing is known of any production at Spilsby although it was certainly stocked. It re-appeared from Autocom in September 1993.

NU031/NC119 LNER/BR Sentinel Railcar

One of Nu-Cast's most distinctive models, the LNER Sentinel steam railcar, would appear to have arrived with the minimum of advance notice in the Summer of 1979. The first illustrated advert was in September which indicated "New" but there were some earlier listings, although no review has been traced. Unlike

(above) Nu-Cast NC115 NER/LNER/BR B16/2/3, built as a B16/3 on a scratchbuilt chassis
Photo: Tony Wright, courtesy Tony Wright

(below) Nu-Cast NC119 LNER/BR Sentinel Railcar
Photo: Richard Sawyer, courtesy Railway Modeller

other Nu-Cast kits of the period, the kit contained wheels, motor, gears, transfers and pre-printed window strip. The transfers certainly provided car 2133 *Cleveland* - how appropriate a choice! The prototype was built in September 1928 and withdrawn in October 1943.

The LNER had 80 Sentinels, along with some jointly owned specimens and some steam rail-cars made by Clayton of Lincoln. They came in a complex assortment of types and bore four distinct colour schemes. *Cleveland* was part of the H series of 100 hp horizontally engined rigid (as opposed to articulated) units that started to appear from 1928. The most obvious livery choice is that used by Nu-Cast's own model, which was green and cream. Such a railcar is a very useful item for a 1930s LNER prototype, and with little 4mm competition, the kit remains important to this day.

It has undergone at least two major revamps. Being cast in whitemetal, the body is exceedingly heavy, with each side and the roof being cast in two halves for a manageable casting. In the initial design, drive was to one pair of wheels only, and you were lucky to see much movement seems the verdict on that arrangement! By June 1983 the kit had been revised - a four-wheel drive motorbogie driven by an Anchoridge DS10 motor was supplied and was more effective. The kit was made at Spilsby around 1991, and it re-appeared from Autocom in April 1994. This latest incarnation features a Romford wheeled Tenshodo motor bogie. Some brief notes on the model and rather more on the prototype appeared in June 1999 *Railway Modeller*.

NU032/NC126 GNoSR/LNER/BR D40 + SECR/SR G 4-4-0

Next into the shops was the Great North of Scotland Railway class V/F prototypes. The 1899 origin design remains in the consciousness, despite the general withdrawal of the class being achieved by 1958. One survivor, the proudly named *Gordon Highlander* joined the Scottish Region operational preserved fleet before then being passed on to the Glasgow Transport Museum.

Previewed from December 1979, the model was first priced in the April 1980 RM advert. An illustrated advert followed in July 1980, and the kits that year appear to mark a general specification change by being released with everything bar motor and paint - something the Sentinel railcar had started. The gears and wheels used were by Romford, and by the 1983 W&H listing the majority of kits were so packed.

The D40 was well detailed, and fine cast coal rails and brakegear appears to have featured from the outset. The chassis seems likely to have been one of the last cast examples - only a couple of models on and we have the first brass chassis. This model is likely to have gained a brass chassis in April 1987 when it was re-released, having been withdrawn in the previous July list. There was a new production run during the Spilsby era, and the kit was back in

Autocom's adverts from August 1993, still creating two prototypes.

This feature of the kit is rather unusual - it can model a SECR class G as well. The same design was bought by the SECR looking for a fast solution in 1899. Five came south lasting until between 1925-27, at which point the newest of the Scottish based engines were only six years old. On the Scottish prototypes, the detail of whether a superheater was fitted or not informed the exact location of the smokebox. The Nu-Cast model has alternative smokeboxes for both saturated and superheated versions.

The kit provided name and numberplates for both GNoSR and SECR examples. More details about exactly which are sought, but surely *Gordon Highlander* was included, although Autocom didn't receive any plates at all when the tooling moved to them. *Gordon Highlander* was not really the Victorian antique she may have appeared in 1958 - she was only built in 1920.

Back in 1980, in conjunction with the D40, Nu-Cast released NC401 and NC402 to provide two whitemetal kits of GNoSR wagon prototypes. They are worthy of mention here because they commenced the Nu-Cast wagon list.

NU033/NC107 GNR/LNER/BR J6 521 0-6-0

NU034/NC108 GNR/LNER/BR J6 536 0-6-0

There were various designs of Ivatt 0-6-0 to go beside his 0-8-0. The 0-8-0 by now existed in the Cotswold range and would, like the K's J3, in time come to be a running mate in Nu-Cast's own list. Nu-Cast's own design efforts for a Great Northern 0-6-0 went for a class of 110, built between 1911-22, and all deceased by 1962. The class leader was numbered 521 (note well).

Nu-Cast had been announcing the model in the Modeller advert from February 1980, and it was priced in April alongside the equally fresh D40. Release was just about contemporary with the D40, and using a statement in the W&H 1983 catalogue, MAY have preceded it. The relevant words are "This kit is the first that includes Romford driving wheels, axles and gears". An illustrated advert was present in June, but no review has been traced.

Two separately referenced kits are involved. The distinguishing feature was whether the leading sandboxes are combined with the front splashers. The first engines were not so fitted, but the Gresley build from 536 was. NC107 therefore represents the Ivatt, and NC108 the Gresley engines. On the model the sandboxes and splashers are cast separately, and the variant is created with the inclusion of the additional part. Additionally, the 521 version has a slightly different length of boiler which requires surgery, with the instructions giving guidance to help the builder.

What the chassis was initially made from is not

clear and neither is the exact timetable for its transition to brass. Both models were current in 1983, but by 1986 only NC108 was in the catalogue and price list. The year before an advert had announced the kit's withdrawal, and I suspect that gap is the transition point to brass for the chassis. Ever since then, as so in Autocom's adverts from May 1993, only NC108 has featured. The 1990s instructions supplied advice on how to model each option.

NU035/NC253 GWR/BR Manor 4-6-0

The Manor was the first Nu-Cast designed Great Western prototype to reach the market, and very few GWR kits would ultimately be originated by Nu-Cast. Its reference number is a poser - NC251 was the ex-Poole Pannier and would suggest that the NC251+ series was being reserved for Great Western prototypes. What then was NC252 intended to be? It is a blank in the system yet was surely once filled, if only by intent. However, in the list of proposals with which the narrative concludes, there is no suggestive GWR engine to choose from.

For Nu-Cast to work up a Manor was a major shift in strategy. It was first mentioned in the May 1979 RM advert, then various delays were apologised for and the first priced advert (which at the time equated to availability) appeared in July 1980's Modeller, and the following month included an illustration of 7800 *Torquay Manor*. For the first time the actual advert made much of the change to a "simple to complete solid brass chassis" taking an XO4 type motor. The assumption is that this was milled brass. There were periods of unavailability, but the kit was around for July 1986, and during the Spilsby period.

Search for an Autocom advert and you will be disappointed. In the narrative account, this is the first kit encountered that has not been revived. Alternative RTR provision now tells against it.

NU036/NC122/SP1 GER/LNER/BR F4/F5 2-4-2T

The last of the ex-Poole kits to be revived first appeared in Nu-Cast's advert in September 1980. This was for the GER origin LNER class F4/F5. It had an interesting history with Poole, appearing in May 1971 and advertised as body and chassis kits for class F4/F5. The F4 was a Worsdell design of 1884, thirty of which were rebuilt into F5. A range of boiler mountings could be carried, and assorted members of F5 were fitted for push-pull working or with condensing apparatus. Two members of F4 carried cowcatchers for use on the St. Combs branch in Scotland. Poole also indicated that the kit could be built as the NER A/LNER F8 Worsdell design finally withdrawn in 1938 - the potential for model variety is therefore clear.

Poole noted in his initial adverts that one kit could build either the F4 or F5. The kit was available assembled from Poole as another option - certainly between 1971-72 at least. Reviews appeared for the kit in the Modeller and Constructor for September 1971. In addition to

the chassis, brass was used for spectacle plates, buffers and GER number plates. The Constructor review revealed some of the possible options to include: condensing gear, and GER or LNER cabs in addition to the two core classes. The full range is helpfully revealed in the November Constructor advert adding choices of two chimneys, Ramsbottom or Ross Pop valves, push-pull fittings, optional coal rails and further brass detailing parts, but not cowcatchers!

During 1976, as outlined for other Poole engines, the specification was considerably changed when the loco was brought into the "orange label" series. As such it appeared in the W&H 1977 catalogue where the claim "covers all known versions" was made. I still doubt that this extended to the St. Combs variation. The model was "re-tooled" in the Nu-Cast's era by 1986, but exactly what did this entail? A new brass chassis probably, but no cowcatchers, even with the 1986 Nu-Cast catalogue speaking of the Scottish connection. At Autocom it was re-advertised from September 1993. Their list says F4; the F5 parts for cab roofs, chimneys and safety valves are also still included.

NU037/NC130 LNER/BR A2/1 4-6-2 6w tender

NU038/NC128 LNER/BR A2/1 4-6-2 8w tender

The year 1981 proved a big year in two major ways for Nu-Cast. Firstly, they produced a Pacific engine, and secondly they swallowed up the Cotswold range. When a kit manufacturer reaches Pacifics, then they may be seen to "have arrived", and Nu-Cast produced their only homegrown designed example to see the light of day in the first half of 1981. There were four members of A2/1 built under Thompson - essentially they were his Pacific version of the Gresley V2, allowing Nu-Cast to share some components.

In Nu-Cast's October 1980 Modeller advert, the Thompson Pacifics were first mentioned in the "coming soon" listing. Since Millholme had only just released their own kit for the A2/2 and A2/3, one has to guess at how much this influenced subsequent events. Right at the outset, Nu-Cast actually announced kits for all three classes: A2/1, A2/2 (the Thompson Pacific rebuilds of the Gresley P2) and A2/3. In early adverts the reference used for the A2/3, which was NC129, was being shared with the A2/2. That idea proved totally stillborn - NC129 was never released.

The first of the Thompson Pacifics to actually appear was NC130, which was priced from the January 1981 Modeller advert. One guesses that this came out first because, whilst Nu-Cast were still developing the eight wheeled tender, they could justify issuing the locomotive with the Gresley standard tender already available in the range. Three of the engines worked with these well into BR days. The eight-wheeled tendered NC128 appeared that May. No reviews of either kit have been traced - in line with previous models, it looks as if Nu-Cast ceased submitting new models for review. The A2/1 kit included a choice of chimney. Despite the move elsewhere to a brass chassis, the model had a cast example at the outset leading to a Tony Wright (published) comment that the original Nu-Cast chassis was "a joke". The front of the frames showed some rivet detailing in 1981 adverts that reveals the cast frame.

In the W&H 1983 edition catalogue, NC128 and NC130 were priced but NC129 was annotated as not available. Both were available by 1986, and at that stage they had gained brass chassis. Around 1991 they appear to have been made at Spilsby, and in July 1993 Autocom commenced advertising them. At that point etched plates were provided, with *Waverley*, *Robert the Bruce* and *Duke of Rothesay* being possibilities, although the latter two were incorrectly spaced. Autocom has not altered the kit, despite some published evidence suggesting differently.

NU039/NC127 GNoSR/LNER/BR D41 4-4-0

The final engine to slip in from Nu-Cast's own hands before the Cotswold Armada sailed in from the North was the predecessor of the D40, most notably lacking the side windowed cab of that prototype. The LNER D41 came out on the GNoSR six years before the D40 prototype - 1893 instead of 1899. The majority of dimensions were similar, but in addition to the cab, the splashers showed differences. The D41 kit was withdrawn in 1986 but was back in 1987, and whether there were chassis changes at that point is not known. There was a new production at Spilsby around 1991 and the kit was back with Autocom from October 1993.

The ex-Cotswold Models

NU040/NC208/Cotswold 11 LMS/BR 3F 0-6-0T

In the Nu-Cast Modeller advert for June 1981 an eye-catching "Stop Press" announcement revealed that Nu-Cast had acquired Cotswold whose background has been described earlier. This advert also spoke of a new combined list of kits. Assuming that all the Cotswold models were current in June 1981, we shall endeavour to describe them within the chronological order of release that Cotswold had achieved, starting with their first loco kit - the ex-R&J LMS Jinty. Cotswold's catalogues provide the Cotswold references that are quoted,

Talk of the Jinty kit will take the narrative back as far as October 1970. R&J Supplies operated from 26 Alexandra Street in Narborough near Leicester, this being the residential address of Rob and June Hamp. Rob decided to model the Jinty; he would make the patterns but turned to Cotswold when it came to casting. Subsequently, he made patterns for five of the later Cotswold models such as the F1 and the Tilbury Tank.

In October 1970 R&J advertised as new their first loco kit, the LMS Jinty, and the following January there was a Modeller review. R&J offered a separate body and chassis kit, both being cast, but no wheels or motor. At the outset the side rods were simply drilled bullhead rail.

After about nine months, the kit passed to Cotswold. Development was carried out in the Autumn of 1972 by which time Cotswold had three locos on their books, and the Lanky saddletank and GWR 42xx/72xx on the way. This development saw the removal of the Jinty's cast chassis and its replacement with a solid brass milled block. It is not thought that the bullhead rail coupling rods had quite gone at this stage, but they probably did by the Spring of 1973.

Not a lot is known about the kit in Nu-Cast's hands beyond its continued availability, although at some point an etched chassis was fitted. The kit was made at Spilsby, and it was back from Autocom for May 1993 with their first releases. Otherwise, there were no changes until in 1999 when new moulds were made, and there is an intention to provide etched coal rails.

NU041/NC209/Cotswold 12 LMS/BR Fowler 7F 0-8-0

The second loco in the ex-Cotswold range offers R&J ancestry too - they had been developing the "Austin Seven" but never released it. Exactly when Cotswold released the kit is not yet known, but it was reviewed by the Modeller in September 1972. It is placed before the Cotswold 2-4-2T in this chapter (next entry) on the strength of comments in the October 1971 Modeller, but it is possible that the order was inverted. The simple outline of the prototype posed few complications. What would become a Cotswold trademark made its first appearance - the chassis was made from a block of solid ½" square brass. This offered the benefits of great rigidity, ease of assembly, good wearing qualities and assisted tractive effort. Despite which, the solution was crude in terms of scope for chassis detail. Early models followed the Jinty in having coupling rods made out of bullhead rail. They appear to have been improved during 1973.

Beyond its appearances in Nu-Cast's own lists, relatively little is known about it after the takeover. Autocom commenced advertising it in October 1993, and at some point etched and fluted rods were substituted.

NU042/NC211/Cotswold 18 L&YR/LMS/BR 2P 2-4-2T

NU043/NC212/ Cotswold 19 L&YR/LMS/BR 3P 2-4-2T

The third Cotswold loco to be released (or possibly their second - see above) can be traced back to the R&J brand. There are few advertisements from R&J, although one particularly important example was placed by them in the May 1971 Constructor. At that point the Jinty was available, the 7F was to come shortly, and the Aspinall 2-4-2T was new and priced in a combined body and chassis kit. That R&J truly did release some of these is shown by a Howell Dimmock advert in the August 1971 Modeller - the R&J Aspinall 2-4-2T was under the heading "New and in stock". What undid R&J was the 1971 Postal

(above) Cotswold 12 LMS/BR 7F Fowler "Austin Seven"

Photo: Tony Wright, courtesy of Rob Kinsey

(right) Cotswold packaging, with the oldest (Western Precision Castings) to the top

Photo: Tony Wright, courtesy Nick Gillman

(below) Cotswold 18 L&YR/LMS/BR 2P 2-4-2T, completed with Romford wheels and Airfix motor

Photo: Colin Hey, courtesy Eric Robinson

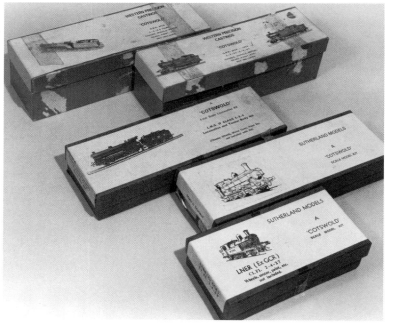

Strike - it became impossible to stay in business, and Rob Hemp sold all the patterns and rights to Cotswold who were doing the casting anyway. On that basis some R&J examples are out there for the finding. R&J only offered a round top firebox 2P model.

The Modeller report on the Cotswold take-over specifically said in distinction to the 7F which was coming soon, that the 2-4-2T would be available later. It was Cotswold's May 1972 advert that seems to have launched the 2-4-2T. What can explain this? An unconfirmed but reasonable assumption is that the R&J version had a cast chassis, and Cotswold wished to replace this in brass, and that the time until May was occupied on this task. An additional explanation revolves around the alternative parts for which the Cotswold version clearly had a number. What little evidence has been seen for the R&J model does not suggest there were any alternative parts. Perhaps the delayed re-introduction was influenced by additional development work in the kit.

This now brooks the question which prototypes could be modelled? That is answered by the Modeller review provided in July 1972. As is clear from our header, as far back as Cotswold's own references (i.e. 1976), and from their own July 1972 advert, the Aspinall tank model was divided into two kits, a division that has been retained by Nu-Cast subsequently. The Modeller review and these adverts make clear that you either purchased the unsuperheated round topped firebox 2P or the superheated Belpaire firebox 3P. For both, a long or short bunker could be fitted, but had R&J released both bunker options?

After this complicated birth, the kit seems to have become part of the scenery. It was current through the 1970s and 1980s. At least NC212 was stated to be in production at Spilsby. Both were current at Autocom for 1994, and by then the chassis was etched brass.

NU044/NC210/Cotswold 13
L&YR/LMS/BR 2F 0-6-0ST

Having cleared the matters arising from the R&J take-over, Cotswold could now turn to entirely fresh developments. In the Summer of 1972 a complete kit for a Hawksworth tender had been given some attention. That October the advert revealed two new additions to the programme which were developed over the coming months. These were the L&YR 0-6-0ST and the GWR 42xx/72xx. The saddle tank was shown at the 1973 Toy Fair, and Cotswold own adverts seem clear that release took place in February 1973.

No review has yet been traced, although various pictures in the trade press suggest that the manufacturers held onto a model of LMS 11325 for a long time. The prototype has largely remained in the memory thanks to one example now on the K&WVR. The kit had a milled brass chassis block from new (survives in 1999), which should be taken as the norm for Cotswold kits from now on. Availability at Nu-Cast seems general and Autocom advertised it from June 1993.

NU045/NC256/Cotswold 15
GWR/BR 47xx 2-8-0

Using Cotswold's own adverts as a reference, it is clear that they managed to spring a completely different engine in before the large GWR eight coupled tanks - the kit being the 47xx 2-8-0; a class of nine 5'8" wheeled express engines. The March 1973 Modeller mentioned the 47xx in both the Toy Fair report, and the Cotswold advert. The advert allows no room for confusion with the eight-coupled tanker.

Again a review is lacking, but the kit assuredly existed along with a solid brass milled chassis and lost wax crossheads and slidebars. Somewhere along the line after 1983 this model died at Nu-Cast. Various references over 1985-87 reveal that the kit was withdrawn or "coming soon" and the best intelligence is that it never did. The kit has not been in any Autocom list, and since Mike Griffiths believes that the original tools no longer exist, that situation is unlikely to change!

NU046/NC255/Cotswold 14
GWR/BR 42xx/72xx 2-8-0 or 2-8-2T

Announced in October 1972, the kit for the big GWR eight coupled tank was clearly new from the May 1973 Modeller Cotswold advert, and a review was furnished in the November Modeller. Both the main interpretations of the class could be modelled, along with options on safety valve cover, steam pipe and cab shutters. Chemically etched side rods were now adopted and made standard across the range. For the first time, these GWR engines required Cotswold to produce outside motion. According to the review of this engine and Mike Griffiths, this was cast in a silver-based alloy.

The kit was widely available from Nu-Cast at Hartlepool, and was back from Autocom by June 1993. In that incarnation it has beaten the K's offering - both kits had ended up in the same list potentially, and it was decided that Cotswold's was better. However, the etched chassis and rods available from the deleted K's kit have been substituted for the inherited Cotswold components.

NU047/NC131/Cotswold 22
GCR/LNER/BR F1 2-4-2T

After the burst of effort that 1973's releases represented, no more locos came from the Bristol base. There were serious space issues and what development there was, went into the bus range and then into taking over Pirate. In 1974 there was a stillborn intention to produce an LNWR steam railmotor kit - this actually got as far the production of masters which are still available for Autocom to use. Then in 1975 there was the move North, and 1976 had to arrive before new loco kits were generated.

Anyone familiar with the F1 prototype will realise how similar the thirty-nine examples of the GCR 2-4-2T were to the L&Y 2-4-2T already in the Cotswold range. Despite this, both the body and the chassis were newly tooled up.

Alternative parts for a Belpaire boiler version, with or without superheat, were fitted, but the original round topped firebox was not supplied. The kit was displayed at the 1976 Toy Fair and was on sale soon enough afterwards to feature in W&H's April 1976 advert, and the Constructor reviewed it in June. There was an attempt at brakegear with this kit, the suggestion being that this was the first Cotswold model so fitted. The kit marks the point at which provision of a separate chassis kit was abandoned, with the mainframe now being included in the one kit.

At Nu-Cast one guesses sales were not enormous, after all the prototypes were not terribly well known. It was not priced in 1986 (having been so in 1983). Apparently Spilsby did not advertise it, but Autocom did from July 1993.

NU048/NC216/Cotswold 24 HR/LMS 39 0-6-4T

The second introduction from 1976 was in some respect prototypically even more obscure, but it had considerably more charisma, and its appearance was wholly appropriate to a company now based in Sutherland. The Highland Railway had only eight 39 class 0-6-4T engines designed by Peter Drummond - they earned their fame as banking tanks for the notorious HR gradients.

One of the incentives behind the October 1976 issued catalogue was the chance to feature this new model, which was advertised by W&H as new in November 1976's Modeller. December's Constructor ran a review; in this instance no chassis was supplied. The design was intended to fit the standard Tri-ang Hornby Jinty chassis with a 6" overscale compromise, and a cast whitemetal trailing bogie was included in the kit.

Attractive nuances of detail featured an opening smokebox door with detailed interior, and the cabside tablet catcher. The casting process often produces thick slab edges to components, but on this model efforts to taper down the edges were made.

In subsequent Nu-Cast listings no individual chassis was generated for the model. There have been sustained periods when the kit was not available, but it has been current at Autocom since 1994.

NU049/NC257/Cotswold 25 M&SWJR/GWR/BR 1334 2-4-0

The October 1976 catalogue previewed a further three loco kits using pictures of their prototypes as illustrations. The first was promised for November 1976 delivery, a target which seems to have been met, and December's trade press carried release adverts with the actual model shown. The subject was a GWR 2-4-0, but reviews did not appear until July and August 1977 in the Modeller and Constructor respectively.

Originally the prototype had been built as a class of three by Dubs in 1894. The customer was the Midland & South Western Junction Railway, so the engines passed to the Great Western.

Swindon rebuilt them in 1924, and the three lasted until 1952/4. Their post-rebuild GWR state was modelled, but no numbers for 1334-1336 were furnished. Cotswold may still have been cautious about choosing prototypes with complicated outside gear, but the detail of an opening smokebox door and interior was repeated from the HR 0-6-4T. At the other end of the engine a detailed boiler backhead was provided. It was back to a brass chassis block on which there was no brakegear, but there was an ATC shoe and steam heating pipes. Such things allowed various alternative GWR conditions to be modelled.

Like several other manufacturers, Cotswold was caught by the replacement of the K's Mk II motor with the HP2M unit. They responded by producing a new motor cradle which was available from the Summer of 1977. Its absence in the packaging can therefore indicate an early kit. There appears little to say about its Nu-Cast career, save that it was present at Autocom's outset from May 1993, and at some stage gained an etched chassis.

NU050/NC218/Cotswold 26 LT&SR/MR/LMS/BR 4-4-2T

After the 2-4-0, new releases did not follow the pattern previewed in the October 1976 catalogue. A relatively intense programme went forward with a complete, yet welcome, surprise for February 1977.

The surprise was the first of two successive 4-4-2Ts, in this instance for the London Tilbury and Southend Railway. These may have been geographically limited in operation, but they had a very affectionate following on the eastern fringe of the capital. Cotswold's model filled a clear hole and has not been challenged since in 4mm scale. Advertised in the trade press from February 1977, there was a Modeller review that September. The kit was well thought out - there were dummy chassis frames to extend forward of the main brass unit, and the bunker was weighted to balance the engine. A detail such as arranging the connecting rods inside the coupling rods was shown.

Review, adverts and catalogues showed the model in LMS finish as 2137, and since the distinctive LTSR safety valve cover was not enclosed, the modeller was guided to the LMS finish. The Tilbury tanks were in reality a series of considerably varying classes with further batches being built by the LMS between 1923-30. Cotswold's own adverts suggest (but not later Nu-Cast literature), along with the review, that the kit is really for an LMS build.

Turning to the real LMS 2137 we find that this was one of the small 1P engines, originally LTSR number 28 *Romford*. I would assert that various pictures and references describing 2137 as a 2P are somewhat misleading. As far as I can see, LMS 2137 never resembled the kit, and if one wants to model one of the LMS built large 3P engines, then an example should be selected between 2110-2134 and 2151-2160. As a model of the LMS build, the kit has to be a 3P. If faced with building or buying a ready finished example, do one's homework to ensure correctness! The kit itself was widely available during the Nu-Cast era and was back from Autocom in October 1993.

NU051/NC132/Cotswold 27 NBR/LNER/BR C16 4-4-2T

Hard on the heels of the Tilbury tank, April 1977 saw the availability of a model of North British class L for a Scottish 4-4-2T for which a review has not been traced. We can, however, trace its availability through 1983/86/88 and re-release in June 1993. The adverts showed LNER 9438, which was the class leader as NBR 438 back in 1915. No element of the chassis was shared with the Tilbury tank.

NU052/NC213/Cotswold 21 L&YR/LMS/BR 7F 0-8-0

June 1977 marked the next addition to the Cotswold range. There were three generations of Hughes L&YR 0-8-0 - outstandingly ugly prototypes. Cotswold produced another L&YR 0-8-0 - see NU063. The 7F large boilered L&YR Q4 built from 1912-20 was the third prototype and forms the present model. The prototype looked totally out of proportion; cab and boiler seemed to tower over the eight-wheeled tender.

The kit itself contained two designs of cab, and no review has been discovered thus far. The kit has probably not been a best seller despite 115 prototypes, some of which lasted until 1951. The kit was withdrawn sometime during 1985-6, although there must have been some further Hartlepool production since adverts from 1988 exist. Under Autocom, more comment is called for - the kit re-appeared in their advert from June 1993, only the second Autocom advert. Then in December 1993 Autocom indicated that a new chassis was being fitted to the kit.

As will become evident with further models (and especially those from K's), Autocom has undertaken a lot of work on chassis replacement. Their basic specification uses etched brass, screw together, full-length mainframes. These are correctly profiled and feature spring detail, and such was designed in one unit to fit both the L&YR 0-8-0 kits.

NU053/NC262/Cotswold 28 BR (WR) 16xx 0-6-0PT

Later in 1977, and virtually a year since first indicated, it was time to return to the plans of the October 1976 catalogue. Therein a BR built 16xx had been promised - these were lightweight pannier tanks which only started to appear in 1949, and were destined for a short life with only number 1638 preserved. The adverts for the new model commenced in October 1977. Cotswold made much of the class's ability to penetrate beyond the WR, and they had even substituted for former Highland locomotives on the Dornoch branch - something that was bound to be a pull in Cotswold's new home. This time the kit came complete with everything accept a motor; wheels were from

K's. Reviews appeared in the Constructor for February 1978 and the Modeller for March 1978. A two-page test report was afforded by the MRN in September 1978.

One alternative part provided a spark arresting chimney - several engines being so fitted for duties that included the Worcester "Vinegar" branch and the Cleobury Mortimer and Ditton Priors Light - suitable engines for this work would be 1616, 1623, 1629 and 1661. Cotswold's own loco was numbered 1638, but there were no plates included in the kit. However, the opening firebox gimmick remained, and there was much praise for the kit's design including arranging the motor to drive on the rear axle and so allow a fully detailed cab.

Subsequently, the kit has proved popular and has not met a lot of competition. So it was current at all the datum's already mentioned which included being made at Spilsby around 1991. It was amongst the first releases from Autocom in May 1993.

NU054/NC219/Cotswold 36 LMS/BR 4P Compound 4-4-0

The first release of 1978, by choosing the LMS Compound, entered a rather more crowded field than the 16xx. It was previewed in the January Modeller wherein the transition to "wheels and gears" was confirmed. At this point two 4-4-0s were promised as the 1978 programme. An illustrated advert was placed from March of the kit, but no review has yet been traced. In distinction to Gem's example which provided a Midland Railway origin Deeley era Compound, the Cotswold example was modelled on the LMS build. The 195 engines of LMS origin were numbered from 1045 upwards. Cotswold's own example was finished in LMS Crimson Lake as 1089 which was a 1925 engine.

Demand for the kit has been considerable leading to it being in at the datums mentioned, and there was stated to be a production run at Spilsby in 1991. When the kit re-appeared from Autocom in November 1994, it was with a new chassis. This was to the new standard specification detailed at NU052, but with the added refinement of an etched cylinder stretcher.

NU055/NC217/Cotswold 38 HR/LMS/BR Small Ben 4-4-0

Previewed beside the Compound back in January 1978 was an engine for the Highland home ground. The release adverts for the Highland Railway Small Ben started in July 1978, with reviews in the Modeller for October 1978 and the Constructor for January 1979. Several years on and Allan Sibley furnished a detailed account in the December 1985 *Your Model Railway*.

The kit went further than before by including an ECM motor. Other interest derives from its prototype for which the only other 4mm models are in etched brass. Like Nu-Cast and their

(above) Cotswold 42 GNR/LNER Q1 0-8-0 "Long Tom", with the worm clearly showing
Photo: Dave Wheatstone, courtesy Dave Wheatstone Collection

(left) The key *Railway Modeller* Cotswold advert for the Cotswold 31 RR/GWR AR class 0-6-2T. Identification of this prototype proved troublesome and the story needed some unpicking! To cut a long story short, this kit is in fact modelled on the RR R1 class

(bottom) Further fun and games with this Cotswold 33 L&YR/LMS/BR 6F 0-8-0; as stated in the text, this kit really represents a L&YR 5F, and in this case the kit builder has numbered it accordingly
Photo: Dave Wheatstone, courtesy Dave Wheatstone Collection

Gordon Highlander, the kit was used as an excuse to release some related HR wagons which in due course would swell Nu-Cast's own wagon range. There was a difference in that the Cotswold wagons were composite plastic and whitemetal, whilst the Nu-Cast wagons were solely whitemetal.

Back with the engine - its marriage to a six-wheeled tender made it quite specific in prototype. All the review and advert engines were finished (correctly) as *Ben More* in HR livery. This engine was HR 4 built in 1899 and in traffic until 1946. It was one of the first eight turned out by Dubs in 1898-99, and attached to the small tender. Boiler fittings were only supplied appropriate to the Highland era and this batch. As ever, the kit was extremely well detailed, such that the lack of brakegear was glaring and commented upon, particularly when compared to the cab which was full of lost wax brass fittings and had a simulated wood floor.

Due to the complications of boiler fittings, and changes with tender allocation (for an eight wheel watercart), it is particularly important to work from photos when finishing a model. With this kit (and surely this was for the first time?) etched Highland number plates for four engines, and etched worksplates and lamps were included. The kit was dimensionally complimented, and along with the detail provision, represented a first class example of what the classic whitemetal kit could achieve. Hence it bore the detailed attention Sibley gave it seven years later, where his major work was to replace the chassis for something better, something which Autocom also did in 1995 with the introduction of their own etched chassis.

Hopes that Cotswold would provide an eight wheeled watercart tender option never materialised. Nu-Cast removed the motor from the package, and unfortunately their own comments in their 1986 catalogue strain one's credulity. There is no preserved example of this engine, and the implication that an example ran in the ScR historic fleet is not right. *Ben Alder* was stored for a number of years in the hope of preservation but was eventually scrapped. The kit has been unavailable at times (for example 1986), and no production at Spilsby is known, but Autocom re-introduced it from October 1993.

NU056/NC220/Cotswold 39 LMS/BR Stanier 3P 2-6-2T

Cotswold released five loco kits in 1978, three from the Autumn. Next in line was the Stanier standard 3P 2-6-2T design of 1935 for the LMS. Despite the relative familiarity of the engine and the fact that Cotswold/Nu-Cast were to have the field to themselves for many years, I have not traced a great deal of attention given to the model. An illustrated release advert appeared in the October 1978 Modeller, and there was a reversion to "complete less motor" specification.

Some alternatives were allowed for, so there was "a choice of Vortex or standard chimneys, and top feed for domed or domeless boilers". To unpack this requires some prototypical background. The Stanier 2-6-2Ts were numbered 71-209. With number 145 there was an important break - before that number, the engines had domeless boilers, and after that domed boilers. These engines came two years after the first example was outshopped. All engines were withdrawn by 1962 which meant none surviving to be preserved.

The model was made around 1991 at Spilsby and features in the Autocom list from 1994.

NU057/NC215/Cotswold 37 L&YR/LMS H3 0-6-2T

An old stager from the Lanky came next, and produces probably Cotswold's most obscure choice. The format for what was a relatively simple inside cylindered 0-6-2T was proven and despite getting an illustrated release advert in December 1978, I have not been able to trace much more attention spent on the newcomer. These class H3 engines (identity taken from the number 11617 on Cotswold's own model) were a class of 54 built in the early 1880s. They were withdrawn by 1932, and so do not seem very familiar today. The kit was not current at times in the mid-1980s, but there are adverts in 1988, and it was apparently made at Spilsby around 1991. In October 1993 it made its first appearance in an Autocom advert. A new etched brass chassis replaced the milled version in 1995.

NU058/NC261/Cotswold 41 GWR/BR 2021 0-6-0PT

Cotswold's final efforts for 1978 were to offer a model suitable for the standard GWR 4'1½" driver six-wheeled tank that existed in abundance between 1875 and 1959. This was bound to be a good idea, and Cotswold elected to focus on the 2021 batch in both saddle and pannier tank forms. These engines were Wolverhampton built from 1897, being an updated version of the earlier 850 class. At the time K's had promised an 850, Wills offered an '1854' and Hornby's 2701 was not revealed until 1980. Anyway, the two latter examples were for the larger wheeled classes. The basis of such a kit as this 2021 class pannier was bound to be simple, but the exact execution for a prototype which knew so many variables would be more complicated.

Suffice to say that Cotswold released the pannier version in time to be mentioned beside the Lanky H3 in December 1978 adverts. An illustrated advert for the kit followed in the February 1979 trade press. Alternative components were important, and a spark arresting chimney was one rather specialist component for certain engines (examples were 2034, 2051, and 2144) which had duties similar to that option as applied to the 16xx discussed earlier. Of wider applicability were the parts that could create a flared or straight-sided bunker, an open or closed cab, and an alternative smokebox. What Cotswold supplied does not exhaust all options, and any model should only be finished against photographic evidence.

The detailing above the running plate was once

again so good that the undetailed slab of brass that was the chassis was really very obvious. Unfortunately as yet, no review for either saddle or pannier kit has been traced. Nonetheless, they proved popular for both Cotswold and Nu-Cast, being current in 1983 and 1986, and some time that decade an etched brass chassis was adopted. Both pannier and saddle tank kits appear to have been made at Spilsby around 1991, and the pannier kit re-appeared from Autocom from the Summer of 1993. For further details on the saddle tank, move on to NU061.

NU059/NC133/Cotswold 42 GNR/LNER Q1 0-8-0

The Q1 was the "Long Tom", all fifty of them. Designed by Ivatt in 1901 for heavy freight on the Great Northern, these 0-8-0 engines were not especially long lived - all had gone by 1935, as had the related Q2s. Cotswold's kit had an illustrated release advert showing a model finished as LNER 3425 in the April 1979 Modeller, but no review has been traced. A prominent amount of daylight is visible under the boiler, but this means that the motor intrudes into the cab. In the 1986 Nu-Cast list this model was withdrawn, but two years later Nu-Cast "had a few", and apparently the loco was made at Spilsby in 1991. From October 1993 Autocom advertised it. Newer generations of motor allow a boiler backhead to be fitted, but the milled brass Cotswold era chassis remains.

NU060/NC258/Cotswold 31 RR/GWR AR (sic) 0-6-2T

Only two loco kits were released in 1979, so by the time this next kit arrived in September, one wonders with only four more loco releases to come, whether the wisdom of the move to Bonar Bridge was becoming questionable?

A visit was made to the South Wales Valleys for a model of the Rhymney Railway class AR 0-6-2T, at least that is how the Cotswold Modeller advert of September 1979 and the Nu-Cast catalogue of 1986 described the model. As yet I do not have a great deal of supporting evidence, so take a deep breath as we try to assess precisely what is modelled. The material available to me includes these two references - firstly, the advert has a GWR model which is numbered 38 and the comment "many parts are included to allow the construction of the locomotive in several of the many forms it took from Rhymney days to late BR ownership"; and secondly the catalogue has an indistinct photo of a prototype in what is probably RR works grey. W&H's 1983 catalogue sat on the fence and simply referred to the kit as RR 0-6-2T.

To assess these comments, Casserley's lists of the grouped and 1948 stock are available, as are four relevant Modeller references. Back in May 1968 Freezer had drawn up both the MSWJR 2-4-0 1334 and an ex-Rhymney 0-6-2T number 67. It seems likely that these drawings were before the Cotswold interest, but Freezer did not give a class allocation (for completeness - it was a Hurry Riches class A). Finally, three Beattie

profiles consider Rhymney 0-6-2T engines in the Modeller: December 1985 for class R, August 1988 for class A1, and February 1994 for the rebuilt AP.

If we start our investigations with GWR number 38, this had been Rhymney number 42. Rhymney 42 had been a Hurry Riches R class. To quote from Beattie, the ten built in 1921 were "distinguished by leading sandboxes slung under instead of atop the running plates". The kit in the advert was so (but the prototype picture in 1986's catalogue showed an earlier engine) and number 38 is correct for a 1921 engine. Casserley's Grouping list calls these engines R, whilst in 1948 the batch 35-44 were R1. This may simply be a way of distinguishing the 1921 build from the earlier R class engines which had a slightly reduced front framing. Of the R1 (the 1921 engines), all entered BR service; three (not including 38) had received taper boilers but all had been Great Westernised with boiler fittings as shown in the Cotswold advert.

So what's the problem? Is not the kit simply a model of the ten strong 1921 batch of R class engines with provision for GWR boiler fittings but only a parallel boiler? Other GWR changes altered the location of the front springs and the coalbunkers. However, we are left with this AR description and the knowledge that the alternative parts do include domes, buffers, steps, tank fillers and safety valves. Mike Griffith's view is that models of the following GWR numbers are possible: 30-32, 34-44 and 46.

The confusion is because I as such have not traced the class AR, but Hurry Riches did design the largely similar classes A/A1 and AP, and one AP was even Rhymney 38. With catalogue entries that seem deliberately vague, it is not difficult to imagine that the kit's different makers and owners may not have been 100% certain exactly what it is. Nu-Cast's 1986 list avoids any class description at all. At Autocom it had re-appeared in February 1994 and that listing had another cackhanded piece of evidence calling the model an R/R1 class 0-6-0T. Nonetheless, with that we rest our case: that the model is and always has been of the TVR R1 0-6-2T class (and, if the parts are there to change the front framing and sandboxes, the R class). Phew!

NU061/NC263/Cotswold 30 GWR/BR County 4-6-0

In the first part of 1980 Cotswold released an engine which has a rare fate. Presently we can trace only one loco kit which Cotswold generated and which then is lost to view at Nu-Cast - it is a GWR County 4-6-0. There were stockist's adverts from as early as February 1980, and a major illustrated release advert was placed in the April Modeller. Construction followed usual Cotswold principles and produced a somewhat bare looking chassis compensated by "lots of lost wax castings". For instance, there were three types of copper chimney - two types of double and one single. The kit benefited from the long-standing Cotswold model of the Hawksworth tender. There actually is a review, in the August 1980 Modeller.

So what became of this engine? W&H in 1983 manage much confusion by pricing a NC263 County 4-4-0. Actually that must have been the old Cotswold stock of the 4-6-0. The 4-6-0 as NC263 is illustrated in the 1986 catalogue but the accompanying list shows it as withdrawn. M&L had released a competing kit in 1980 and did Nu-Cast decide not to compete further? It will certainly not appear from Autocom.

On the subject of mystery Cotswold models, proposals for a GWR Manor and an LNWR railmotor have been mentioned. Another engine lost without trace, and which was intended, is the LMS Fowler 2-6-4T (c.1977).

NU062/NC260/Cotswold 41S GWR/BR 2021 0-6-0ST

After Cotswold's County came the saddle tank version of the GWR 2021 which has already had some discussion under NU058. The differences to bear in mind are that this kit is for the as-built state with a saddle tank, the last example of which (number 2048) survived until 1948.

The kit arrived in about September 1980, and there was an illustrated advert for it along with the next release in that peculiar one-off Modeller published to replace the "lost" May issue that year. Cotswold stated that it could be made in four versions - "tall or short boiler fittings, Swindon or Wolverhampton cab". Even in saddle tank form the engines existed with several other elements (especially bunkers and cabs). Using the illustrations available, the saddle tank engine model has a flush smokebox, and some prototypes had extended versions. Some engines started life with domes, but there is no dome in the kit. At least one of the manufacturer's models was numbered 2156, and it would be good to have that tied back to a specific image. The saddletank was made at Spilsby around 1991 and Autocom released it from June 1994.

NU063/NC214/Cotswold 33 L&YR/LMS/BR 6F (sic) 0-8-0

Back at loco NU052 in 1977, Cotswold had offered the Hughes L&YR Q4 7F 0-8-0. A straightforward variant would produce a smaller Aspinall 5F design built between 1900-08 and numbered 12700-759 by the LMS. The last engine was withdrawn in 1950.

The original advert called the kit an "LMS ex L&YR small boiler goods loco", and the model illustrated appeared to be numbered either 12748 or 12749. Subsequent catalogues are no more specific than the label "small boiler" or 6F. Nu-Cast's 1986 catalogue showed a prototype engine numbered 12719 ascribed to Hoy, but using Casserley's *Locomotives at the Grouping*, there are no Hoy 0-8-0s. The only L&YR 6F 0-8-0 that the LMS inherited was the Hughes Q3. Engine number 12719 was an Aspinall 5F from L&YR class Q1, as was 12748. The model therefore is of that class, the first L&YR 0-8-0, and it really should have been better described. Like its big sister, the kit was withdrawn in the 1986 listing. The kit re-appeared from Autocom in June 1993 and as narrated under NU052

received a new chassis. Two chimneys and sets of safety valves are also enclosed.

NU064/NC264/Cotswold 29 GWR Flower o/f 4-4-0

The last but one kit to be originated at Bonar Bridge first appeared in the Modeller with a launch advert for January 1981, showing 4150 *Begonia*. Amongst the legions of GWR 4-4-0s, both the Flowers and the preceding Cities (see NU066) formed two compact and clearly defined classes. The Flowers were 20 engines of 1908 whose deep frames aided recognition. All sorts of innovations came in the new kit for which typically no review is known. For the first time Cotswold supplied a one-piece boiler. As usual the coupling rods were etched, but so were the dummy outside frames. Brass, copper and nickel castings supplied other details. The kit was soon in Nu-Cast's hands and was available through the 1980s. Autocom re-released it in June 1993.

NU065/NC259/Cotswold 32 TVR/GWR rebuilt A 0-6-2T

Some irony was present in the final kit to come from Bonar Bridge, filling the slot occupied by the last model previewed in the October 1976 catalogue to reach production. What was amongst the last adverts to come from Bonar Bridge at all was the one in the *Model Railway News* of April 1981 that launched the GWR rebuilt ex-TVR class A. This time there are none of the traumas of identity. Description, numbers and model all tie up.

The GWR, having inherited the Taff class A, rebuilt them with a taper boiler and Swindon fittings, in which state Cotswold modelled the engine. The engines either retained their round-topped tanks (which is what the kit has) or had modified straight edged tanks fitted. The advert's example was GWR number 364, and a point of detail would seek to clarify which tanks 364 had. Certainly if faced with finishing a model, then check this detail.

The tradition of fine detail stayed with Cotswold to the end, and the milled brass chassis block stayed too, but notable on this model was the underframe detail that included sandboxes and brakegear. Photos reveal extensive rivet detail on the model. The kit seems to have been available through the 1980s, to have been made at Spilsby around 1991, and to have come from Autocom in 1994. A new etched and correctly profiled chassis was fitted from 1995.

Back to Nu-Cast's Own

NU066/NC120 LNER/LMS/GWR/BR Sentinel Shunter 0-4-0T

After this long Cotswold excursus, progress resumes with the models that Nu-Cast generated. NU031 described Nu-Cast's Sentinel railcar; to offer the four wheeled Sentinel shunter was an obvious step, and this was done from September

1981. The kit was marketed as an economy kit, and came with an Anchoridge DS10 five-pole motor. The body was moulded in plastic, and castings were used for detail and chassis. Adverts and catalogues over some years showed made-up examples finished as LNER 148, GWR 13 and LMS 7161. There were some detail differences visible on the GWR example.

Further analysis is required to determine the prototypes associated with these numbers. LNER 148 was a single speed engine classified as Y1. LMS 7161 was the second of four turned out in 1930 - the LMS preferred diesels so watch out for a later re-numbering of the Sentinels to make way for those diesels. GWR 13 was an engine purchased in 1926 and used until 1946 - working mainly around the Slough Trading Estate. The kit best represented the later type of LNER loco with double chimney, compared with which GWR 13 showed several differences.

By 1986 the model's purchaser was left to buy the motor. The shunter then played an interesting role during the Spilsby era. It appears to have been the first item of renewed Nu-Cast production, and being advertised with a pre-assembled motor bogie from February 1990, it actually progressed to an illustrated advert that October. There was even a review in the November 1990 *Model Railways* - this was quite scathing, noting that the model was now fitted with a Tenshodo motor bogie, but sold with no instructions save an exploded drawing showing the earlier arrangement. The kit was back for the start at Autocom in May 1993, and in their hands is sold with or without a Tenshodo motor bogie.

NU067/NC265 GWR City o/f 4-4-0

Unlike so many Nu-Cast models, the GWR City class appeared with the minimum prior warning. It was advertised by Nu-Cast as available in the September 1981 Modeller, and progressed to an illustrated advert in the November issue which predictably enough featured 3440 *City of Truro*. Clearly such a model could have shared its development with a Flower, and in addition in the months before the merger, Cotswold and Nu-Cast had been working together - something about which more detail is needed.

That the City was begot by the Flower is further suggested by the detail of the frames whose etched outside frames and machined brass chassis block smacks of pure Cotswold influence. The shallower frames reveal a set of brakegear and rigging which were also present on the Flower. The tender also seems to have plentiful underframe detail.

Availability was general through the 1980s, but nothing is known of any production at Spilsby. Autocom started to advertise it from 1994.

NU068/NC254 GWR Steam Railmotor

With 1982 upon our narrative, Nu-Cast turned back to products more conventionally in their thinking. The GWR list had grown, and what the Sentinel was to the LNER, a GWR steam railmo-

tor was to that line, if a decade or so earlier. Nu-Cast had planned the model well before Cotswold was absorbed, and adverts since September 1980 had put it in the "coming soon" territory, and allocated the reference number.

The January 1982 advert priced it for the first time along with the D2. Precedence in this account is being given to the railmotor on the basis that the illustration sequence first features this model, which happened from the March 1982 advert. Despite being back in the Nu-Cast flow, no review is yet to hand. There was an increasing tendency in the 1980s for fewer kits to receive detail reviews, and it should be assumed from now on that no mention of a review implies that none has been traced.

Construction followed the principle of the Sentinel car, but the outside valve gear power bogie called for more refinement in a set of etched nickel silver valve gear. The model, however, remained a heavy affair. I have a verbal source that advises that the tooling was undertaken by Anbrico. Interior fittings and a well-detailed underframe were apparent. The prototype that was taken was a 70' car with the Nu-Cast example numbered 67 - that was a car that entered traffic in 1906, was withdrawn in 1927, whereupon without its engine unit it became autocar 152.

The kit was withdrawn around 1985, but was re-released with some fanfare in March 1987. It is unlikely that this release involved any re-engineering along the lines of the Sentinel, and the motor specified (as an Anchoridge DS10) was no different.

The kit was advertised for March 1994 by Autocom. An interesting variation has been available since that year - kit NC254Z is described as "GW trailer car". As mentioned above (and as widely recorded in sources) many of the former steam railmotors were turned into unpowered autotrailers. Such a variation is an obvious step, and to implement this the sides have been altered, and new ends, roof and bogies created. Work was put into the railmotor itself during 1997 when a new etched four-wheel drive power bogie was introduced.

NU069/NC109 GNR/LNER/BR D2 4-4-0

A model of Ivatt's 4-4-0, later to be LNER D2, had been "coming soon" since April 1980. It was priced from the January 1982 advert, but only from August 1982 is there a series of illustrated adverts. The kit provided for the 64 out of 70 engines with the curved running plate, in which state they were widely recognised as a most attractive engine. No production at Spilsby is known, and release from Autocom took place in December 1993.

NU070/NC221 LMS/BR Stanier 4MT 2-6-4T

The model of Stanier's 2-6-4T design seemed to have a short gestation - unless it owes anything to Cotswold's 1977 announcement of the Fowler

(top) K's BL2 GNR/LNER/BR J50 on Hornby Dublo chassis
Photo: Tony Wright, courtesy Autocom Collection

(right) Miscellaneous late preiod K's packaging
Photo: Tony Wright, courtesy Autocom Collection

(below) K's L22 GWR/BR AEC Railcar
Photo: Tony Wright, courtesy Ted Kanas

(over, top) K's L36 rebuilt LNER P2, finished as *Mons Meg*, with Romford Wheels and added brakegear

Photo: Tony Wright, courtesy Autocom Collection

(over, middle) Nu-Cast NC014 GWR/BR Dean Goods, with 1999 production etched chassis 3,000 gallon tender

Photo: Tony Wright, courtesy Autocom Collection

(over, bottom) Nu-Cast NC024Z GWR/BR Duke, with post-1998 2,500 gallon tender

Photo: Tony Wright, courtesy Autocom Collection

(above) Nu-Cast NC128 LNER/BR A2/1 4-6-2 ready for the paintshop

Photo: Tony Wright, courtesy Tony Wright

(below) Wills F115 LMS/BR original Stanier 3 cylinder 2-6-4T displayed on the genuine Wills exhibition display unit

Photo: Tony Wright, courtesy South Eastern Finecast Collection

L.M.S. CLASS 4
3 cylinder passenger locomotive

(left) South Eastern Finecast F124
(rightmost) Belpaire and F185
round top Flatirons built by Allan
Sibley
*Photo: Tony Wright, courtesy South
Eastern Finecast Collection*

(below) South Eastern Finecast
F154 SR/BR E1R 0-6-2T
*Photo: Tony Wright, courtesy South
Eastern Finecast Collection*

(bottom) South Eastern Finecast
F160 LNER/BR A2
*Photo: Tony Wright, courtesy South
Eastern Finecast Collection*

design. The February 1982 advert revealed it as "coming soon", and indeed it seems to have done so, being priced from the following month, and illustrated from June. Reference to a milled brass chassis could hint at a Cotswold ancestry, but Nu-Cast themselves had specified this on their Manor in 1980. Brakegear and rigging were present for the drivers.

The kit became the subject of a detailed analysis in that rare magazine, *Loco Modeller*, for November 1983. That spoke positively of the model except in respect of the valve gear which was found to be challenging. The kit was available through the rest of the 1980s, but no production at Spilsby is known. At Autocom the kit was advertised from September 1993.

NU071/NC154 LBSCR/SR/BR C2X 0-6-0

It was time next to fulfil a long-standing promise. As far back as December 1976 and the 1977 catalogue, a Brighton C2X 0-6-0 had been promised. Now, just as DJH managed to release theirs, so did Nu-Cast, and the launch adverts started in December 1982. Nu-Cast were certainly proud of their kit, and I just wish some additional commentary beyond the adverts could be traced.

As a prototype, the class had a following on the former LBSCR system. That was well explained by the noted and now deceased D. Fereday Glenn (in the June 1979 Modeller). He lamented the lack of a model for "the handsomest pre-grouping 0-6-0 of them all". A trifle partisan perhaps, but they were certainly interesting enough, and some lasted until 1962. They were rebuilds of the C2 "Vulcans" with a large boiler; the name coming from their original builder. The engines managed all sorts of detail differences, notably whether they sprouted one or two domes. Casserley claimed that the second dome was a second top feed apparatus, yet Glenn put it down to sanding equipment.

Furthermore, in Southern days, they strayed from the Central section, and to cope with this, chimneys and domes were cropped. Quite a number of alternative fittings were needed, and Nu-Cast certainly supplied most if not all. Brakegear even on the tender would appear to have been *de rigueur* on the Nu-Cast specification now. Matching LBSCR wagons came as an accompaniment.

At times a number of kit manufacturers advertised their wares ready-to-run; Jidenco and DJH being examples. Nu-Cast had advertised batches of the B1, and the practice was revived with the C2X. The basic kit cost £36, ready-to-run she was £159.67 and £183.82 for the SR and LBSCR finishes respectively. Nothing is known of any production at Spilsby, and when introduced at Autocom from November 1993, the engine was one of the earlier beneficiaries of the programme of chassis replacement, with a new and more detailed etched brass chassis. Around 1997 provision for alternative SR or BR coal rails was made.

NU072/NC135 LNER/BR K1 2-6-0

The workaday Gresley ex-GNR K2 2-6-0 was already a familiar Nu-Cast model. To complement that with a model of the 70-strong LNER designed Peppercorn two cylinder K1 series of 1949 made sense. Unless you are modelling the preserved 2005, do not paint these in LNER livery! The kit has an illustrated release advert in the April 1983 Modeller. This was yet another finely detailed model - it is known that the masters for the kit came from Michael Sheppard. There seems to have been production at Spilsby around 1991, and Autocom re-released the kit from June 1993.

NU073/NC155 LSWR/SR T14 Paddlebox 4-6-0

Nu-Cast next moved to a Southern prototype which lent itself to future development (see NU081). Drummond's LSWR 4-6-0s never achieved the success of the 4-4-0s that he designed for this line. He managed an assortment of five designs, and there were ten in class T14 which Nu-Cast chose. The nickname Paddlebox came from the splasher shape. In their lifetimes, they existed with three distinct shapes, and Nu-Cast's two kits would provide two of the outlines, and generate a model of an LSWR large 5,800 gallon eight wheeled water-cart tender (not the normal eight wheeled Drummond double bogied inside framed tender used on the T9). Kit NC155 showed the class after Urie had got to them from 1915 - there is a superheater, an extended smokebox, but no firebox water tubes.

The model was new for the October 1983 advert, having been flagged since the Summer, and it followed the usual specification. New engines of this time often were designed (like this one) for an "XO4" type motor which, along with the milled brass frames, was a bit restrictive.

However, it is possible that the chassis for this model requires more comment - the Modeller in April spoke of the T14 featuring "Nu-Cast's new and superb machined brass frames". Precisely how this ties into the Cotswold inheritance, or Nu-Cast's own brass chassis (as designed for the Manor back in 1980) is not yet clear to me. Mike Griffiths described that chassis as "etched chassis, tender bogies and cosmetic spring detail". For an illustrated advert one has to turn to the November 1984 Modeller. This model was withdrawn in 1987, none appeared at Spilsby, but it was produced by Autocom from August 1993, and withdrawn in 1999.

NU074/NC351 Wickham type 27 motor trolley

Can the next model take the award for the most unusual piece of traction that Nu-Cast modelled? How easy it would have been to overlook this kit of an unpowered (in model form) Wickham motor trolley of the Permanent Way gang. These were ubiquitous features of the prototype but are rarely modelled. Nu-Cast's appeared for £4.99 from the October 1983 advert, and gave you the

(above) Nu-Cast **NC154 LBSCR/SR/BR C2X 0-6-0** - compare the boiler fittings and the coal rails to the example on page 42
Photo: Tony Wright, courtesy Autocom Collection

(left) Nu-Cast **NC351 Wickham type 27 motor trolley** Hartlepool era packaging
Photo: Tony Wright, courtesy Autocom Collection

(below) Nu-Cast **NC156 LSWR/SR/BR rebuilt Paddlebox 4-6-0**
Photo: Tony Wright, courtesy Les Spratt

trolley and a trailer. As far back as September 1979 Nu-Cast had produced a Wickham in N gauge.

The Type 27 modelled has open sides with rolled canvas covers, solid ends and a roof. They were built in quantity during the 1950s, and were popular on the Cambrian lines amongst many others. In the partial disintegration of Nu-Cast in the late 1980s, the wagon range went to ABS, and along went the Wickhams to that destination too.

NU075/NC136 LNER/BR V1/V3 2-6-2T

Hanging over from the December 1971 advert of some thirteen years before, there was still an outstanding model to deliver. A Gresley 2-6-2T had been promised back then and subsequently, and it would fit in well with Nu-Cast's ethos of providing locos for North Eastern modellers. Finally the January 1984 Modeller announced its imminent arrival, and I take the priced and illustrated advert in March showing LNER 7684 as my release datum. A maker's plate was prominent on the made-up model which has never been in the kit, but a fine chassis and set of valve gear were etched components. Visually there was little to tell between the two classes of V1 and V3. Engines could vary with regard to their bunkers, and whether a Westinghouse brake was fitted; Nu-Cast provided for these alternatives. The kit was produced at Spilsby around 1991 and was back for Autocom's 1994 list.

NU076/NC266 GWR/BR Hall 4-6-0 3,500g Churchward tender

Following on from the V1/V3 came an ambitious project. Nu-Cast decided to produce (in their own words) "the first scale Hall kit to be produced without any major compromises in dimensions". The existing Wills kit was aged and dimensionally compromised (see Wills' chapter). With the advantage of an existing Churchward 3,500 gallon tender (off the Manor ex-Nu-Cast), and Hawksworth and Collett tenders (ex-Cotswold), a range of Halls could be replicated. It was decided to model both the Collett and the Hawksworth Halls. No names or numbers were provided by Nu-Cast.

The project was revealed in the July 1984 Modeller advert, but coincidentally the same magazine had DJH thirty miles up the road announcing theirs. Five Nu-Cast models were to come, and NC266 of a model in an early state was new for the October advert.

Brakes on the tender suggest either that the Manor tender always had them, or that the tender model had been further developed. The engine also had brakes, and a great host of other details confirm that these are fine kits. The chassis design prevented any thoughts of compensation though, and the way the market was behaving that might have been seen as a drawback. It is certainly a pity no review has been traced for any of these Hall models.

Nu-Cast's own model appeared as 4911 *Bowden*

Hall, a loco BR never owned. According to an M. G. Sharp advert in December 1984, the Hall kits were intended as limited editions of 100 each. All the versions of Hall were re-made at Spilsby (i.e. in October 1991), and all five versions were re-advertised from Autocom in June 1993.

NU077/NC267 GWR/BR Modified Hall 4-6-0 Hawksworth tender

The second Hall model, with the ex-Cotswold Hawksworth tender seen on their County, coupled to a wartime-build Hall, was also new that October of 1984. Availability otherwise is charted under NU076. Wheels were supplied with all Hall kits, and does this mean that the distinctive wheel on these modified engines with an in-filled web below the crank pin was featured? Unfortunately not!

NU078/NC268 GWR/BR Hall 4-6-0 Collett tender

The pre-war Hall coupled to the Collett tender (certainly having brakegear and a water pick-up) off Cotswold's 47xx, was illustrated as a new kit in November 1984's Modeller advert. Availability otherwise is charted under NU076.

NU079/NC222 LMS/BR Ivatt 2MT 2-6-0

Breaking the run of Halls came another model which was warmly requested, and for which patience has been required. A model of Ivatt's 2MT 2-6-0 as designed for the LMS in 1946 seemed attractive. Hornby's model had not lasted long, and otherwise in 4mm there was only the Jidenco model.

A January 1984 advert that one would be made was welcome reading. After some apologies for delay the loco probably appeared just in time for Christmas 1984. It seems to have the usual copious detailing, and two of the several chimneys are provided.

This model was manufactured at Spilsby around 1990 - apparently one of the first so done, but disappeared during the Autocom period for a long time despite being consistently marked as "available later". This absence partially reflected perceived failings with the tender's chassis. These were corrected when from October 1996 a new part-etched tender was introduced, and the full model was re-released in December 1999. This coincided with the release of a 4mm Comet kit, thus competing for a market which up until then had largely neglected these 128 LMS designed engines.

NU080/NC269 GWR/BR Modified Hall 4-6-0 Collett tender

The Modified Hall fitted with a Collett tender arrived in March 1985. Availability otherwise is charted under NU076.

(above) Nu-Cast NC004 GWR/BR 44xx 2-6-2T showing clearly the new chassis detail
Photo: Tony Wright, courtesy Autocom Collection

(right) Nu-Cast NC020 LBSCR/SR/BR Terrier 0-6-0T in post-1995 form with etched chassis, showing clearly that the model doesn't have an extended smokebox, thus the kit is an A1 engine
Photo: Tony Wright, courtesy Autocom Collection

(below) Nu-Cast NC028 GWR/BR 26xx Aberdare o/f 0-6-0 in post-1993 condition
Photo: Tony Wright, courtesy Autocom Colection

NU081/NC156 LSWR/SR T14 rebuilt Paddlebox 4-6-0

A lot of 1985 then passed without much activity on the loco front. The next move was to offer the ex-LSWR T14 as heavily rebuilt in Southern days, so losing their paddleboxes altogether. The May 1985 advert flagged this version as "coming soon". Exactly when this kit did appear has eluded me, but it was in time for the 1986 catalogue. October 1985 is being hazarded as a guess whilst we lack more information.

NU082/NC271 GWR Armstrong 388 o/f 0-6-0

As we move into the last year of "classic" Nu-Cast's activity in Durham as far as releasing loco kits are concerned, there were only two entirely new prototypes to come. Both of them were most attractive examples as kits of distinctive mid-Victorian prototypes. The first went to the GWR as Armstrong's 388 or Standard Goods. The prototype was a straight framed engine of which 310 were turned out from 1866, and can be seen in distinction to the similar vintage curved frame 322 or Beyer Goods which K's had produced. Both led the way to the well-known Dean Goods. Nu-Cast intended their kit as a contribution to GW 150 which was being celebrated in 1985, and they achieved this with a release announcement in the June 1985 Modeller, and actual release adverts in the November and December issues.

The kit focused on the variables that could be modelled for the engines as running in the 20th century. To finish an engine exactly, reference to textbooks would be essential, but generally speaking Nu-Cast's options allowed for round top or Belpaire fireboxes, short or extended smokeboxes, and alternative boiler fittings.

Various tenders could be fitted, but Nu-Cast offered a kit for an 1800 gallon version where the springs were hung externally above the framing, which was very antique in appearance. The outside frames were etched, and the level of rivet detail throughout was appealing. The trademark of Cotswold heritage in an opening smokebox door was present. Autocom was able to release this kit for their June 1993 advert.

An additional variant came from Autocom in May 1998. Known as NC271Z, this provided an option with a 2,500 gallon small tender having an etched underframe and brakegear, and this was then applied to four suitable GWR models.

NU083/NC138 NER P1/LNER/BR J25 0-6-0

In February 1986 the next two releases appeared in a nicely ambiguous "coming soon" yet priced category in the advert. One was for the NER P1 or LNER J25 class. This was in many respects the J21 which was a long-standing member of the range (see NU014), but with smaller driving wheels for goods work. Since the kit included driving wheels, further detail about them and any amendments from the first J21 kit is sought. It seems likely that both this and the next kit

were available in time for the Easter Show at York. It is not thought that the kit was made at Spilsby, but it has been in the Autocom range since the outset in May 1993.

NU084/NC137 NER/LNER/BR N8/N9 0-6-2T

A similar process of amendment produced a full kit with a new chassis for the NER 0-6-2T of classes N8 and N9 (see NU013). Now an entirely new kit, both body and chassis was generated. Stock was seemingly sold at Spilsby, but production there is unlikely. At Autocom the kit was back in the advert from June 1994.

NU085/NC139 NER/LNER BTP G6 0-4-4T

The last substantive entirely new loco kit to come from Nu-Cast, seen as I write in 1999, has now to be discussed. It was appropriately enough (though I guess no one appreciated its valedictory setting at the time) a pukka NER engine, and a worthwhile yet neglected prototype to boot, just the recipe that Nu-Cast had adopted for the Q6 at the outset. The engine was the BTP tank or Bogie Tank Passenger. Fletcher had built these from 1874, and of 130, 46 came to the LNER, with the class being extinct by 1929. Two matters made them distinctive: like the MR 0-4-4T, their tanks were well hidden; and many were fitted for auto working, nineteen of which came to the LNER. Their unusual outline and typical duties turned them into an indispensable shape for many an NER branch line.

There are a considerable amount of etched components on the kit. These included brakegear, firegrate and a choice of splashers. The model was out in August 1986, and available from Autocom in July 1993. The obvious partner for this distinctive engine would be a porthole windowed clerestory autocoach, and the April 1986 announcement advert had promised one. I am not sure that it progressed further however.

NU086/NC270 GWR/BR Hall 4-6-0 Hawksworth tender

NU086 stands in this narrative for the final new loco kit from Hartlepool in providing the pre-war Hall as sometimes partnered with the later Hawksworth tender. Little fanfare announced its arrival beside the G6 in August 1986. Availability otherwise is charted under NU076.

The K's Influx

The strange period of the Lincolnshire residence now intervened. The public evidence of new ownership for K's was first seen in Brian Emberton's HMC group. Practically speaking this meant that Nu-Cast, what was now called Nu-Kays, and M&L Premier were all bedfellows. Despite the shared ownership, K's kits were not integrated into the Nu-Cast range until the next move which took the business to Autocom in Andover in May 1993.

(right) Nu-Cast NC039 LMS/BR 0-6-0T Dock tank

Photo: Dave Wheatstone, courtesy Dave Wheatstone Collection

(below) The 1995 production of the Nu-Cast NC006 NER/LNER/BR J72 0-6-0 with the new etched chassis

Photo: Tony Wright, courtesy Autocom Collection

(bottom) Nu-Cast NC013 GWR/BR Grange 4-6-0 as modelled after 1991 with a Nu-Cast Hall chassis, and with added detailing

Photo: Tony Wright, courtesy Autocom Collection

The following block of kits therefore describes the K's range during the period of Nu-Kays and during the Autocom ownership. The dates quoted in the tables at the end of the chapter will reflect the date of introduction at Autocom as traced through their regular Modeller advert. We shall not repeat the prototypical information as described in the K's chapter to which the reader is referred. The NC references appear from Autocom, and since the original Nu-Cast range started at NC101, it was a simple matter to re-use the K's number with a prefix.

NU087/NC003/K's L3 GWR/BR Bulldog 3252 (sic) o/f 4-4-0

Leading the way on this analysis is K's Bulldog, one of the nine ex-K's kits that featured in Autocom's May 1993 advert. The new Nu-Cast's description does prompt some discussion of the prototype, since for both this kit and the Duke they list the engines as "3252". That number is correct for the Duke, but I suspect a mistype under the Bulldog entry. Number 3352 was the first Bulldog, but the problem with that is that it had curved frames, and the ex-K's model is still one for the shallow straight framed engines only. Therefore the description should read 33xx.

A Spilsby-made Bulldog has not been noted. Autocom put the Bulldog into their initial May 1993 list, and from April 1994 the kit enjoyed a new chassis. These have the specification encountered in discussing the upgrading of some of the classic Nu-Cast range (see NU052). In other words, etched brass screw together frames which differed from the inherited K's version in showing the correct frame profile, along with dummy springing. For the three GWR 4-4-0s from the K's range, the one new chassis included an etched drawbar and bogie tie-bar. There was provision to fit brakegear which had been a notable omission on many K's locos.

In 1999 a new model of a 3,000 gallon tender was fitted which had become available from work on the Dean Goods.

NU088/NC004/K's L4 GWR/BR 44xx 2-6-2T

Back at the outset of Autocom in May 1993 came the 44xx which gained a new etched chassis by August 1994. The loco is not thought to have been made at Spilsby. Etched connecting rods have been used since March 1994, the first so introduced by Autocom and shared with the 45xx.

NU089/NC008/K's L8 LMS Karrier Ro-rail bus

Most of the K's range was stocked at Spilsby, and as the Modeller advert in February 1990 shows, gained the Nu-Kays brand. I am minded to believe that any actual production came later. So neither Mike Griffiths nor I believe the Karrier was made in Lincolnshire. It was a member of Autocom's first advert, and at that point it was a body only kit (and I wonder whether that still indicates ex-K's stock, after all these were hardly

best sellers?). Genuine new production of the kit awaited the January 1996 Modeller advert. At this point a new batch most emphatically had appeared for the body only, using new moulds. Behind it was to come a motorising kit, but plans for which have now been abandoned. Instead, instructions for motorising the kit with a Tenshodo bogie are furnished within the packaging.

NU090/NC010/K's L10 GWR/BR 1361 0-6-0ST

Another in from the outset at Autocom was the 1361 dock tank which lacks any specific information regarding Spilsby production. New frame sets for this kit were first advertised from September 1994, and these corrected the loco height and wheel spacing, and comparing old and new models clearly shows the difference. Additionally, by March of 1995, new etched valve gear and brass cylinders were being fitted. Etched connecting rods were used from the same time.

NU091/NC012/K's L12 MR/LMS/BR Kirtley o/f 0-6-0

The lovely Kirtley outside framed 0-6-0 is not recorded as produced at Spilsby, but it was with Autocom at their outset. Quite soon, by December 1993, a new etched chassis had been originated.

NU092/NC016/K's L16 MR/LMS/BR Johnson 0-6-0

The Kirtley's Johnson relative was similarly quiet, we think, in Lincolnshire. It reappeared beside the Kirtley and shared the new etched chassis that Autocom produced for the Kirtley. The springs provided on the one etch are kept for the Johnson and cut off for the Kirtley.

One element of the K's legacy Autocom inherited were those plastic inside frames for tenders which earned K's few friends. A gradual programme to replace these with an etched chassis and brakegear is a second major strand in the upgrading of former K's kits. A tender suitable for the Johnson (and for the Spinner) was released for October 1996.

NU093/NC024/K's L24 GWR/BR 3252 Duke o/f 4-4-0

NU094/NC026/K's L26 GWR/BR Earl/Dukedog o/f 4-4-0 3,500 gallon tender

The Duke and Dukedog class locos' tale at Autocom parallels that of the Bulldog already described. From April 1998 a new etched chassis 2,500 gallon small tender kit was available, and this was followed in May by a full kit version (NC024Z) using this tender attached to a Duke.

(above) The leftmost locomotive is the body-only kit Nu-Cast NC015A of the LMS/BR Fowler 3P, as produced from October 1993; the loco to the right is the body of ex-Poole Nu-Cast produced NC121 GNR/LNER/BR N2
Photo: Tony Wright, courtesy Autocom Collection

(right) Nu-Kays components as supplied and packed from Spilsby; L47 is NC047 LMS/BR 8F 2-8-0
Photo: Tony Wright, courtesy Nick Gillman

(below) Nu-Cast NC035 LMS/BR Stanier Mogul
Photo: Dave Wheatstone, courtesy Dave Wheatstone Collection

NU095/NC032/K's L32 LMS/BR Beyer Garratt 2-6-0+0-6-2

With the Garratt, an engine is encountered that was produced at Spilsby, being so advertised from January 1991, and more new production allowed it to be featured in Autocom's initial advert. A new etched chassis and valve gear has been produced and is sold separately, since to use them requires surgery to the main kit.

NU096/NC007/K's L7 GER/LNER/BR J70 0-6-0T tram

Initially, Autocom adverts introduced the full range of what was available in batches. In the second advert (June 1993) there were six ex-K's models including this tram. Prior to that, the J70 tram engine had been made at Spilsby. Around May 1994 a few were advertised and sold assembled but unpainted, and with the motor bogie ex the factory. In the Autocom list, it is sold either as a body only kit or with a Tenshodo motor bogie.

NU097/NC019/K's L19 LSWR/SR/BR Adams Radial 4-4-2T

The Adams radial tank had been made around 1991 at Spilsby, and was therefore ready to be advertised in June 1993. From October 1994 the kit has been available in a substantially updated form - the core of this being the new etched chassis which included etched spring hanger plates and a bogie tie-bar. A substantial amount of additional changes provide brass cylinders, lost wax and etched details including alternative chimneys and domes. K's kit originally had Drummond fittings, and at this point Adams versions were added. What used to be a cast whitemetal cylinder crosshead became a lost wax nickel silver casting.

The etched nickel silver detailing fret includes *inter alia* coal rails, brakegear and lamp irons. Normally the kits come with wheels, but the detail of motor choice and gearing is left to the buyer - in the Nu-Cast era, an additional package including the DS10 motor was an option, and these days a separate motorising kit is retailed by Autocom.

NU098/NC020/K's L20 LBSCR/SR/BR Terrier 0-6-0T

No Terrier production has been noted at Spilsby, and apart from the June 1993 Autocom advert and its subsequent presence in Autocom's list, the Terrier appears to have led a surprisingly quiet recent life. The only changes noted were during 1995 when a new etched profile chassis with corrected axle spacings and new coupling rods were fitted.

NU099/NC025/K's L25 GWR/BR 4575/55xx 2-6-2T

As Nu-Kays L25, what was billed as a 55xx was newly produced at Spilsby in January 1991. This was the sloping tank top small Prairie variety numbered above 4575. Despite the Spilsby pro-duction, the initial listing in 1993 from Autocom was a further new batch. From March 1994 etched connecting rods were available. The kit was listed by Autocom in 1994 and 1996, but in the Modeller full list advert for the range in December 1997, it had been dropped. Existing stocks have become low with the next move being to provide a new chassis.

NU100/NC028/K's L28 GWR/BR 26xx Aberdare o/f 2-6-0

Nothing is known of Aberdare production under Nu-Kays, but Autocom were able to revive the model in June 1993. A new etched chassis and drawbar were applied from December 1993. K's had never taken the obvious step of offering the class with a ROD 2-8-0 tender which they had available. Nu-Cast did this from February 1994 using the NC028Z reference for this option.

NU101/NC039/K's L39 LMS/BR Fowler Dock tank 0-6-0T

Apart from being reported in the June 1993 advert and being in subsequent Autocom lists, the Fowler Dock tank had led a sheltered existence both in Lincolnshire and Hampshire. What was quite a good model in the first instance has not yet merited changes.

NU102/NC006/K's L6 NER/LNER/BR J72 0-6-0T

At Spilsby there was new production of the J72 around 1991, and this probably enabled the engine to feature as one of the five ex-K's locos in the July 1993 advert. The new etched chassis was advertised from January 1995.

NU103/NC009/K's L9 GWR/BR 14xx 0-4-2T

The 14xx has had an eventful time with Autocom. New production was advertised in July 1993, and a new etched chassis was advertised from December 1993. Integration of chassis and body waited until early 1995, when from February a new kit was available. The revised chassis was supplemented by new fittings for the brake gear, a retooled running plate structure, new buffers, whistle and top feed, and added detail to the spectacle plates.

NU104/NC013/K's L13 GWR/BR Grange 4-6-0

The Grange, which appeared in the July 1993 advert, had been made at Spilsby around 1991. After 1991, production used the Nu-Cast Hall chassis, and one benefit of Autocom's ownership was an etched set of connecting rods from April 1995. The kit was in the 1996 list, but not in the December 1997 datum, having been withdrawn pending reworking of the masters.

NU105/NC041/K's L41 LMS Turbomotive 4-6-2

Nu-Kays issued the Turbomotive and otherwise

(above) Nu-Cast 1998 production NC011 MR/LMS Spinner o/f 4-2-2

Photo: Tony Wright, courtesy Autocom Collection

(below) Original instructions artwork from K's for the Nu-Cast NC011 MR/LMS Single 4-2-2

Photo: Tony Wright, courtesy Autocom Collection

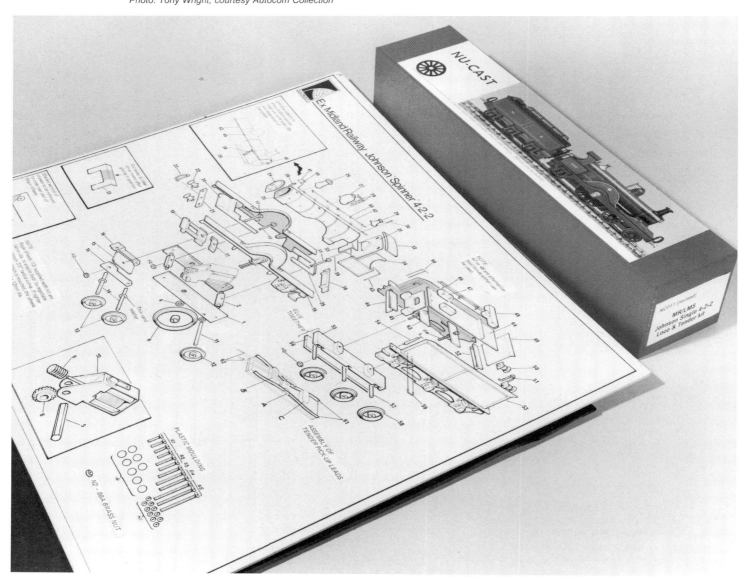

apart from its re-appearance from July 1993, there appears little to add.

NU106/NC046/K's L46 LMS/BR Duchess 4-6-2

We are not aware of the Duchess actually being made at Spilsby although inherited examples were certainly advertised, and whether these old stocks were the kits mentioned in later Autocom adverts of July 1993 is not known. The model was listed through to the Autocom 1996 list but was not present in December 1997, having been deleted.

NU107/NC002/K's L2 LNWR/LMS/BR Coal Tank 0-6-2T

New production of the Coal Tank took place around 1991 at Spilsby, and further stock was produced for the August 1993 Autocom advert. A new etched chassis was available by February 1995.

NU108/NC005/K's L5 GCR/ROD/LNER/LMS/GWR/BR 2-8-0

The ROD 2-8-0 was made around 1991 at Spilsby. It was advertised by Autocom in August 1993, and new etched connecting rods and an etched chassis with etched cylinder stretcher and drawbar came in 1994. A revised tender with etched chassis was fitted by the Winter of 1997.

NU109/NC023/K's L23 GWR/BR 28xx 2-8-0

The 28xx was in the August 1993 advert as new production, and by 1996 this loco had an etched chassis/slotted stretcher and drawbar. A year later the kit was not listed - there are complications relating to the K's running plate which suits early builds only, despite which both types of cab were included. As a result, pending a revision, the kit is now withdrawn.

NU110/NC029/K's L29 GNR/LNER C1 4-4-2

Much the same applies to the GNR Atlantic as said for the 28xx about initial production. Additionally, the tender now included is the Ivatt type designed by Nu-Cast.

NU111/NC037/K's L37 MR/LMS/BR Johnson 1500 series 0-4-0ST

Again, except for an initial mention in the August 1993 advert, and subsequent appearances in the company's list, little detail is known about the Johnson tank subsequent to 1988. A new etched chassis was available in 1995.

NU112/NC043/K's L43 BR (WR) 15xx 0-6-0PT

For the 15xx, beyond this August 1993 appearance and subsequent listings, there is neither known Spilsby production, nor the advent of an etched chassis to distract.

NU113/NC044/K's L44 GNR/LNER/BR J3 0-6-0

Comments as for the 15xx mentioned previously, except that an etched chassis has been introduced and the Nu-Cast Ivatt tender is now used.

NU114/NC015/K's L15 LMS/BR Fowler 2-6-2T

Matters are more complicated for the Fowler 2-6-2T. Spilsby production around 1991 is recorded, and the loco was advertised by Autocom from September 1993. So it appears in the 1994 list, but it then disappeared from list adverts only to re-appear from October 1996 as a body only kit NC015A. The K's chassis and gear are not felt to be acceptable, and a new etched chassis is under development.

NU115/NC017/K's L17 GWR/BR 57/87xx 0-6-0PT

The classic GWR Pannier was made at Spilsby around 1991, and so appears from Autocom in the September 1993 advert. A new etched chassis appeared from February 1994.

NU116/NC030/K's L30 LMS Ivatt 2P/BR 84xxx 2-6-2T

Apart from the appearance in the September 1993 advert and subsequent lists, the Ivatt 2-6-2T seems to have led a quiet existence since 1988. However, a new etched and profiled chassis was fitted in 1995.

NU117/NC033/K's L33 LBSCR/SR/BR K class 2-6-0

No Spilsby production is recorded, but new Autocom production put the K class Mogul into the October 1993 advert. In May 1994 etched connecting rods became available with marine type big ends. The kit is in the 1994 list, but had disappeared from the full list published in June 1995. A new tender with etched chassis was advertised from October 1996, and this probably led to the loco being priced in the December 1996 list; against which evidence however the loco was still not available a year later. The loco itself remains the subject of an ongoing reworking of the masters and chassis, the result of which was scheduled to see daylight at the Warley Show in November 1998. Certainly a pre-production example was displayed there but there still remained work to do.

In the Summer of 1999, the new model was imminent. The new model has all alternatives including LBSCR and SR cabs, a new running plate, one-piece cab floor, smokebox and firebox castings. The tender can be made with or without etched coal rails, and the chassis and valve gear are new and both are etched brass.

NU118/NC014/K's L14 GWR/BR Dean Goods i/f 0-6-0

No evidence is before us that the Dean Goods was made at Spilsby. Autocom were advertising it from November 1993 with a new etched chassis, but why is the chassis not detailed in the 1996 Nu-Cast list? The answer is that policy is now to use a modified NC017 57xx chassis.

Nu-Cast has used the reference NC014Z for the outside framed variant that K's had originated. From April 1998 a new etched chassis 2,500 gallon small tender was advertised which could be applied to the two types of loco. In May 1998 full kits fitted with this were advertised as NC014Y and NC014YZ.

For NC014 itself, a new etched nickel silver chassis 3,000 gallon tender with a wholly new cast body was originated in 1999. This was then applied to other suitable locos.

NU119/NC034/K's L34 LMS/BR Jubilee 4-6-0

The Jubilee was made at Spilsby around 1991 and was back at Autocom by November 1993. Otherwise it has simply plodded on.

NU120/NC042/K's L42 LMS/BR Princess 4-6-2

The Princess was made at Spilsby around 1991. Apart from appearing in the November 1993 advert and subsequent lists, no other developments are known until the kit was withdrawn in 1998 pending re-tooling.

NU121/NC035/K's L35 LMS/BR Stanier 2-6-0

Having been made at Spilsby so it seems, the Stanier 2-6-0 was in Autocom's advert from January 1994. No other developments are recorded.

NU122/NC047/K's L47 LMS/BR Stanier 8F 2-8-0

Having been made at Spilsby, the Stanier 2-8-0 was in Autocom's advert from January 1994. At some point during 1997 the kit was dropped from the list. Despite that, some stock was available in 1998 but it will not be advertised again until a new chassis is developed.

NU123/NC048/K's L45 TVR/GWR/BR S class 0-4-0ST

Between the end of K's and its appearance in the February 1994 advert, the production history of the TVR class S is not known. Subsequently, it had received its own etched chassis by 1996.

NU124/NC021/K's L21 SR/BR Q1 0-6-0

The distinctive Q1 was turned out from Spilsby around 1991. It is in the Autocom advert from March 1994 when the kit was supplied with

Gibson wheels, and by the 1996 list the wheels used were the Markits variety. That change probably occurred as early as September 1994 when a number so fitted were advertised from Autocom ready-built. The kit was not in late 1997 listings. From April 1998 a new etched chassis tender was advertised. New masters are required for the loco itself.

NU125/NC040/K's L40 GCR/LNER B2 Sir Sam Fay 4-6-0

The B2 was made at Spilsby around 1991. It re-appears from Autocom in their August 1994 advert, and a new tender with brakegear and etched chassis has been introduced.

NU126/NC036/K's L36 LNER 1936 build P2 2-8-2

The year 1994 saw the release of both versions of the P2. Both had been made at Spilsby around 1991. Their re-release was previewed in the Summer of 1994, and the Streamliner arrived to feature in the October advert with its new etched chassis. This revision saw the tender comprehensively upgraded with an etched chassis, and the fret had the tender brake shoes and rodding too.

NU127/NC038/K's L38 NER/LNER/BR Y8 0-4-0T

The Y8's production history at Spilsby is not recorded, but it was back for Autocom's 1994 list and their October 1994 advert. A new etched chassis was produced for the engine in 1994.

NU128/NC051/K's L51 LNER original P2 2-8-2

Apart from arriving for the November 1994 advert, comments apply as made for NU126. As seen in 1999, this was the final full kit re-introduction from K's. In 1999 lost wax crossheads were about to be fitted.

NU129/NC001/K's L1 LMS/BR Black 5 4-6-0

The Black Five was made at Spilsby around 1991. It was present through Autocom's own lists in 1994-1997 but otherwise little is known of recent changes - if there have been any at all. For this, and the three succeeding entries, no date for a first advert has been traced, hence they are placed at the end of the 1994 programme, but they were quite possibly available in 1993.

NU130/NC011/K's L11 MR/LMS Spinner o/f 4-2-2

It is not thought that the Spinner was made at Spilsby, but kits were priced in 1994. The full kit was not priced in 1996 or 1997, instead from October 1996 a new tender appeared. This has an etched chassis and full brakegear. Over the Winter of 1997/98 progress on a revived full kit with a new etched loco chassis and Gibson drivers was made. From April 1998 the new etched mainframes and bogie were advertised followed in May by the full kit.

NU131/NC118/K's L18 GWR/BR 63xx 2-6-0

Churchward's Mogul was made at Spilsby around 1991 which is probably how the model comes to be priced in Autocom's 1994 list. In 1995 suitable etched connecting rods were marketed separately, but the loco kit disappeared. Despite which, the loco was priced in the 1996 list only to be missing again in 1997 adverts, the background being that in 1995 a new etched chassis was made. New cylinders appeared in 1999 along with a new etched tender chassis, etched sidebars and crosshead, and a boiler backhead was added at this point also. The new etched tender chassis is being widely applied to suitable GWR prototypes.

NU132/NC049/K's L49 BR Bulleid rebuilt Merchant Navy 4-6-2

Some evidence suggests the rebuilt Merchant Navy loco was made at Spilsby around 1991, although this is doubted by those close to the business. In any event, Autocom cast some additional stock and the kit was being advertised again in 1994. The kit was then dropped in 1996, although as part of an intended upgrade, a new etched chassis for a 6,000 gallon tender was released in October 1996.

NU133/NC272 GWR/BR 57xx 0-6-0PT

Over 1995-1996 the Nu-Cast's reference series grew by four numbers, each requiring some special pleading. Back in February 1994, a new etched chassis had been produced for the 57xx. It was realised that this would in addition fit the Replica 57xx, and from January 1995 a complete package was advertised for this option comprising chassis, DS10 motor, gears and body (GWR or BR finish to choice).

NU134/NC273 BR 2251 0-6-0

The same process was adopted from October 1995 for the 22xx, but only BR black bodies from Replica were available which were numbered 2203. The etched brass frames in this case were specially originated.

NU135/NC052 GWR Bird class 4-4-0

The only free standing introduction in 1996 was NC052 for a GWR Bird. K's had actually created this deep-framed Bulldog variant years before by providing a deep frame casting that was sold separately. All that then happened is that the components were packed to form a full kit, with a 3,500 gallon Churchward tender being packed too.

NU136/NC048/K's L48 LMS/BR Streamlined Coronation 4-6-2

We have not traced specific evidence confirming any Spilsby production of the *Coronation*, and it has been shy of adverts at Autocom. In the 1994 list it was marked "shortly"; it is priced in the 1996 list, but was not present in our December 1997 datum. The explanation is possibly given by the "A" suffix in 1996 and the comment "body and tender". Nu-Cast have written off the inherited K's chassis, yet a stock of some bodies has been hanging around for which it was felt worth pricing in 1996. The full kit will not reappear.

At least one of these bodies ended up sold and provides an insight into the Wrenn, K's and Nu-Cast *Coronation* models. Bill Woods in *Model Railway Enthusiast* March 1999 compared all three models. When details were compared (such as the provision of an integrally cast chimney), it was clear that the model Nu-Cast had was closer to the Wrenn casting than the K's. It lends credence to the argument that K's produced their model, then altered it for the Wrenn contract, and that those patterns passed to Nu-Cast.

NU137/NC031/K's L31 GWR 322 class o/f 0-6-0

The 322 class is another "shortly" engine; there was no attention paid to the model for many years, until a new etched chassis came in 1998 correcting inherited K's failings. With the 1998 2,500 gallon tender available, this engine was displayed at the Warley Show later in that year, and re-release took place in 1999.

Nu-Cast Proposals

All kits above for which no withdrawal date is cited in text or table have been checked as being in production against the December 1997 Modeller advert full list. The following models relate to proposals that never entered production. The glory of K's proper was that there were only two kits which never made it - the 850 class GWR tank and the same tank with the crane attachment. With Nu-Cast the story is rather different - there is an absolute forest of proposals from Nu-Cast pre-1986. Some of these gained references that we have traced, others probably occupy some of the missing numbers in the table, and a few were really just whims. For a handful it seems possible that considerable development work was carried out, about which it would be of interest to know more.

Finally, this category has to describe the K's models that so far have not reappeared from Autocom, and amongst those are some models which Autocom have a genuine intention in producing. No Nuxxx numbers have been generated.

NC106 LNER/BR D49/1 Shire 4-4-0
Never produced

NC107 NER/BR D49/2 Hunt 4-4-0
Never produced

The project to produce both versions of Gresley's 4-4-0 was announced back in June 1972. Reference numbers were quoted in November 1974 and the plan was still on the stocks in 1977. Did the proposal get to a drawing board or any further? DJH's kit released in 1974 was likely to dissuade production.

NC106 NER/LNER/BR T1 4-8-0T
Never produced

An idea for a T1 4-8-0T inherited one of the 4-4-0 references in 1983. It was "coming soon" in a number of places into 1984. Box labels were produced, but was anything else done?

NC129 LNER/BR A2/2+A2/3 4-6-2
Never produced

Under the entry for NU037/NC128 the detailed background was given to the failed attempt to offer models of Thompson's rebuild of the P2 and his own from-scratch Pacific design.

NC134 LNER U1 Beyer Garratt 2-8-0+0-8-2 *Never produced*

What a model the Worsbrough banker would have been, and both DJH and Nu-Cast announced it in 1982. It was "coming soon" in numerous Nu-Cast sources through to 1984, but really DJH beat them to it. The reference number is culled from box labels that were prepared.

NC153 LSWR/SR Adams T3 4-4-0
Never produced

The T3 is another comparatively little known model. In 1980 Jidenco/Falcon would offer one in 4mm, so Nu-Cast's model was probably dealt a body blow by that. The kit had been announced in several locations between October 1976 and 1983, but it was not in the Nu-Cast 1986 catalogue nor any subsequent lists. Despite all this, Mike Griffiths would like to release the kit and production of masters was underway in 1999.

NC201 LMS/BR Princess 4-6-2
Never produced

Possibly the most compelling "might-have-been" was a Nu-Cast Princess. From January 1976 the Princess was proposed, and a picture of 6201 at Shildon in 1975 formed the 1977 catalogue cover wherein the kit was fully described to the extent that this source taken in isolation would suggest production. But the kit never made it, and nowadays the Nu-Cast range has a different Princess model.

NC202 LMS/BR Patriot 4-6-0
Never produced

The Patriot proposal was present in the December 1976 Modeller advert, and the 1977 catalogue described it in the same solid vein with a reference number as the Princess. Nothing more has been traced thereafter.

NC203 S&DJR/LMS/BR 2-8-0
Never produced

From a mention amongst a list of seven proposals on the last page of the 1977 catalogue, only one engine (the C2X) made it. Of the others, the S&DJR 2-8-0 must have gone some way before DJH's model perhaps suggested that the effort would be wasted. In 1978 Nu-Cast advertised the project, and the reference appears in 1980 adverts. The kit was listed in the W&H 1983 catalogue such that you would think it current, but check the pricelist and there is no price. Nu-Cast's own 1986 list stated that the kit was "withdrawn". Conceivably this evidence alone might suggest that the model had been made. Until someone finds more evidence I do not believe any kits were sold.

The remaining pre-1988 Nu-Cast proposals have not had any reference numbers traced.

SR/BR Battle of Britain 4-6-2 *Never produced*

A Nu-Cast model of an original Bulleid Light Pacific would have excited interest. The profile of the loco is shown on the 1986 catalogue with a streamlined LNER B17 (which itself was never mentioned anywhere else). Evidence that this WC/BB loco could be more than just wishful thinking comes from at least two adverts.

Puffer's, in the middle of 1979, unambiguously hyped the new release of a "Nu-Cast Bulleid Pacific" which was Big D's kit of the month (Dave King of Crownline fame). After quite a chase, I now believe that anyone who relies on this advert should actually reckon that there was some confusion here with the Millholme Models kit which was actually appearing at the time.

The following locos were proposed in the Nu-Cast 1977 catalogue, but allocation to a known reference number has not yet been achieved:-

LMS/BR 2P 4-4-0

CR/LMS/BR Dunalastair 4-4-0

GCR/LNER/(BR) B2 or B3 Lord Faringdon or Sir Sam Fay 4-6-0

LBSCR/SR/BR B4 4-4-0

Nothing more is known about these proposals save that Nu-Cast would now like to progress the B4 venture which would share some components with the LBSCR K.

NER Z/LNER/BR C7 4-4-2

In addition to being in the 1977 catalogue, it is known that Stott particularly wanted to see this NER Z loco kit made. Published references to the proposal exist elsewhere in 1975 and 1976, but the release of the DJH version probably killed any further plans.

NER Tennant 2-4-0

The same release promissory comments can be applied to the Tennant 2-4-0, except that the published references extend back to 1974.

The K's Residue

The last group of models to be discussed covers those models for which Autocom possess the tools and which could theoretically enter the Nu-Cast range.

NC027/K's L27 GWR/BR 42xx/72xx 2-8-0 or 2-8-2T

The K's GWR heavy tank model has an NC series number, and has been marked in lists (including some contemporary lists) as "available shortly" but with the ex-Cotswold model in production from Nu-Cast, revival is extremely unlikely.

NC050/K's L50 SR/BR Lord Nelson 4-6-0

From October 1996, two versions of etched tender suitable for the engine have been available, these being the original or the Bulleid rebuild, both of 5,000 gallon capacity. Despite this, it is unlikely that the full kit will reappear.

Some K's models will never re-appear. The long forgotten Caley 0-4-4T's tooling never reached Autocom, nor did the AEC Railcar. That lack does, however, explain the logical omission of any NC022 reference.

Nu-Cast Addresses

1968
As Stott, 29 Newark Close, Peterlee c1968, possibly also at Pennine Way, Peterlee.

1969
Nu-sto Scale Models, 108 Westmorland Rise, Peterlee, Co Durham.

1969-1970
Nu-sto Scale Models, 20 Blackhills Road, Horden, Co Durham.

1970-1974
Nu-sto Scale Models, 17 Murray Street, Hartlepool.

1974-1975
Nu-Cast Model Engineering, 65 Brook Street, Hartlepool, Cleveland.

1975-1982
Nu-Cast Model Engineering, 189 Park Road, Hartlepool, Cleveland.

1982-1987
Nu-Cast Model Engineering, 81 Clifton Avenue, Hartlepool, Cleveland.

1987-1988
Nu-Cast Model Engineering, Unit 8 Hackworth Road, Blackhall, Co Durham.

1988-1990
Nu-Cast Model Engineering Ltd (Sales), Firsby, Spilsby, Lincolnshire, PE23 5PX.

1990-1993
Nu-Cast Model Engineering, Hinstock House, Firsby PE23 5PX.

1993-date
Nu-Cast at Autocom UK Ltd, Alexander Bell Centre, West Portway Industrial Estate, Andover, Hants, SP10 3UR.

(left) An assortment of Nu-Cast packaging with the oldest to the back. Also shown is the 1976 catalogue
Photo: Tony Wright, courtesy Autocom Collection

Nu-Cast Locomotives Table

Text Reference	Previous Reference	Description	New Date	Withdrawal Date	Notes
NC001	K's L1	LMS/BR Black 5 4-6-0	1994		
NC002	K's L2	LNWR/LMS/BR Coal Tank 0-6-2T	8/1993		
NC003	K's L3	GWR/BR Bulldog 3252 o/f 4-4-0	5/1993		
NC004	K's L4	GWR/BR 44xx 2-6-2T	5/1993		
NC005	K's L5	GCR/ROD/LNER/LMS/GWR/BR 2-8-0	8/1993		
NC006	K's L6	NER/LNER/BR J72 0-6-0T	7/1993		
NC007	K's L7	GER/LNER/BR J70 0-6-0T tram	9/1993		
NC008	K's L8	LMS Karrier Ro-rail bus	5/1993		
NC009	K's L9	GWR/BR 14xx 0-4-2T	7/1993		
NC010	K's L10	GWR/BR 1361 0-6-0ST	5/1993		
NC011	K's L11	MR/LMS Spinner o/f 4-2-2	1994		
NC012	K's L12	MR/LMS/BR Kirtley o/f 0-6-0	5/1993		
NC013	K's L13	GWR/BR Grange 4-6-0	7/1993	c.1997	
NC014	K's L14	GWR/BR Dean Goods i/f 0-6-0	11/1993		Further references below
NC014Z		with outside frames	11/1993		
NC014Y		with 2,500 gallon tender	5/1998		
NC014YZ		with outside frames and 2,500 gallon tender	5/1998		
NC015	K's L15	LMS/BR Fowler 2-6-2T	9/1993		
NC016	K's L16	MR/LMS/BR Johnson 0-6-0	5/1993		
NC017	K's L17	GWR/BR 57/87xx 0-6-0PT	9/1993		Both cabs
NC018	K's L18	GWR/BR 63xx 2-6-0	1994		
NC019	K's L19	LSWR/SR/BR Adams Radial 4-4-2T	6/1993		
NC020	K's L20	LBSCR/SR/BR Terrier 0-6-0T	6/1993		
NC021	K's L21	SR/BR Q1 0-6-0	3/1994	1997	
NC022	K's L22	GWR/BR Diesel Railcar			NC022 has never been used by Autocom
NC023	K's L23	GWR/BR 28xx 2-8-0	8/1993	c.1997	
NC024	K's L24	GWR/BR 3252 Duke o/f 4-4-0	5/1993		Further reference below
NC024Z		with 2,500 gallon tender	5/1998		

Text Reference	Previous Reference	Description	New Date	Withdrawal Date	Notes
NC025	K's L25	GWR/BR 4575/55xx 2-6-2T	6/1993		
NC026	K's L26	GWR/BR Earl/Dukedog o/f 4-4-0	5/1993		3,500 gallon tender
NC027	K's L27	GWR/BR 42xx/72xx 2-8-0 or 2-8-2T			NC027 has never been used by Autocom
NC028	K's L28	GWR/BR 26xx Aberdare o/f 2-6-0	6/1993		Further reference below
NC028Z	with ROD tender		2/1994		
NC029	K's L29	GNR/LNER C1 4-4-2	8/1983		
NC030	K's L30	LMS Ivatt 2P/BR 84xxx 2-6-2T	9/1993		
NC031	K's L31	GWR 322 Beyer Peacock o/f 0-6-0	1999		
NC032	K's L32	LMS/BR Beyer Garratt 2-6-0+0-6-2	5/1993		
NC033	K's L33	LBSCR/SR/BR K class 2-6-0	10/1993		
NC034	K's L34	LMS/BR Jubilee 4-6-0	11/1993		
NC035	K's L35	LMS/BR Stanier 2-6-0	1/1994		
NC036	K's L36	LNER 1936 build P2 2-8-2	6/1994		
NC037	K's L37	MR/LMS/BR Johnson 1500 series 0-4-0ST	8/1993		
NC038	K's L38	NER/LNER/BR Y8 0-4-0T	10/1994		
NC039	K's L39	LMS/BR Fowler Dock tank 0-6-0T	6/1993		
NC040	K's L40	GCR/LNER B2 *Sir Sam Fay* 4-6-0	8/1994		
NC041	K's L41	LMS Turbomotive 4-6-2	7/1993		
NC042	K's L42	LMS/BR Princess 4-6-2	11/1993	1998	
NC043	K's L43	BR (WR) 15xx 0-6-0PT	8/1993		
NC044	K's L44	GNR/LNER/BR J3 0-6-0	8/1993		
NC045	K's L45	TVR/GWR/BR S class 0-4-0ST	2/1994		
NC046	K's L46	LMS/BR Duchess 4-6-2	7/1993	c.1996-97	
NC047	K's L47	LMS/BR Stanier 8F 2-8-0	1/1994	1998	
NC048	K's L48	LMS/BR Streamlined *Coronation* 4-6-2	1996		
NC049	K's L49	BR Bulleid rebuilt Merchant Navy 4-6-2	1994	1996	
NC050	K's L50	SR/BR *Lord Nelson* 4-6-0			NC050 has never been used by Autocom
NC051	K's L51	LNER original P2 2-8-2	6/1994		

Text Reference	Previous Reference	Description	New Date	Withdrawal Date	Notes
NC052		GWR Bird class o/f 4-4-0	3/1996		
NC101		NER/LNER/BR Q6 0-8-0	12/1971		
NC102		LNER/BR B1 4-6-0	1/1973		
NC103		NER/LNER/BR G5 0-4-4T	11/1973		NC103B new 3/75 was a variant for N8/N9/N10
NC104		LNER/BR V2 2-6-2	12/1974		
NC105		NER/LNER/BR J21 0-6-0	4/1975		
NC106		LNER/BR D49/1 Shire 4-4-0	Never Produced		Reference used twice
NC106		NER/LNER/BR T1 4-8-0T	Never Produced		Reference used twice
NC107		LNER/BR D49/2 Hunt 4-4-0	Never Produced		Reference used twice
NC107		GNR/LNER/BR J6 521 0-6-0	4/1980	c. 1986	Reference used twice
NC108		GNR/LNER/BR J6 536 0-6-0	4/1980		
NC109		GNR/LNER/BR D2 4-4-0	1/1982		
NC110		GCR/LNER/BR A5 4-6-2T	3/1978		
NC111		GNR/LNER/BR K2 2-6-0	12/1975		
NC112		GNR/LNER/BR O2/2 2-8-0	12/1977		
NC113		LNER/BR O2/3 2-8-0	c.12/1977		
NC115		NER/LNER/BR B16/2 & B16/3 4-6-0	2/1979		
NC116		NER/LNER/BR J26/J27 0-6-0	8/1975		
NC117		NER/LNER/BR Y7 0-4-0T	11/1976		
NC118		GCR/LNER/BR C13 4-4-2T	11/1976		
NC119		LNER/BR Sentinel Railcar	9/1979		
NC120		LNER/LMS/GWR/BR Sentinel Shunter 0-4-0T	9/1981		
NC121	S.Poole 2	GNR/LNER/BR N2 0-6-2T	2/1978		
NC122	S.Poole 1	GER/LNER/BR F4/F5 2-4-2T	9/1980		
NC123	S.Poole 6	GER/LNER/BR Y5 0-4-0ST	9/1978		
NC124	S.Poole 4	GER/LNER/BR J15 0-6-0	3/1978		
NC125	S.Poole 5	GER/LNER/BR E4 2-4-0	c.3/1979		
NC126		GNoSR/LNER/BR D40 + SECR/SR G 4-4-0	4/1980		

Text Reference	Previous Reference	Description	New Date	Withdrawal Date	Notes
NC127		GNoSR/LNER/BR D41 4-4-0	5/1981		
NC128		LNER/BR A2/1 4-6-2	5/1981		8w tender
NC129		LNER/BR A2/2+A2/3 4-6-2	Neither Produced		
NC130		LNER/BR A2/1 4-6-2	1/1981		6w tender
NC131	Cotswold 22	GCR/LNER/BR F1 2-4-2T	6/81		
NC132	Cotswold 27	NBR/LNER/BR C16 4-4-2T	6/1981		
NC133	Cotswold 42	GNR/LNER Q1 0-8-0	6/1981		
NC134		LNER U1 Bayer Garratt 2-8-0+0-8-2	Never Produced		
NC135		LNER/BR K1 2-6-0	4/1983		
NC136		LNER/BR V1/V3 2-6-2T	3/1984		
NC137		NER/LNER/BR N8/N9 0-6-2T	3/1986		See also NC103B
NC138		NER/LNER/BR J25 0-6-0	3/1986		
NC139		NER/LNER BTP G6 0-4-4T	8/1986		
NC151		LSWR/SR/BR Jubilee 0-4-2	9/1976		
NC152		SR/BR Remembrance N15x 4-6-0	4/1978		
NC153		LSWR/SR Adams T3 4-4-0	Never Produced		
NC154		LBSCR/SR/BR C2X 0-6-0	12/1982		
NC155		LSWR/SR T14 Paddlebox 4-6-0	10/1983	1999	
NC156		LSWR/SR T14 rebuilt Paddlebox 4-6-0	c.10/1985		
NC201		LMS/BR Princess 4-6-2	Never Produced		
NC202		LMS/BR Patriot 4-6-0	Never Produced		
NC203		S&DJR/LMS/BR 2-8-0	Never Produced		
NC204		CR/LMS/BR Pickersgill 4-4-0	9/1978		
NC208	Cotswold 11	LMS/BR 3F 0-6-0T	6/1981		
NC209	Cotswold 12	LMS/BR Fowler 7F 0-8-0	6/1981		
NC210	Cotswold 13	L&YR/LMS/BR 2F 0-6-0ST	6/1981		
NC211	Cotswold 18	L&YR/LMS/BR 2P 2-4-2T	6/1981		
NC212	Cotswold 19	L&YR/LMS/BR 3P 2-4-2T	6/1981		

Text Reference	Previous Reference	Description	New Date	Withdrawal Date	Notes
NC213	Cotswold 21	L&YR/LMS/BR 7F 0-8-0	6/1981		
NC214	Cotswold 33	L&YR/LMS/BR 6F 0-8-0	6/1981		
NC215	Cotswold 37	L&YR/LMS H3 0-6-2T	6/1981		
NC216	Cotswold 24	HR/LMS 39 0-6-4T	6/1981		
NC217	Cotswold 38	HR/LMS/BR Small Ben 4-4-0	6/1981		
NC218	Cotswold 26	LT&SR/MR/LMS/BR 4-4-2T	6/1981		
NC219	Cotswold 36	LMS/BR 4P Compound 4-4-0	6/1981		
NC220	Cotswold 39	LMS/BR Stanier 3P 2-6-2T	6/1981		
NC221		LMS/BR Stanier 4MT 2-6-4T	3/1982		
NC222		LMS/BR Ivatt 2MT 2-6-0	12/1984		
NC251	S.Poole 3	GWR/BR 54xx 0-6-0PT	12/1977		Further reference below
NC251Z		GWR/BR 64xx/74xx 0-6-0PT	by 1994		
NC253		GWR/BR Manor 4-6-0	7/1980	c.1990	
NC254		GWR Steam Railmotor	1/1982		Further reference below
NC254Z		GWR Railmotor Trailer	by 1994		
NC255	Cotswold 14	GWR/BR 42xx/72xx 2-8-0 or 2-8-2T	6/1981		
NC256	Cotswold 15	GWR/BR 47xx 2-8-0	6/1981	c.1984	
NC257	Cotswold 25	M&SWJR/GWR/BR 1334 2-4-0	6/1981		
NC258	Cotswold 31	RR/GWR AR 0-6-2T	6/1981		Actually an R1 class
NC259	Cotswold 32	TVR/GWR rebuilt A 0-6-2T	6/1981		
NC260	Cotsw'd 41S	GWR/BR 2021 0-6-0ST	6/1981		
NC261	Cotswold 41	GWR/BR 2021 0-6-0PT	6/1981		
NC262	Cotswold 28	BR (WR) 16xx 0-6-0PT	6/1981		
NC263	Cotswold 30	GWR/BR County 4-6-0	6/1981	c.1985	
NC264	Cotswold 29	GWR Flower o/f 4-4-0	6/1981		
NC265		GWR City o/f 4-4-0	9/1981		
NC266		GWR/BR Hall 4-6-0	10/1984		3,500g Churchward tender
NC267		GWR/BR Modified Hall 4-6-0	10/1984		Hawksworth tender

Text Reference	Previous Reference	Description	New Date	Withdrawal Date	Notes
NC268		GWR/BR Hall 4-6-0	11/1984		Collett tender
NC269		GWR/BR Modified Hall 4-6-0	3/1985		Collett tender
NC270		GWR/BR Hall 4-6-0	8/1986		Hawksworth tender
NC271		GWR Armstrong 388 o/f 0-6-0 with 2,500 gallon tender	11/1985		Further reference below
NC271Z			5/1998		
NC272		GWR/BR 57xx 0-6-0PT	1/1995		Part Replica
NC273		BR 2251 0-6-0	10/1995		Part Replica
NC351		Wickham type 27 motor trolley	10/1983	c.1988	

(below) K's L10 (rightmost) and Nu-Cast NC010 GWR/BR 1361 0-6-0ST versions showing clearly the improved buffer height of the later Nu-Cast example

Photo: Tony Wright, courtesy Autocom Collection

Further Notes
The 6/1981 catalogue was the first Cotswold / Nu-Cast combined issue.

Nu-Cast Catalogues Table

Date	Cover	Price	Notes
late 1976	Orange and 6201 at Shildon	18p	
6/1981		40p	In listing format
12/1983		75p	
10/1986	Many loco drawings	£1.25	
c.1989		£1.25	Advert in MRN 3/1989
c.1990			Advert in RM 10/1990

Issued Manufactured Nu-Kays Models

Further Notes
The table to the right illustrates those Nu-Kays models believed to have been manufactured (and not merely retailed).

K's Ref	Later Nu-Cast Ref	Date of Modeller Advert
L1	NC001	1/1991
L2	NC002	9/1991
L5	NC005	3/1991
L6	NC006	1/1991
L7	NC007	3/1991
L9	NC009	1/1991
L13	NC013	1/1991
L15	NC015	1/1991
L17	NC017	1/1991
L18	NC018	1/1991
L19	NC019	3/1991
L21	NC021	1/1991
L25	NC025	1/1991
L32	NC032	3/1991
L34	NC034	1/1991
L35	NC035	1/1991
L36	NC036	3/1991
L40	NC040	1/1991
L41	NC041	11/1991
L42	NC042	11/1991
L47	NC047	11/1991
L49	NC049	11/1991
L50	NC050	1/1992
L51	NC051	3/1991
LM2 (Problem Class)	(na)	10/1991

Advertised Nu-Sto Super 'P' Plan Locomotives

Description	First Advertised
NER/LNER/BR N10 0-6-2T	1/1969
CR/LMS/BR McIntosh 0-6-0	2/1969
GNR/LNER C1 4-4-2	3/1969
LBSCR/SR/BR H1 or H2 4-4-2	3/1969
GWR De Glehn Large Atlantic 4-4-2	4/1969
GER/LNER/BR F3 2-4-2T	4/1969
LNWR/LMS/BR G2 0-8-0	5/1969
NER/LNER/BR Q5/Q6 0-8-0	5/1969

Further Acknowledgements

This chapter has been aided by *inter alia* Mike Griffiths, Rob Hamp, David Geen, Graham Bean.

Wills

A long with K's, the name Wills represents both a pioneer and one of the longstanding players in the field of UK 4mm scale cast whitemetal locomotive kits. The parallels extend further; both ranges became wide-ranging in extent, with Wills finally offering 46 prototypes. For neither concern did these kits represent the full extent of their involvement in the hobby. Moreover, the core of each concern's kits remains available in 1999, though in both cases with a new owner, new name, and extensive updating. Despite these considerable parallels, two related substantial differences exist. The generation that established K's has died, and the Keyser family have had no commercial involvement with the hobby during the 1990s. Robert Wills, whose baby the Wills' range was, sold the Wills Locomotive Kits in 1988. However the new proprietor in David Ellis, trading as South Eastern Finecast, operates from the same settlement of Forest Row in Sussex. By 1988 Bob Wills had established a successful parallel range of injection moulded plastic kits known as the Wills Scenic Series. Unlike K's, his use of plastic seemed to gel in the market and his provision of plastic accessories for model railways continued to thrive through the 1990s.

Today's operations are a far cry from the back room of the model shop in Coulsdon from which Bob Wills' first kit emerged in 1955. This was launched at the Model Railway Hobby Show in October 1955. Wills' manufacturing endeavours had started with some O gauge whitemetal castings, and OO components were added at the show, along with the first cast whitemetal wagon kit. This was a GWR shunting truck, and by the standards of the time, it was a very detailed rendition with interlocking lugs to ease assembly.

More wagons followed up until 1962 when there were eight in the range, and these have continued to be available with interruptions - they still feature in 1990s' South Eastern Finecast catalogues. However, the wagons were really only testing the water, and that range was not developed after 1962. These vehicles deserve to be appreciated - the Shunter's Truck had as companions the equally idiosyncratic Folkestone Harbour branch track-cleaning wagon which really worked, and a tiny four wheeled bullion van.

Initially, although the first wagon kit predated K's offering, development was quite restrained. A second kit for the simple match truck followed late in 1956 - other wagons followed but it was 1959 that really marked lift-off for Wills' range. That was the year, that in addition to more wagons, the first two locomotives appeared. Following that, each year from 1960 to 1963 was marked by intense activity with between four and six locos released annually. The year 1964 thus started with 22 loco models available,

and by then the Wills pattern was established. A large number of the kits, starting with the second introduction (the GWR 94xx) were body only, designed to fit onto proprietary chassis and these could confidently appeal to beginners. A number of other kits of popular prototypes, which could never fit such chassis, had an additional and separate chassis kit which Wills manufactured. To this the kit builder had to add the suggested motor and wheels. This was quite a different approach to K's and probably helped spread the market efficiently. Wills' kits also manifest a definite but not exclusive preference for Southern and Great Western prototypes. The trio of LNER Pacifics became a distinctive exception.

Such a bias gave room for the likes of GEM to arrive with their own favourites in the mid-1960s. That period saw the pace of releases from Wills slacken - from 1964, one or two new kits a year was the norm (1965 excepted). In 1970 there was actually no new release, and this was repeated in 1980. By then the steam pressure was dropping, but the actual new kits when they arrived were finely regarded, such as the SECR trio which appeared between 1974 and 1981. The last of these, for the class H 0-4-4T became the final Wills loco kit, thus between then and 1988 no new prototypes appeared, but note that the range as a whole was still retailed until the sale of the concern.

Whilst nothing else in Wills' story can rival his own version of the frantic frenetic swinging sixties achieved in the first half of that decade, the company as a whole remained very innovative, even during the years when the OO loco kits were not in the limelight. During 1961 what had previously been purely Robert Wills' own business, essentially derived from his activity as a model shop owner, became a limited company called R. Wills (Scientific Hobbies) Ltd, and Bob became Managing Director. Soon thereafter the manufacturing operations became a separate company, also with Bob as Managing Director, known as Industrial Display Company Limited. This latter company remained the legal basis for the Wills Scenic Series until 1997. The formation of the companies was followed in 1962 by the move to premises in Thornton Heath which was more suited to manufacturing. The same period also saw the adoption of the "Finecast" brand name which adorned the 1961-issued second catalogue

Wills' move to the country at Forest Row followed in 1964, and it was from Forest Row that other innovations appeared. In brief order: from 1968 what became a considerable range of whitemetal motor car kits (now with South Eastern Finecast too); during the late 1960s and early 1970s co-operation with Peco in the production of N gauge loco kits; in 1970 co-operation with W&H in the production of the Steam

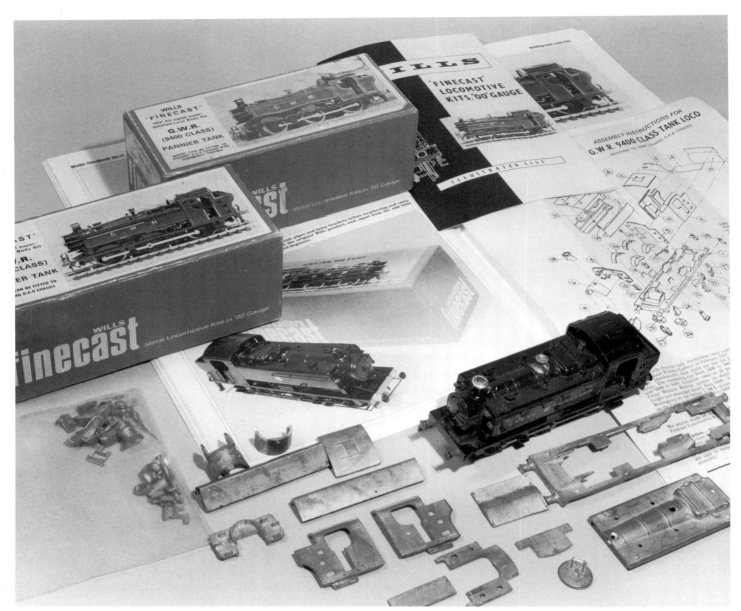

(above) The generations of the Wills F110 GWR/BR 94xx started by using the Tri-ang chassis, and evolved over time to use Wills' own CK1/FC100 chassis by the mid-1970s. The above picture shows body castings and instructions for an example probably from about that time

Photo: Tony Wright, courtesy South Eastern Finecast Collection

(right) Wills SECR/SR/BR P class with some fine detailing and early packaging

Photo: Tony Wright, courtesy Les Spratt

Era series of locomotive paperweights; and the acquisition around 1975 of the Stephen Poole wheel range.

Then in 1977 Wills released an etched nickel silver chassis kit designed to be used in his kits instead of the former Tri-ang, now-Hornby Railways, Jinty chassis. This became part of a steady programme by which Wills produced etched chassis for their own kits. At the same time Wills had moved into using spark erosion technology for producing plastic kits, and in 1979 the first Scenic Series kits appeared.

The twin demands of upgrading the loco range with etched metal components, whilst also developing what became the very successful Scenic Series in a totally different media, influenced the decision that Bob took in 1988 to pass the whitemetal loco kits to his near neighbour Dave Ellis. Since then, Dave's South Eastern Finecast has followed the same philosophy of upgrading the older kits with the benefits of etched components, and introducing some new prototypes. A concluding chapter to Bob Wills' involvement in the hobby was the sale of Industrial Display Ltd and the Wills Scenic Series thereby on 24th April 1997. Despite this, Bob's visits down the road to Dave Ellis at South Eastern Finecast were still very much on the agenda of life in his mid-70s. In March 1999, it was reported that all Wills Scenic Series production was to take place in the Ratio factory at Buckfastleigh by which means Wills in effect became part of Peco.

That is by way of the preamble, now it is time to return to the Spring of 1959 in the capital city, amongst whose many different locomotive classes, one large group of small tank engines was guaranteed an appreciative audience. We refer to the Holden designed backbone of the Liverpool Street Suburban services, the so-called Buckjumper 0-6-0T, an example of which was then acting as Liverpool Street pilot adorned in full GER blue livery. With this prototype the Wills loco kits commenced.

List of Locomotive Kits

W01/F113 GER/LNER/BR Holden Buckjumper 0-6-0T

Being the first of the range and proving very popular, never having a ready-to-run model to supplant it, the Buckjumper kit is worth some attention. The Easter 1959 Model Railway Club Show marked the great moment, and the kit certainly received a warm welcome shown in the reviews which appeared in June's Modeller and July's Constructor. In more ways than one, the Buckjumper marked the beginning and end of the Wills Loco Kit range in its 29-year life. Right at the outset there had only been a 50-part cast whitemetal body kit for 35/-; a separate chassis kit followed closely behind. This was workman-like cast whitemetal with little prototypical detail, but splined brass bushes were fitted in which the axles ran. A Romford Terrier motor and wheels had to be sourced, as well as the characteristic GER cast plate if required, and

suitable examples were sold by Kings Cross Models. There was no rivet detail and no handrail holes, and these were never added.

Despite the rapture there were complications. The kit was presented as a "J69". However, the prototypes existed in a wide number of variations encompassed in the two LNER J67/J69 classifications, and in other earlier GER conditions. What Wills sold could not actually be finished as a J69! Wills had derived his kit from the Roche drawing, and those drawings are now seen as less than perfect - incidentally this problem afflicts other Wills kits. What then was the Wills kit? One cannot do better than quote an authority of 1980s and 1990s kit design and construction, Iain Rice, who investigated the model and the prototype in *Model Railway Journal* issues 35/36.

Rice's investigation was painstaking and his conclusion is that the original "Wills kit was really all about a post-1893 R24 with stepped up side-tanks concealing the condensing chambers". Most of the R24 class (basically the later LNER J67) was in this condition for no more than 12 years. These complications were in the enthusiasm of the moment overwhelmed by the sheer originality of the new kit. It took critical eyes in the 1980s to unlock the difficulties that the kit could really only be finished as a GER model. Even then the kit still contained errors/omissions carried over from the Roche drawing.

Iain Rice persuaded Bob Wills that the model was worth redesigning, and the Modeller reported the project in January 1987. Rice redesigned the patterns in order to provide a much more flexible kit, providing the key choices of the J67/69 prototypes, and Rod Neep designed a new etched chassis for the model. Meanwhile, the arrangements to sell the range to South Eastern Finecast were being made. As a Wills kit (and notwithstanding the name on the chassis components) the revamped Buckjumper never appeared; instead it became the first new product under the SEF name, being so advertised in the months after August 1988.

W02/F110 GWR/BR 94xx 0-6-0PT

Back in 1959, the October Model Railway Hobby Show saw Wills' second loco kit on display. The prototype was the GWR 94xx, a design only just over a decade old at the time. With this kit the twin-track approach of Bob Wills became clear. A 49-part body only whitemetal kit was provided, designed to fit the standard Tri-ang 0-6-0 chassis. Certain compromises were involved, and this was also a route whereby chassis detail was bound to be minimal. Again a Roche drawing was used (W.L.16), and by featuring steps on either side of the bunker, the kit was firmly located as representing one of the first six prototypes.

There are reviews in the December 1959 *Model Railway News* and in the January 1960 *Model Railway Constructor*. Handrail holes appeared on the kit from the outset, but no cast number-plates were supplied, and except where noted differently, none were supplied for Wills models.

(top) **Wills F104 LMS/BR Crab 2-6-0 on a (non-RTR!) chassis of unknown pedigree**

Photo: Dave Wheatstone, courtesy Dave Wheatstone Collection

(above) **Wills F103 LNER/BR K3 2-6-0 on a scratchbuilt chassis, thus avoiding the pitfalls of the Tri-ang offering. A comparison against the South Eastern Finecast retooled K3 (F161) on page 117 clearly shows the inaccuracy of the cab detail with the original kit**

Photo: Tony Wright, courtesy Tony Wright

(below) **Wills F102 LNER/BR J39 0-6-0 with additional detail such as the sanding gear**

Photo: Tony Wright, courtesy Tony Wright

The kit existed throughout the Wills era without alteration, but once Wills' own etched nickel silver CK1 chassis materialised, it was suggested that this should be used. At the latter's outset in 1977 it was known to Wills as the CK1, but in W&H catalogues (1977 and 1983) this had become the FC100.

Production records have never been kept for any of the Wills kits, but Bob Wills recollection is that this kit proved the most popular. He estimates that typically several thousand formed the average sale per kit over its Wills lifetime, and that for some lengthy time demand outstripped supply for the range, despite running four casting machines full time seven days a week, and having an army of out-workers to do the packing.

W03/F109 LBSCR/SR/BR E2 0-6-0T

Magazine reports suggested that demand for the easy to complete 94xx was very encouraging. With the Spring of 1960 and the Easter Show upon him, Wills took out an illustrated advert in the April Modeller showing a range of four 0-6-0Ts. The two newcomers were both Southern and both used a proprietary chassis. The Modeller reviewed the E2 that April (wherein the G6 and additionally the P classes were noted as forthcoming in that order). Designed around the standard Tri-ang chassis, the 31-part E2 kit was really very straightforward. A removable chimney was required to align with the Tri-ang chassis' screwhole, and from 1977 the model could use Finecast's own FC100 chassis.

It is strange that a model of such a small class, which lacked the charisma of some of the other Wills tanks, could be viable. Awdry's *Thomas* was however based upon an E2, yet it took Hornby Railways' model for that link to become common coinage. Trix offered a near contemporary to the Wills model, and Bob must have been grateful for the weird scale Trix chose. In actuality only half of the class resembled the Wills kit - those were the five LBSCR engines (100-104) built with the short side tanks of the Wills kit itself.

W04/F108 LSWR/SR/BR G6 0-6-0T

The parallel (but actually appearing some weeks later) introduction was the basic LSWR 0-6-0T. Here there were rather more prototypes: 34 in all. Even in BR days there was still a choice between the Drummond or original Adams boiler fitted examples. Wills went for the Adams boiler shown in the August 1960 Modeller review, with a stovepipe chimney. This time the suggested chassis was the Hornby Dublo R1, but latterly it could fit onto Wills' own etched chassis. This was not the Tri-ang replacement CK1 but a later Wills introduction instead of the Dublo/Wrenn R1 product, known as the FC101.

W05/F107 SECR/SR/BR P 0-6-0T

The third in the trio of Southern tanks that Wills released in the Spring of 1960 was amongst the most endearing of Wills' engines. The model was first illustrated in an advert in that May's Modeller showing all three Wills SR tanks. What the Terrier was to the LBSCR and K's, the P was to the SECR and Wills, and it can be seen as Wills' counterblast to the K's offering. Unlike the numerically strong Terriers, there had only been eight Ps originally intended as railmotor engines, but destined to spend much of their life in shunting yards or on light railways. Four of the original eight are in preservation and split between the K&ESR and the Bluebell (where the first arrived only a matter of weeks after the Wills model appeared). Unlike the E2 or the G6, this choice has remained very much in the limelight ever since the model's introduction, which can have done no harm for sales.

Aside from the intrinsic appeal of this tiny 0-6-0T, that very matter of size posed Wills some challenges. The wheelbase was only 11', and so no proprietary chassis could be used. When the Modeller reviewed both the G6 and the P in its August 1960 issue, and you might have thought that the profile picture of the two bodies posed together showed 4mm and 3mm scale models - the P really is a tiny prototype. Wills provided his own chassis styled after the J69; a whitemetal casting with brass bushed bearings for the axles. To power the model Wills suggested the Tri-ang XT60 motor (designed for TT gauge), and the fitting of Romford wheels.

The little engine was exceptionally well detailed for the period - handrails, a Westinghouse air pump (these were perhaps expected), brake pipes, brakeshoes and sanding gear were *avant-garde*. However, they would not appear again from Wills for years after. In the remainder of its life as a Wills product, no further alterations were made.

W06/F101 LBSCR/SR/BR E5 0-6-2T

Southern tanks were not left when the next Wills engine arrived in December 1960. The thirty-strong E5 class of 1902 was back to bodyline style, fitting over the Dublo R1 chassis. The necessary pony truck and wheels were included within the kit, but only the original of several possible safety valve options was supplied in the kit. The review model shown in the January 1961 Modeller was finished as *Woldingham*, and presumably the same engine, but with different shots, graced the catalogue. Apart from latterly fitting the FC101 chassis, I am not aware of any significant changes to the model during the Wills regime.

W07/F112 GWR/BR 2251 Class 0-6-0

Along with the E5 review, the Modeller carried news of Wills' planned 1961 programme. What would become F105-106/111-112 were envisaged. All would be relatively simple bodyline kits but in offering two 0-6-0s, a South Wales 0-6-2T, and a Southern Mogul, a rich variety of popular prototypes could be anticipated. First off was ready for a review in the March Modeller. Collett's standard 0-6-0 was intended to fit the overlong wheelbase of the Tri-ang chassis. The splashers had to be slightly moved from scale to

(top) Wills F114 LSWR/SR/BR *King Arthur*, this example being completed with the later Wills FC114 chassis rather than the earlier Tri-ang *Britannia* option

Photo: Dave Wheatstone, courtesy Dave Wheatstone Collection

(above) Wills F115 LMS/BR Stanier 4MT on Dublo chassis with Romford wheels. It would appear this particular model has been finished as a 2 cylinder example

Photo: Dave Wheatstone, courtesy Dave Wheatstone Collection

(below) Wills F116 LNER/BR A2 on Tri-ang *Britannia* chassis but fitted with scale wheels and Jamieson valvegear

Photo: Tony Wright, courtesy Tony Wright

prototype to fit this chassis, which created a knotty problem to undo for anyone so determined, such as fitting the correctly scaled Dean Goods chassis from K's (see the *Model Railways News* in October 1963).

At the outset Wills recognised that some customers would prefer a better chassis. With the Tri-ang chassis, although some daylight under the boiler was present, the worm was extremely visible and the cab was filled with motor - indeed the bottom of the boiler was actually cut off to accommodate the mechanism. An optional piece of boiler was supplied for those who could do better! Late in the Wills era the 1977 W&H catalogue stated that the Wills FC100 fitted, then in 1983 it was allocated the FC102 chassis (there truly were three Wills 0-6-0 chassis: CK1 or FC100, FC101 and FC102).

As far as the tender was concerned, a 3,000 gallon flared top GWR design was fitted. The cab was side windowed which represents the usual state, but thirty built from 1940-44 were not at first so fitted. Incidentally, in the early 1970s the Collett 0-6-0 became the most prominent in the intended series of Peco/Wills N gauge collaborations, but it never progressed beyond prototypes.

W08/F106 SR/BR Q 0-6-0

Hard on the Collett's heels in April 1961 was a second 0-6-0 for the SR Maunsell equivalent. This had a similar specification and was reviewed in the June Modeller. Both 0-6-0s could be greatly improved if the modeller was prepared to wield a saw on the pronounced chassis block at the front of the Tri-ang unit. Whilst the Collett could run in green, how many of the Q models were finished in a SR green? Wills own catalogue model was even so adorned whilst reminding its readers that these 1938 locos were finished in unlined black! The kit was fitted with a 3,500 gallon flush sided SR tender. Chassis provision followed the 2251 class pattern.

W09/F111 TVR/GWR U1 0-6-2T

The next release used the same principles as the E5 to produce the Taff Vale Railway U1 0-6-2T. The kit had appeared for reviews in the August 1961 Modeller and *Model Railway News*. Like the E5 in the final part of the Wills era, their own FC101 etched chassis was preferred. This 1896 engine for a pre-grouping Welsh Valley's prototype was certainly something different back in 1960s, but it would go nicely with the Trix 56xx of the same period.

W10/F105 SECR/SR/BR Mogul 2-6-0 classes N/N1/U&U1

The last model previewed back in January 1961 required the use of another Tri-ang chassis, this time taken from the BR Standard 3MT 2-6-2T. By the time it appeared in the Autumn of 1961, it occasioned some excitement for it became the first of three successive Mogul releases from Wills. It also was capable of representing a variety of SR prototypes - the original was the 5'6"

wheeled N of 1917, so the 18mm diameter Tri-ang wheels were right for that if you could otherwise stomach them. The N1 of 1922 was similarly wheeled and the Tri-ang chassis helpfully provided the necessary Walschaerts gear, but the kit was then committed to the Tri-ang 3MT cylinders, and these were incorrectly inclined for all these engines. The alternative parts for the SR designed 6' wheeled U/U1 bodies were provided, but the modeller had to source wheels. To accommodate these, the larger wheeled U/U1 had a different running plate with small wheel splashers. The N1/U1 versions were three cylinder machines and this showed in their front profile which the kit provided.

So although welcomed in the Modeller's review of October 1961 and by many modellers themselves at the time, the model was still compromised, added to which there were tender variants and further body alterations, which meant that an accurate model needed to be tightly checked against reference material. The kit came with the 4,000 gallon curved top SR tender. Reliance on the Tri-ang chassis was maintained throughout the Wills era, but that is now a thing of the past for today's SEF offering.

W11/F104 LMS/BR Fowler/Hughes Crab 2-6-0

The SR Mogul review made clear that those kits were available before that September's Model Railway Hobby Show, and held out the prospect that the next in the series, which was to be the LMS Crab, would be released at the event itself. Wills was advertising it in the October and November Modeller and it was reviewed in the January 1962 issue. The Crab was conveniently 5'6" wheeled and had Walschaerts gear. Its cylinders were also markedly inclined, and Wills provided a wedge to further incline those taken from the Tri-ang chassis. As a further refinement Wills provided a replacement cast crosshead with all the Mogul kits (although the earliest SR Moguls may have escaped). On the Crab the 3MT cylinder block and gear remained quite a weak representation of what the real thing carried. No alterations are known to the model in the Wills era.

W12/F103 LNER/BR K3 2-6-0

In fact, the January 1962 review was a twin billing with the third Mogul which took the LNER K3 prototype, having been advertised by Wills in December. This prototype had 5'8" wheels and did not use Walschaerts gear. It was the weakest of the three in modelling terms, and proved to be the first to be thoroughly renovated in the SEF era. Its deficiencies even extended to the body which seemingly combined the original GNR design cab width with the profile of the LNER build's cab - these mistakes are apparently perpetrated from the Skinley drawing. The result also created an overlong boiler which, just to finish matters, was undersize in diameter. It needs bearing in mind that the first K3s were GNR build and had totally different cabs, whilst the Wills kit is modelling the 1924 LNER build from Darlington works with a cab derived from

NER practice.

W13/F102 LNER/BR J39 0-6-0

As 1962 dawned, Wills' pace remained undiminished as a trio of 0-6-0s was completed with this 1926 Gresley design. Both this kit and the next release were announced in the January Modeller, wherein for the first time the idea that Wills would release their own chassis kits in lieu of the proprietary units was floated - a hope that was never entirely fulfilled in the Wills era. In fact, as with the Q and the 2251 class, the J39 required a Tri-ang Jinty chassis.

At the outset it was recognised that re-wheeling the Tri-ang chassis was advantageous. The review model in the February 1962 Modeller and the catalogues of the time were so altered. The March Constructor had a more extensive review, and along with the Modeller, was effusive. Leave the model with the Tri-ang wheels and you could have a J38 into the bargain and a boiler that was six inches too short; this the Constructor had done and they even painted the result unlined BR black. Actually some J38s did use J39 boilers later, so this dodge could be justified.

Alan Gibson's examination of the kit in the April 1974 Constructor was a little different - expectations of accuracy had changed in 12 years. Gibson reckoned to have spent six months working out which prototypes the model could fit, along with the consequent range of necessary alterations.

Like the Holden tank, in still later life this model excited the critical eye of Iain Rice with a detailed feature in Model Railway Journal 34. He was able to identify many shortcomings, some arising from use of the Roche drawings, others from the commitment to the Tri-ang 0-6-0 chassis. The chassis had destroyed the daylight under the boiler and any hope of cab fittings.

By 1986, Rice's lobbying had persuaded Wills that the model had to be reborn. Indeed Railway Modeller in January 1987 announced that the J39, K3, SR Mogul and the J69 would all get the treatment. As recorded for the J69, the result was not available until the models moved to their new owners. That process has now spawned three kits where once there was one, and the injunction not to paint the result anything other than black, when had one followed the example of one's betters in 1962, LNER Apple Green would have been chosen!

W14/F114 LSWR/SR/BR King Arthur 4-6-0

The wisdom behind Wills choices may be evidenced by the manner in which decades later the ready-to-run manufacturers followed suit. Of these first 14 engines modelled by Wills, seven gained ready-to-run representation by 1976. Wills' first 4-6-0 was reviewed in the May 1962 Railway Modeller when the kit was by some margin the largest offered in its genre, having 90-plus components. The boiler came in two castings with another one for the smokebox. The

intended chassis was taken from the Tri-ang Britannia; but unfortunately the latter has incorrect valvegear and makes the driving wheels sit too far forward.

Despite chassis shortcomings, the body did provide the parts to deal with the two major prototype variants. The two versions were the original Urie design of 1918 and the later 1925 Maunsell design. A massive eight-wheeled watercart tender was provided but nameplates were not. When in 1976 Hornby Railways introduced their own (rather inadequate) King Arthur, no attempt was made by Wills to use the latter's chassis since that had been adapted from the old Tri-ang B12. An etched nickel silver chassis kit FC114 was designed for the kit around 1978, which along with scale wheels and better valvegear, improves the kit markedly.

W15/F115 LMS/BR Stanier 4MT 2-6-4T

The next kit was ready for reviews in the September 1962 issues of both the Modeller and Constructor. Wills stuck firmly with Home Counties traction in his choice. The general outline of the Stanier designed LMS 2-6-4T may have been common across the LMS, but Wills chose a three cylindered version encompassing 37 prototypes - these being closely associated with LT&SR services. By 1962 many of Wills prototypes faced sudden extinction, and the Constructor noted that the same post that brought the review kit, brought too the official BR notice announcing the condemnation of the final 30 survivors, leaving class leader 42500 alone for preservation.

As is often the case, there were subtle variations within the class. Wills' bodyline kit, which was always sold to fit the Hornby Dublo/Wrenn 2-6-4T chassis, was properly speaking modelling only engines 2500-2507. These were the only examples having both the full height cab door and the parallel sided bunker. At least in this instance the chassis had some definite relation to the prototype! The kit remained unmodified in the Wills era.

W16/F116 LNER/BR Peppercorn A2 4-6-2

Wills was certainly not finished with 1962, there were another two releases to go. The Model Railway Hobby Show saw the arrival of a Pacific, something which confirmed that 1962 marked Wills' arrival in the Big Engine market. The prototypes were modern, having only entered service in 1947-48. They were Peppercorn's stylish refinement of Thompson's preceding A2/3. Despite this, 1962 nevertheless saw the first example condemned.

The kit was reviewed in October's Modeller and Constructor, and it has to be remarked that when one compares a series of Modeller and Constructor reviews, the latter is usually a more detailed and critical affair. Wills' use of the Britannia chassis was relatively acceptable, since the wheelbase, diameters, cylinders and valvegear of the former were appropriate. Appropriate and not perfect - there are differences between the Riddles and Peppercorn Walschaerts gear. The builder had to lower the cylinders, and the one feature of the A2 that was radically different to the *Britannia* below the footplate was attended to - this was the provision of the Cartazzi pony truck.

Wills packed what was a prestige model full of detail, which included detailed cab, turbo-generator, and electric lights. Cast nameplates for 60525 *A H Peppercorn* were included. Due to detail differences, the kit most accurately represented the single chimneyed 60525/7/8/30/1/4-7.

Notwithstanding which, a number of errors were present. The tender was more of a pastiche than an accurate reproduction, the consequence of errors in the Roche drawing. Fitting a banjo dome was wrong, and cab roof and cab side windows were poor too.

The length of boiler necessitated its reproduction in several sections. That and the fact that, no matter the changes Tri-ang and later Hornby Railways themselves instituted to their chassis, by the 1980s modellers expectations of what constituted quality had changed somewhat, all this added up to South Eastern Finecast putting the kit through a major rebuild in 1991.

W17/F117 LSWR/SR/BR O2 0-4-4T

November 1962 witnessed the final arrival for the year and with it another wheel arrangement. The O2 0-4-4T certainly could not use a proprietary chassis. A separate chassis kit was offered along with the appropriate bunker parts for the mainland or the Isle of Wight based engines. There were also Westinghouse brake fitments and twenty-one name castings for the Island locos. Perhaps a pity Wills did not push on to more chassis detail? The Modeller review loco of January 1963 was completed but still looked naked. There was an MRN review the following month.

Wills probably felt that they had invested some effort getting the chassis to where it was. The turn of 1962/63 saw them work up two 0-4-4T chassis - one for the O2 and one for the forthcoming M7 kit. Both resulted in a jig drilled cast mainframe with riveted and reamed brass bearings, a special bogie unit, and cast coupling rods and power collectors. In the catalogues for the mid-1960s, a whole page was devoted to this. Either the Modeller loco was not complete or swift alterations did at least provide front guard irons. An early small change to the O2 kit certainly improved the chimney.

What a difference work below the running plate could make, and this was shown in a detailed article by Frank Crudass published in the March 1966 Constructor. He discarded the Wills chassis and made up a brass strip chassis which was then detailed. Come SEF, and the kit was completely reworked, there being no further changes under Wills.

W18/F118 LSWR/SR/BR M7 0-4-4T

The first release in 1963 offered the larger LSWR M7 0-4-4T which graced that year's catalogue cover. There is a review in the February Modeller, and one solely devoted to the special chassis in the July Constructor. From the latter it can be seen that the M7 chassis did incorporate some extra detailing. Scale size cast coupling rods and the sprung bogie impressed the reviewer. Sandboxes were prominent beneath the running plate (unlike the Tri-ang model).

The class had been introduced in 1897 and grew in length by 1'2¾" after the first 55 examples. Wills endeavoured to model the longer version. We say endeavour because the model suffered from a common failing of whitemetal products - whitemetal shrinks by about 1.5% after casting. This kits' patterns may have been spot on, but the assembled result was typically between the two prototype sizes. This phenomenon is another factor in the challenge that a whitemetal chassis often poses.

Wills did not provide push-pull fittings, and other options would have to await South Eastern Finecast.

W19/F119 CR/LMS/BR McIntosh 782 class 0-6-0T

Apart from the Taff Vale U1, hitherto all Wills choices could have had some Home Counties connection, and there were to be very few exceptions to this rule, but a model of a Caledonian Railway 0-6-0T was certainly one. This was ready before the Easter Show and there are reviews in both the April 1963 Modeller and Constructor. It was designed to use the faithful Tri-ang chassis, but it was recognised that a special chassis would be preferable, and Wills had provided this option by later in 1963. It was supplanted by the introduction of CK1/FC100 in 1977.

The prototype (about which Wills was rather reticent) was the McIntosh 782 class dating from 1898. They became the standard CR shunters with 138 examples. Extinction took place in 1962, so as hard as Wills modelled prototypes, BR withdrew them. Alternative safety valve, dome and chimney parts to allow CR and typical LMS/BR conditions were provided, the latter of which saw many of the locos carrying an unattractive stovepipe.

W20/F120 LBSCR/SR/BR D1 0-4-2T/E1 0-6-0T

Wills had already introduced multi-prototype models (the SR Mogul) but the D1/E1 kit allowed two different wheel arrangements owing to the fortuitous nature of this 1873/74 Stroudley LBSCR design. The locos may not have had quite the charm of the Terrier being that much larger, but the kit was however an effective partner to the K's Terrier. Since the two D1/E1 classes accounted for 204 locos, the last of which was withdrawn in 1961, they were a key feature of an SR layout. The most basic difference was that the D1 was an 0-4-2T and the E1 an 0-6-0T.

(top) Wills F122 LMS/BR Fowler 4F with scratchbuilt chassis and tender cab, Romford wheels and heavily weathered!
Photo: Colin Hey, courtesy Eric Robinson

(above) Wills F123 GWR/BR original Hall with the original chassis
Photo: Tony Wright, courtesy South Eastern Finecast Collection

(below) Wills F128 LNER/BR A1/A3, finished as A3 *Sandwich*, on scratchbuilt chassis
Photo: Tony Wright, courtesy Tony Wright

The model was released for sale at the Easter Show in April 1963. Reviews in both the Modeller and Constructor took place in June 1963. For the E1, use of the Tri-ang chassis was suggested. A special chassis for the D1 was designed and this was reviewed in the August Constructor. In principle it followed the specification of the two 0-4-4T chassis, but as an innovation dummy inside motion was said to be fitted, a rumour Bob himself denies. The chassis thankfully showed the prominent guard irons, and the air reservoir behind the rear axle. This axle, as on the prototype, was not a pony truck - the D1 simply had a third carrying axle and a set of 4'6" trailing wheels. The D1 had relatively large 5'6" drivers whilst the E1 was entirely 4'6" wheeled. The very minor body differences between the two were covered by an alternative smokebox door faceplate and splasher castings.

The prototypes not surprisingly had a complex history. There was a Billington derivative, boiler fittings changed over the years, and the needs of war even dragged some to Scotland. Some D1s were push-pull fitted, ten E1s became 0-6-2T, and others went to the Isle of Wight. Then there were the fire fighting, oil fuel pumping and stationary boiler conversions. Wills' kit did not cover these oddities, but did allow for the basic differences between the as-new and typically inter-war state of the engines. The kits' only development was to accommodate the CK1/FC100 chassis upon its release for the E1. In SEF hands, three entirely separate kits have been created, and even then you will have to model the fire engine conversion yourself.

W21/F121 GWR 1804/1854 class 0-6-0ST

The prototypes of the Wills GWR 0-6-0ST were entirely 19th century and must have seemed to many modellers altogether more unfamiliar than the preceding model - the last had been converted to pannier tanks by 1932. The models were released for the Autumn 1963 Model Rail & Road Hobby Show and reviews follow in the September 1963 Constructor and Modeller.

Wills went to some effort to capture the prototype. Full rivet detail was very apparent on the tank which enabled the result to be defined as a three course (as opposed to five course) saddle tank. With the open cab prototype, Wills elected to provide its own cast chassis with the motor driving the front axle, which lasted throughout the Wills era. This meant that full cab detail was fitted, but why did the bunker show no coal? One guesses Wills thought that the modeller would glue some material to the flat surface provided, but this always looks odd in the review and catalogue examples.

Fun and games are there to be had about the prototype. The Wills catalogue was clear that the locos were built from 1890. Initially the model was labelled as an 1804 or 1854 saddle tank. Latterly it became a plain 1854 class, but Wills actually provided cast numberplates for 1853. The Constructor welcomed the model as a Dean engine, whilst October's MRN called it an Armstrong engine of a class first built at Wolverhampton from 1874. Behind this lies a fantastically complicated prototype history.

The effective summary is that this three course boiler (it is pretty key) and a central dome which Wills modelled, along with 4'6" (later 4'7½") drivers shows the 1854 series of 1701 class saddle tanks in the condition as rebuilt with an S4 boiler. This group consisted of 100 Swindon engines built 1890-95.

However this begs many questions. Is the dome correct for this rebuild? It is the MRN that states (and various pictures support) that the model was numbered 1853. It is the Wills catalogue that holds out the idea that the 1804 class could be an option. Now neither 1804 nor 1853 had anything intimately to do with the 1701/1854 class. Engine 1853 was actually the final loco of the Dean 1813 class and was built in 1884. These progressed through side, saddle and pannier tanks in their life. The latter were to accommodate the Belpaire boilers of the rebuilding programme. According to Jim Russell's *Great Western Engines*, to have modelled 1853 the Wills kit would have needed a uniquely small motion access step. Yes, in general terms 1853 might have resembled the model at some stage in its career, but that could never have made it either an 1804 or 1854 series engine, and nor was it then made in 1890.

What of engine number 1804? That came from the 1501 series and I surmise that it dated from 1881. With 1,109 of this generic type built between 1870-1905 Wills should be excused this pedantry. What the kit was in essence, was a model of a typical GWR 4'6" wheeled inside framed 0-6-0ST of the late 19th century. If however these nuances fascinate, earlier in the September 1963 Modeller the magazine's editor published his drawing of 1751 as finally running in 1932 as the last survivor of the saddle tanks. Number 1751 was part of the 655 series built from 1892. The interest is excited because Freezer stated that he worked the drawing up for Bob Wills to model his kit from. If so all our fluster could have surely been excused with a cast plate reading 1751?

Having said all this, it is very important to note that the capable modeller armed with accurate prototype pictures and drawings could turn this kit into something like six distinct classes covering hundreds of engines. Buried deep in the literature of the West Mercian EM Group is their own review of the kit (August 1978), wherein with precision the detailed possibilities are outlined (if for instance you are prepared to re-rivet the tanks for anything between three and six courses!).

W22/F122 LMS/BR Fowler 4F 0-6-0

Before 1963 ended another loco was released. Some of the required development work had already been completed, and so the tender used for the Crab kit found a new home on the 4F. Reviews in the model press were provided in November 1963. There is an alternative release date of January 1964 available which was quoted in the late 1963 catalogue wherein it was the newest kit. Surely the Christmas trade was too appealing?

The many detail variations of the prototypes mean that these older Wills' models are correct only for LMS engines built between 1925-28. Although Wills was often prepared to use Tri-ang chassis, a slightly shorter running plate and the 8" difference in wheel diameters between the Jinty prototype and the 4F suggested avoiding that solution. From the outset a separate pur-pose-designed chassis kit was sold by Wills, and this provided proper daylight detail under the boiler into which dummy valvegear could be fit-ted. Thus the firebox became home to the motor, which it was suggested should be the trusty Tri-ang XO4. A set of Romford gears and wheels were the final requirement to get the model run-ning. Thereafter the kit survived unaltered through the Wills era.

W23/F123 GWR/BR original Hall 4-6-0

With 1964 and 22 locos already released, Wills pace of activity changed. Between now and 1981 only three years broke the one or two releases per year rule - 1965 when there were three and 1970 and 1980 when there were none. The Easter Show release in 1964 justified any patience, for it was another prestigious choice with the very popular GWR Hall class. This was modelled in its Collett form as built 1928-44. Ultimately, a possible contributing fac-tor to Wills' decision to quit locos was the increasing output of high quality ready-to-run prototypes, and in 1966 the Hall kit became an early victim - Tri-ang released an acceptable Hall model, followed the next year by an M7.

Wills' kit was reviewed in the April model press, and by the standards of the day produced a sophisticated model. The body kit came com-plete with the front bogie frames and the cylin-der/crosshead set up. It was possible to provide a detailed backhead in the cab. The modeller either used a re-wheeled (to 6') Tri-ang B12 chassis or Wills provided their own chassis kit in the now-typical style. The latter enabled an extra segment of boiler to be used, and thus a fully rotund boiler to be completed; two chimneys and sets of buffers were also supplied. A flared 4,000 gallon tender was excellently modelled and would be useful to Wills in the future. The cast chassis lasted throughout the Wills era.

Wills decided to be very specific about proto-type, and cast name and numberplates were pro-vided. Ironically, the level of detailing was even at the time regarded as too crude, etching being a far better process for such fittings. Any rate, 6942 *Eshton Hall* was the chosen loco - this example was still in traffic in 1964, and the Constructor could advise that she was running with the shorter chimney and parallel shank buffers. Condemnation followed that very year.

When Iain Rice wrote about the model in the *Model Railway News* in March 1982, opinions were no longer complementary. Designing a loco around a B12 chassis had necessitated com-promises that led Rice to declare that "rather than building a Wills 'Hall' kit. I would build a model of a 'Hall' from a Wills kit". Fundamental errors, which would be none too easy to correct, were found in the wheelbase, cylinders and front bogie/framing - even though Wills had offered their own chassis, matters like splasher location reflected the Tri-ang dimensions.

W24/F124 MR/LMS Flatiron 0-6-4T

At least the next model looks likely to be safe from RTR competition. In general, short to medi-um life pre-grouping prototypes prove to be less likely to be aped. This kit was for the forty 1907 built MR 0-6-4T prototypes which became extinct by 1938. Most unusual engines, they had been built for passenger work but their output did not match their mammoth profile. Some had put in an appearance on the LT&SR, so a Home Counties connection was established. In the far distant past there had been a Marklin model, but otherwise they have not proved wildly exciting to manufacturers.

Bodyline style was followed with the kit designed around the Tri-ang Jinty chassis, a rear bogie frame was provided. The kit modelled the class in their rebuilt state - this process com-menced in 1920 and the major visual conse-quence, which Wills reproduced, was the extended smokebox and the Belpaire firebox. Reviews are in all three major model railway press magazines in October 1964, and the Constructor confessed to some surprise at the prototype! The MRN was able to point out a handful of detail divergences from prototype. They followed the kit up in May 1966 with a detailed article by Bob Essery which addressed providing a better chassis than the Tri-ang option, using a K's Kirtley, and correcting the few other errors. Latterly the Wills CK1/FC100 chassis was recommended.

W25/F125 GER/LNER/BR N7 0-6-2T

It was back to a Home Counties favourite for the next kit. The GNR London Suburban 0-6-2T had been done to death by the likes of Hornby Dublo and Tri-ang, but the GER equivalent was virgin territory - this was the LNER class N7. Wills had indicated that this would be in the programme as far back as March 1962; release actually took place in the Spring of 1965 with reviews in the Modeller and Constructor that June. It was programmed as the Easter Show release, slated to be beside the T9, but the latter suffered some delay.

The trusty Tri-ang 0-6-0T chassis was relied upon, so latterly the CK1/FC100 combination could be used, and parts for the rear bogie frame came with the body kit. After some of the uncer-tainties of previous locos, it was specifically advised that the loco had been based upon LNER 8006. This was GER 1006 when new in 1921, and the kit was firmly based on the origi-nal GER condensing version with its Belpaire boiler and without any parts for the various alter-natives. There were three further LNER builds, each given a sub classification. Rebuilding with round-topped boilers further increased the variety so that classes N7 and N7/1-5 had all existed. This wealth of choice had to await the SEF intervention.

W26/F126 LSWR/SR/BR T9 4-4-0

Wills had not manufactured a 4-4-0 before the T9, although others would follow. Having completed an 0-4-4T, the techniques of chassis manufacture only required reversing. No, that did not happen! The chassis was quite different and really resembled an 0-4-0 with the bogie unit fitting separately under the smokebox, although some fine tuning was still required by the builder. Wills advertised the model for the 1965 Easter Show, but it was September before stockists advertised it, with reviews in November and December magazines. By 1965 Wills choices were inescapably becoming past history, and the last T9 had gone into preservation in July 1963.

The class had sixty-six members all built in the two years 1899-1901. Not all were identical even then, and as the years passed a variety of tenders were fitted, and a rebuilding programme instituted between 1922-29 produced further changes. Fifteen were built in the form Wills modelled (300-5/7/10-4/36-8) - these had a wider cab and splashers, and were fitted with the eight-wheeled tender. The Wills kit showed this group as running post-rebuilding with an extended smokebox and superheater. The kit and its matching cast chassis kit were not altered in the Wills era.

W27/F127 GWR/BR Star 4-6-0

The 1965 programme became conflated, and hard on the heels of the T9 came the GWR Star, such that they were both being reviewed in the November and December magazines beside one another. For the third time in a row a prototype that could have benefited from some judicious alternative parts was presented in one form only, rather sad compared with previous kits and noted by the reviewers. The Star class dated from 1907 and helped put the GWR 4-6-0 tradition on the map. These were four cylinder engines and later begot the Castles, in parallel to their two cylinder Saint contemporaries begetting the Halls. Wills would model all four classes.

The excellent Hall tender was re-used and the same principle of using the B12 chassis was adopted. Unlike the Hall, no special Finecast chassis was ever developed by Wills, but like the Hall, the model was given a unique identity with 4051 *Princess Helena* being chosen. Since Castle design steampipes and the 4,000 gallon tender were fitted, the model was firmly placed in its final years, 1944-50. The proficient modeller wanting other options was left to source alternative parts and get out the craft knife.

W28/F128 GNR/LNER/BR Gresley A1/A3 4-6-2

Alternatives were at least on the agenda for the only release of 1966. The model was slated for release during March but adverts appeared a couple of months later, with all three modelling press magazines carrying reviews in June 1966. This time the challenge was to provide the classic Gresley Pacific in the various conditions they operated in, and which merited the dual A1 and A3 classifications. The kit was offered as a bodyline with separate chassis kit; the latter being reviewed in the August Constructor. The key alternatives offered in the body kit were the cab sides, chimney, dome, cab seating, and left or right hand drive. Detailing was particularly extensive, for instance lubricating equipment, and the fire iron tunnel on the tender were both modelled. Cast whitemetal nameplates for seven examples were supplied. One was incorrectly rendered as *Columbus* for *Columbo*, and this was never corrected. The others were *Gay Crusader*, *Windsor Lad*, *Blink Bonny*, *Flying Fox*, *Spearmint*, and *Flying Scotsman*.

Beneath the running plate the modeller was required to assemble the leading bogie and trailing truck from the body kit, obtain the Wills chassis, and the proprietary motor and wheels. Additionally, a set of Tri-ang *Britannia* Walschaerts valvegear was required, and this was probably the weakest element of the kit. The tender was the typical non-corridor LNER design. The model was actually of corridor tender width and when shown, as Wills did, attached to a loco finished as LNER 4472, a work of fiction was created. The option for the earlier and smaller GNR version had to await the SEF era (which amongst other alterations has entirely changed the chassis and cylinders etc.).

W29/F129 GWR/BR King 4-6-0

The reign of the Wills King started at the Easter 1967 MRC Show. A separate chassis kit was provided and full reviews of both occurred in *Model Railway Constructor* that May and June, and Modeller and MRN reviews are in the June issues. The detail included a fully detailed cab interior and the rocking gear components to the front of the cylinders. The distinctive King bogie was formed from seven castings in the body kit, as were the cylinder components. Optional fittings included a double chimney suitable for the last seven years of their BR life (not the most popular of options) and the *King George V*'s bell. Cast name and numberplates for 6000 came too, as did the familiar Wills 4,000 gallon tender. No revisions were undertaken during the Wills era.

W30/WF167 LMS/BR Fowler Dock tank 0-6-0T

The narrative now reaches without doubt the most unusual loco kit in the line-up. It is one that I cannot as yet trace any catalogue entry for, despite which at least two illustrated reviews exist (the December 1967 *Railway Modeller* and the January 1969 *Model Railway Constructor*). The model was evidently newly available in the Autumn of 1967. It was a bodyline kit for an LMS Fowler Dock tank expressly designed for, and indeed supplied with, a Fleischmann chassis. The latter were highly regarded for their mechanisms, and its outside valvegear had some

(above) Wills F129 GWR/BR King 4-6-0

Photo: Tony Wright, courtesy Aberhafren Layout

(below) The box top for the unusual Wills body kit WF167 representing a Fowler Dock tank, supplied with a ready-to-run Fleischmann 0-6-0 chassis.

Photo: Dave Wheatstone, courtesy Dave Wheatstone Collection

(below) Wills F131 LMS/BR original Scot built on a scale chassis

Photo: Tony Wright, courtesy Ian Rathbone

similarities to the LMS prototype. Even so, both body and chassis were significant compromises. One felt the trade press were not quite sure what to make of this initiative, and even getting it to couple effectively to British stock must have been a challenge. The model seems to have died an unmourned death after just a few years. The WF167 reference has been seen on a boxed example, but otherwise how it fitted into the Wills numbering system is not understood. The patterns still exist with SEF.

W31/F130 GWR/BR 1854 class 0-6-0PT

The King and the Dock tank were the 1967 programme, and the 1968 programme was even more restrained. The one release of the year was a simple rebuild following the prototype, but one whose value to the Great Western modeller should not therefore be understated. The F121 0-6-0ST prototypes were rebuilt after 1911 into pannier tanks, and Wills' kit took the saddle tank and changed it into a pannier. The existing chassis and even the cast numberplate were replicated. Thus to summarise what was said at length for F121, do not expect utter guaranteed prototype fidelity to number 1853, but if prepared to undertake some homework, the kit could provide an excellent model of the generic group. The kit was released at the Easter 1968 MRC Show, although it was intended to play second fiddle there to the A4. The latter's development became extremely complex and its release was still two kits and another year into the future. The GWR pannier was released and by June 1968 the Modeller could review it, and the Constructor followed that August. Wills never altered the kit further.

W32/F131 LMS/BR original Royal Scot 4-6-0

Wills was quiet in the remainder of 1968. He was beavering away at what had become the challenging task of the streamlined A4, yet for the Easter Show of 1969 sprung a different big engine surprise. An original Royal Scot model was displayed at the Toy Fair, with release at the Easter Show. A full review followed in the June 1969 Modeller and Constructor. The whitemetal body kit fitted an altered Tri-ang A3 chassis. A 3,500 gallon Fowler tender was provided (from the Crab/4F) and thus the model leaned towards the earlier years of the prototype, although smoke deflectors were provided for fitting if desired. Body scaling was good, and so too was detailing provision above the running plate, but below was a different matter with wrong cylinders, valvegear, wheel spacing and wheel diameters inherited from the Tri-ang chassis.

Although the kit lasted unchanged throughout the Wills era, its reliance on the proprietary chassis had created some fundamental problems, and as will be narrated in the SEF account, the model went into abeyance with the new owners.

W33/F132 LNER/BR A4 4-6-2

It has already become clear that this kit had a lengthy gestation: "very much more tricky than anticipated" as Bob Wills told the Modeller. After much anticipation it was available to be advertised in September 1969, and not long afterwards Trix would follow the same path with a ready-to-run model. Both became very acceptable models but it still must have been frustrating to find competition so soon with what was potentially such a desirable choice.

The reviews followed in the Modeller that December and in the Constructor the following January. The kit was cleverly designed to offer the two fundamental choices that the prototype required, and to be motorised either with a Tri-ang A3 chassis, or for the experienced modeller, with Wills' more accurate own chassis. The basic prototype choice was pre- or post-war, i.e. with or without valvegear valences. These were provided in the kit as optional cast panels, and another choice allowed a double or single chimney. Unlike the A3, no names were provided. It had originally been hoped that the deceptively simple body and cab outline could have been cast in just two units, but eventually they had to become four pieces, although this challenge was later won by SEF.

The eight-wheeled tender was not drawn from the A3, but was a newly generated design complete with the prototype's streamline fairing. It could be finished in corridor or non-corridor form but had shortcomings - the corridor tender had no flange at the base of the tank and the turn-in was too sharp; the non-corridor tender had no beading, was too wide, and had no turn-in at the front. No changes during the Wills era took place.

Those with a fondness for Wills A4s may want to know that Wills produced a cast paperweight model in 1970. Part of the Finecast Steam Era series, 1000 models measuring 4 7/16" over buffers and mounted on a mahogany plinth were made, with each model being numbered. The prototype was *Mallard*, and they were supplied in an imitation red leatherette box.

W34/F133 GWR/BR Saint 4-6-0

There now followed a run of four GWR prototypes taking us through 1971 and 1972. The first of these for the Saint was originally announced as the Easter 1970 model, but in the event it was Easter 1971 before the model emerged. On the prototype, GWR Saint led to Hall. With Wills the order was reversed but they shared the option of Hornby B12 or Finecast chassis, the latter being individual to either loco. Wills did decide to generate a new tender for the smaller 3,500 gallon design which would be used on other kits in the future, and the development of this tender was the reported reason for the delay. The original plan would have re-used the Hall's 4,000 gallon tender, but this was not suitable for most of the lifespan of the class, so should the modeller require one, Wills would always arrange a swap.

Certainly the Saint was welcomed, and there was a Modeller review that April (which paired up with the next kit too). Engine 2931 *Arlington*

(above) Wills F132 LNER/BR A4 constructed in post-War form, seen performing on Wolverhampton MRC's Stoke Summit Layout

Photo: Tony Wright, courtesy Tony Wright

(below) Wills F134 GWR/BR 61xx built on the subsequent South Eastern Finecast chassis

Photo: Tony Wright, courtesy South Eastern Finecast Collection

Court featured in the Modeller was not a Wills provision - they provided neither numbers nor names. The model remained unchanged through the rest of the Wills era, and within the Saint class it specifically represented the series of "Court" named locos.

W35/F134 GWR/BR 61xx 2-6-2T

The result of the Saint's delay was that Easter 1971 was actually graced by two new models, along with the announcement of the GWR 4-4-0 County, the LBSCR I3 and the GWR Castle. The other release was the GWR 61xx, and here Wills really went to great efforts. The preserved Great Western Society 6106 built at Swindon in 1932 and located at Didcot was used as a pattern, and an ex-Swindon designer checked Wills' drawings. An individual cast chassis was provided, so designed that the motor cleared the cab into which a full set of backhead detail was fitted, although no cast numbers were supplied. The chassis however, with plenty of empty space between the drivers, began to emphasise the fact that brakegear was lacking. A Constructor review rather late in the day was published in November 1971 which was also positive about the kit. The kit was not altered during the Wills era.

That elusive periodical *Loco Modeller* gave the Prairie the full treatment in February 1984 - "one of the most satisfying [kits] I have had the pleasure to construct". Even so, that suggested that the standard Wills cast coupling rods were now passé, and replacement with Gibson's etched product was desirable. Nonetheless, Paige reckoned that the kit eclipsed the newer RTR Prairie from Airfix with which Wills had to contend from 1976. That comment struck me as slightly baffling insofar as the Airfix model reproduced brakegear, and other under-the-running-plate details, that Wills ignored.

W36/F135 GWR County 4-4-0

Full advantage of the smaller 3,500 gallon GWR tender was taken with the next kit. With only one 4-4-0 behind them, the final years of releases from Wills would offer another three. First away in this group was the GWR County, a model well known to the older modeller with the famous Hornby O gauge example. The kit was planned for the Autumn of 1971, but once again Wills found themselves bunching two releases, this time in the Spring of 1972. "Finest Finecast" proclaimed W&H in February 1972, and with rivet heads along the running plate valance, and a fully detailed and very visible cab, the claim was well made. Despite this, cast numbers were not supplied. The Modeller and Constructor both reviewed the model in May 1972 and were equally impressed.

The prototype was significant as the first outside cylindered GWR 4-4-0, and dated from 1904. Their model, with a section of curved running plate at each end, represents one of the final ten built in 1911-12 and numbered 3821-30. The representation of the final ten meant that they were not destined for a long life as the last one went in 1933.

A special Wills chassis was required, and after release there were no further changes in the Wills era. Thus what was beginning to become a dated feature such as the two part-boiler remained - in parallel, K's were upgrading their own specifications to single piece boilers.

W37/F136 GWR Metro 2-4-0T

Only a few weeks later, and a rather different little GWR loco ended this quartet. The Modeller reviewed the Metro tank in July 1972. Its 2-4-0 wheel arrangement shared with the County the requirement put upon Wills to design a special cast chassis, but there the resemblance ended. These engines were originally designed in 1874 for through workings over London's Metropolitan Railway and then built over the next 25 years. However, in the passing of time their appeal for use in country pastures grew, and by the 1920s they were closely associated with country byways.

Wills allowed for two main choices - open or closed cab. Wills did not supply condensing gear so subterranean operations were ruled out. Indeed the model is "late" in period; even the open cab is not a mere weatherboard. The one bunker option supplied is the enlarged design typical of later years. Moreover, the class had long, medium or short side tanks. The Wills model has short tanks and should therefore be numbered 3-6, 455-470, 613-632, 967-986, 1445-64, and 1491-1500 - a total of 90 engines. As so often is the case, this is to skate over a myriad of changing details, and an accurate model needs reference photos and the distillation of knowledge of something like Russell's book. The small size of the model virtually made it inevitable that the motor would have to invade the cab space which it did. No alterations are recorded.

W38/F137 SR/BR Schools 4-4-0

After all this Great Westernry, and much of it rather antique, Wills changed focus and opted for the final SR 4-4-0 design in the famous Schools class. Having been trailed several times through 1971 and 1972, it became the Easter 1973 release, and there was a Modeller review that July. At its advent this kit was extremely highly regarded, which is well evidenced in a very detailed review afforded by the MRN in August 1973 (down to pointing out that the spoked tender wheels supplied would only suit numbers 900-909). The usual Finecast choices were present - the kit could be modelled as-built, as soon fitted with smoke deflectors, or as altered by Bulleid with a large Lemaitre chimney. Two options for cab sides were also offered because the first ten engines had a slightly different design.

The kit's arrival marked some product development - the innovation came with the chassis. Whilst it was still cast, it was ready fitted with brass bearings. Yet the etching revolution warranted investigation by Wills, and the Schools initiated this process with a set of etched nickel silver Walschaerts valvegear. Wills never provided an etched chassis for the Schools, but brake shoes and sandboxes were supplied from the outset. The high regard for the kit was maintained, when after ten years, *Loco Modeller* reviewed the kit in detail in their November 1983 issue, summarising it as "still one of the best of the whitemetal kits and remains the only true replica of the Schools in 4mm".

W39/F138 SECR/SR/BR D 4-4-0

Southern rails would now be followed for a further three releases. The 1974 model took one back to 1901, and the SECR Edwardian elegance of the Class D 4-4-0. Hitherto, there had only been one SECR kit from Wills, two more were to come and others from the SEF stable later. The April 1974 release date in the table is at present an informed guess - it was reported as due for Easter, and W&H did advertise it from May.

However, this was the year of the miners' strike and all sorts of chaos was around. At present no reviews have been traced and so our coverage is sketchy. The kit was, however, written up in the *Airfix Model Trains* magazine in December 1983. The Wills specification relied on an individual cast chassis and a two-part boiler (both would change under SEF). Despite those 1990s amendments, this series of SECR releases proved mighty popular, offering long-lived Victorian classics otherwise unobtainable.

W40/F139 SECR/SR/BR C 0-6-0

Such was also the case with the humble C class 0-6-0 which the Modeller reviewed in June 1975. Typically, the cab was very detailed; there was another factor which contributed to the excellence of these mid-1970s releases - efforts were made to thin the castings at their edges. Despite the 0-6-0 wheel arrangement, the kit was never designed for anything other than its own cast chassis. Like the D class, both boiler and chassis would attract attention from SEF after the take-over.

W41/F140 LBSCR/SR/BR I3 4-4-2T

The last in this Southern group exploited another niche - the classy Brighton express tanks. The kit had been announced back in 1971 but it took until 1976 for it to appear. Despite being a fine model, it received relatively little press attention, yet the Constructor had received a kit for review, and illustrated a completed example in the June 1976 issue. A unique chassis was required from Wills, and alternative parts to build the engine in original LBSCR form or modified SR form were provided. The prototypes had operated from 1907 into the BR era.

W42/F141 GNR/LNER/BR C12 4-4-2T

Another 4-4-2T and another chassis formed 1977's release, which offered a GNR 4-4-2T. Whilst the I3 had Wills' last cast chassis, the C12 soon had its own etched chassis; remember that 1977 marked the release of Wills' first general purpose etched chassis for the 0-6-0s. By 1978 it was being reported (i.e. the Modeller in April) that a new 33mm wheelbase 0-4-0 etched nickel silver chassis was to be available, and that it was targeted at the C12. It was referenced as the FC141.

W43/F142 GWR De Glehn 4-4-2

Staying with 4-4-2s, the elegant French designed GWR De Glehn compound arrived around Easter 1978. This certainly had an etched chassis from new, as well as etched valvegear. However, one is struck that despite what one assumes was the undoubted fine quality of these later releases, relatively little press coverage followed.

The prototype was distinct - there were three GWR De Glehns, and Wills went for numbers two and three in that group, viz. 103 and 104 of 1905, and they only modelled the parallel boiler with which they were delivered. Both 103 and 104 seemed to carry these for a short time only, Swindon taper boilers appeared from 1907. As Evans' *Atlantic Era* shows, the two engines then swapped boilers and changed fittings with alarming frequency between then and 1915. Thereafter, quieter lives followed carrying the taper boilers until their withdrawal in 1927/28. The already available 3,500 gallon tender was fitted. It is a moot point whether 103 *President* ran with the exact combination of tender livery and boiler that Wills' publicity showed. On the model, brakegear was still avoided, but a considerable amount of commendable rivet detail was put onto the bogie frame.

One guesses that the coupled wheelbase must have been stretched. On the prototype the flanges virtually met, a task that would be extraordinarily difficult to transfer exactly into 4mm scale.

W44 & W45 / F143 & F144 GWR/BR Castle 4-6-0

The release for 1979 marked an interesting combination of economy, quality, and a sense of completion to the Wills range. It had been trailed as far back as 1971, and it was an obvious offering in relation to the other GWR express engines Wills sold. A Modeller review of the Castle was provided in May 1979; it may be significant that Wills appeared unwilling to actually send review kits to the Modeller any longer - for both this and the next release the reviewer made clear that a photo and not a model had arrived in the office! The Constructor also ran a report and not a review in their April 1979 issue. They approved of the model, commending the choices within the design. There were no names and numbers for these final GWR offerings.

The twin references reflect a choice of tenders, being the existing GWR 3,500 or 4,000 gallon designs from Wills. The model was a traditional Easter release but Wills' ability to move with the times was clear with the individual etched chassis designed for the model. Full brakegear (even on the bogie) did appear, along with dummy springs behind the drivers. With the etched motion, the as-usual very detailed cab, the choice of double or single chimneys, alternative steam pipes, different inside cylinder front covers, and the kit was surely absolutely up to the standards modellers demanded in 1979 - perhaps unlike a contemporary K's product. It must have been dispiriting that the market from the early 1980s was awash with ready-to-run Airfix Castles.

W46/F145 SECR/SR/BR H 0-4-4T

One wonders what Bob Wills was considering in the early 1980s. His Scenic Series was proving very popular and had taken the business into plastic injection moulding. The apparent error, if K's and Ratio's experience means much, of taking this technology into high quality modeller's loco kits was avoided by Wills. The model railway market suffered in the early 1980s as the economy faltered, and it was laden to excess with quality Far Eastern made RTR product. No loco came from Wills in 1980, but a final one was released for Easter 1981. It was fully up to the new standards Wills was capable of. The very useful SECR class H 0-4-4T was the subject, and for a prototype to model, the short trek to the example preserved on the Bluebell Railway was all that was required. The sandboxes,

brakegear, and etched nickel silver chassis were now supplemented by a one-piece boiler casting; Wills had moved with the times to the last. There was even the novel option of providing a "rolling chassis" option of a complete kit with everything except the motor.

W47/F146 LBSCR/SR/BR Atlantic 4-4-2

One final reference was quoted in the 1983 W&H catalogue, and hopes clearly existed that new Wills releases would come. An LBSCR Atlantic had first been flagged as a possibility in the Modeller's review of the intended 1982 Wills programme. It was not to be. Instead, the range continued in Wills hands until 1988, and then the range shifted home. Thereafter new prototypes and major modifications have followed. Amongst those, this potentially attractive prototype for the LBSCR Atlantic has not yet numbered.

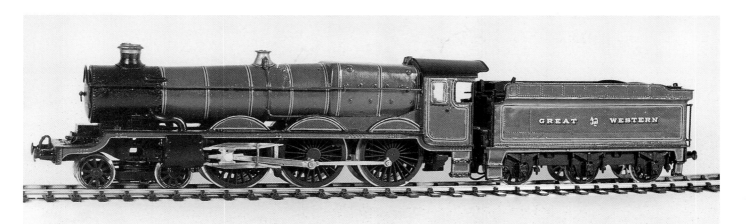

(above) Wills F144 GWR/BR Castle kit made with modest skills and using the original Wills chassis, yet still looking regal with its larger 4,000 gallon tender

Photo: Dave Wheatstone, courtesy Dave Wheatstone Collection

(right) Original Wills Display Case showing top left to top right, F114 *King Arthur*, F115 Stanier 3 cylinder, F124 Flatiron; bottom left to bottom right, F126 T9, F140 I3, and F120 D1 & E1

Photo: Tony Wright, courtesy South Eastern Finecast

Wills Locomotives Table

Text Reference	Wills Reference	Description	New Date	Withdrawal Date	Notes
W01	F113	GER/LNER/BR Holden Buckjumper 0-6-0T	5/1959	6/1988	
W02	F110	GWR/BR 94xx 0-6-0PT	10/1959	6/1988	
W03	F109	LBSCR/SR/BR E2 0-6-0T	4/1960	6/1988	
W04	F108	LSWR/SR/BR G6 0-6-0T	5/1960	6/1988	
W05	F107	SECR/SR/BR P 0-6-0T	5/1960	6/1988	
W06	F101	LBSCR/SR/BR E5 0-6-2T	12/1960	6/1988	
W07	F112	GWR/BR 2251 class 0-6-0	3/1961	6/1988	
W08	F106	SR/BR Q 0-6-0	4/1961	6/1988	
W09	F111	TVR/GWR U1 0-6-2T	7/1961	6/1988	
W10	F105	SECR/SR/BR Mogul 2-6-0 classes N/N1/U&U1	9/1961	6/1988	
W11	F104	LMS/BR Fowler/Hughes Crab 2-6-0	9/1961	6/1988	
W12	F103	LNER/BR K3 2-6-0	12/1961	6/1988	
W13	F102	LNER/BR J39 0-6-0	1/1962	6/1988	
W14	F114	LSWR/SR/BR *King Arthur* 4-6-0	5/1962	6/1988	
W15	F115	LMS/BR Stanier 4MT 2-6-4T	8/1962	6/1988	
W16	F116	LNER/BR Peppercorn A2 4-6-2	9/1962	6/1988	
W17	F117	LSWR/SR/BR O2 0-4-4T	11/1962	6/1988	
W18	F118	LSWR/SR/BR M7 0-4-4T	1/1963	6/1988	
W19	F119	CR/LMS/BR McIntosh 782 class 0-6-0T	3/1963	6/1988	
W20	F120	LBSCR/SR/BR D1 0-4-2T/E1 0-6-0T	4/1963	6/1988	
W21	F121	GWR 1804/1854 class 0-6-0ST	9/1963	6/1988	
W22	F122	LMS/BR Fowler 4F 0-6-0	11/1963	6/1988	
W23	F123	GWR/BR original Hall 4-6-0	4/1964	6/1988	
W24	F124	MR/LMS Flatiron 0-6-4T	9/1964	6/1988	
W25	F125	GER/LNER/BR N7 0-6-2T	5/1965	6/1988	
W26	F126	LSWR/SR/BR T9 4-4-0	9/1965	6/1988	
W27	F127	GWR/BR Star 4-6-0	9/1965	6/1988	
W28	F128	LNER/BR Gresley A1/A3 4-6-2	5/1966	6/1988	

Text Reference	Wills Reference	Description	New Date	Withdrawal Date	Notes
W29	F129	GWR/BR King 4-6-0	4/1967	1988	
W30	WF167	LMS/BR Fowler Dock tank 0-6-0T	c.10/1967	c.1970	
W31	F130	GWR 1854 class 0-6-0PT	4/1968	6/1988	
W32	F131	LMS/BR unrebuilt Royal Scot 4-6-0	4/1969	6/1988	
W33	F132	LNER/BR A4 4-6-2	9/1969	6/1988	
W34	F133	GWR/BR Saint 4-6-0	3/1971	6/1988	
W35	F134	GWR/BR 61xx 2-6-2T	4/1971	6/1988	
W36	F135	GWR County 4-4-0	1/1972	6/1988	
W37	F136	GWR Metro 2-4-0T	4/1972	6/1988	
W38	F137	SR/BR Schools 4-4-0	4/1973	6/1988	
W39	F138	SECR/SR/BR D 4-4-0	4/1974	6/1988	
W40	F139	SECR/SR/BR C 0-6-0	6/1975	6/1988	
W41	F140	LBSCR/SR/BR I3 4-4-2T	6/1976	6/1988	
W42	F141	GNR/LNER/BR C12 4-4-2T	c.3/1977	6/1988	
W43	F142	GWR De Glehn 4-4-2	4/1978	6/1988	
W44	F143	GWR/BR Castle 4-6-0	5/1979	6/1988	3,500 gallon tender
W45	F144	GWR/BR Castle 4-6-0	5/1979	6/1988	4,000 gallon tender
W46	F145	SECR/SR/BR H 0-4-4T	5/1981	6/1988	
W47	F146	LBSCR/SR/BR Atlantic 4-4-2	Never Produced		

Notes:

Some sources intimate that an SR *Lord Nelson* and an LNER L1 would be produced in the 1980s. No Wills reference number is known for these and they were not produced by SEF. A 1962 announcement of the CR Single 123 was also stillborn.

(left) Illustration of the Wills F142 GWR de Glehn 4-4-2 taken from the Wills c.1977 catalogue. The debate is whether the tender would actually have carried such late period insignia?

Courtesy Bob Wills

Wills Catalogues Table

Date	Cover	Price	Notes
c.5/1959	Text only, black on white	FOC	Wagons + J69
c.10/1961	B/W with 94xx	FOC	Dated by Crab and SR Mogul
6/1962	Light blue & white	9d	Fourteen loco kits shown
11/1962	Monochrome leaflet for above	FOC	New: A2/LMS 2-6-4/SR O2
4/1963	Blue cover with M7, additional loose sheet		Nineteen loco kits shown
c.12/1963	Orange/green with M7 357	1/-	Highest release is F122
c.5/1965	Blue with Hall	1/-	Highest release is F125
c.5/1966	Khaki with Hall	1/-	Highest release is F128
c.12/1966	Orange with 4472	1/-	Highest release is F128
c.1967	Blue with 4472	1/-	Highest release is F129
c.1969	Orange with original Scot	2/6	Highest release is F132
c.1969	Red with original Scot	2/6	Highest release is F132
c.Summer 1973	Red with Schools	n/k	
c.1976	Cream with classes D/I3/Metro Tank	n/k	Highest release is F140
c.1978	Olive with classes D/I3/Metro Tank	n/k	Highest release is F142
c.1980	Chester Castle	n/k	Highest release is F145

Wills Addresses

Initial model shop address as R.Wills, 92a Brighton Road, Coulsdon, Surrey.

As Industrial Display Co. Ltd., 14 Green Lane, Thornton Heath, Surrey.

As Wills Finecast, Lower Road, Forest Row, Sussex.

Further Acknowledgements

This chapter has been assembled with the generous help of Bob Wills and Dave Ellis.

(below) An assortment of Wills catalogues

Photo: Dave Wheatstone, courtesy Robert Forsythe

South Eastern Finecast

South Eastern Finecast (SEF) is headed up by David Ellis, and its impact on the model locomotive kit business dates from June 1988 when the Wills Finecast range of rolling stock models was transferred to SEF (see Wills chapter). At the end of 1977, Dave Ellis opened South Eastern Models in The Parade at East Grinstead. He already knew Bob Wills whose operation was at nearby Forest Row. During the 1980s products as well as sales began to carry the South Eastern name, most noticeably the South Eastern Flushglaze concept.

When by 1988 it was apparent that Wills did not wish to operate both a casting and an injection moulding process, with what by now was two very diverse ranges (the whitemetal rolling stock and vehicle kits and the plastic Wills Scenic series), the solution was for the whitemetal based operation to be transferred to Ellis, and the creation of South Eastern Finecast. The fatherly role of Wills remained apparent in his contributing a foreword to the SEF Catalogues. The bonus was that Ellis was prepared to very considerably re-engineer the Wills kits, which in many cases were well over twenty years old and no longer conformed to the standards of the market. This overhaul has involved the expansion of etched components, and the provision of new components, often making a model far more accurate to defined prototypes. The new chassis are generally etched nickel silver, and additional to the upgrading, a series of prototypes forming wholly new kits has been produced. One bonus of Ellis' previous interests was the application of the Flushglaze concept to all new and revised loco kits from early 1990.

In the production table, the references can refer to inherited models that SEF sells (or sold) to the specifications set by Wills. These are all numbered below F145, and it should be noted that the entire Wills range featured in the initial SEF pricelist which dates to June 1988. A second group of models, numbered F146 and above, refers to those models that have been revised or released as entirely new creations by SEF. Within this category the first number allocated to an entirely new prototype was F150, and as of Autumn 1999, thirteen models in this group existed.

One or two caveats attach to these thirteen. One could question F154 (an E1/R) since the E1 class it was rebuilt from was already in the range (see individual notes), but as a model, the E1/R was wholly new. There is something of a prototypical relation between the SECR E class 4-4-0 (F150) and the preceding D class from Wills, but beyond sharing a tender, the E class kit is entirely new. The Q1 (F173) is a solitary example of another manufacturer's prior offering being bought into the range. Only from the LNER W1 (F166) in 1992 is an unambiguously new model produced.

David Ellis has relied on a network of individuals to help him with the revision design work. Names like Neep and Rice were involved around 1988, later Alistair Rolfe of Modeltec and Paul Vine of Precision Miniature Arts were involved, and these names will appear regularly in the entries. Paul Vine had actually started out in the hobby as one of Dave Ellis' "Saturday lads" in the shop. Ray Rogers became involved from the mid-1990s, and in 1999 Alistair Rolfe launched his own No Nonsense Kits range.

The Q1 brings in another name, that of Ron Goult of Little Engines. Little Engines is a range clear in itself, and it might be assumed that save for the sale of the Q1 to SEF, there is no further relationship. However, the reality is really rather different. As will be narrated under the M7 kit, Goult and Ellis struck up a working relationship early on in the SEF era. The *quid pro quo* led to Goult redesigning kits for Ellis, and to Ellis actually casting the Little Engines range. When Goult decided to retire, some consideration was given to SEF taking the entire Little Engines range, but in the event the purchase was restricted to the Q1.

As each loco is considered, the following order will be adhered to:- for each prototype, the first description will cover the un-revised kit as sold by SEF, usually requiring minimal discussion. Immediately thereafter, revision and development of that prototype in the series above F146 will be given so that by referring to one prototype, a full account of its history at SEF should be provided in one location. Reference to the Wills chapter should be made as prototype details are more fully given therein for those engines with a Wills ancestry. Have any Wills models been entirely dropped? The answer is no. A number are in abeyance, having been available at the outset of SEF, and have now been issued revised references awaiting re-appraisal.

The Loco Kits

SEF1/F101 LBSCR/SR/BR E5 0-6-2T

SEF inherited from Wills his full range of locomotive kits, and these were priced by SEF in a list dated June 1988. The old bodyline kit for the LBSCR E5 lasted about four years before being revised.

SEF68/F175 LBSCR/SR/BR E5 0-6-2T

The prime revisions to the E5 were a new fully detailed etched chassis, added cab detailing and alternative parts - these allowed a choice of five different safety valve arrangements. Since the old chassis used the Dublo example which was not accurate, the body of the new model (in particular the splashers) has been altered back to scale dimensions.

SEF69/F176 LBSCR/SR/BR E6 0-6-2T

The E6 prototype was entirely new, but was closely derived from the E5 model. The twelve class members had smaller 4'6" drivers, and consequentially smaller front splashers had to be cast. Four safety valve variants were accommodated. A new chassis in distinction to the E5 was designed by Ron Goult of Little Engines.

SEF2/F102 LNER/BR J39 0-6-0

The old model for the J39 became the subject of a major re-work early in the new decade and spawned three new models. This re-visit had been in the offing for some time, and Wills had previously instructed Rice and Neep to do some of the design work. Reference to the Wills chapter will expose the many shortcomings that had been identified with the old kit. Indeed upon the advent of F162, the old patterns were binned, the dome alone being reprieved.

SEF61/F162 LNER/BR J39/2 0-6-0

The old model had come with a rather crude straight sided 4,200 LNER group standard tender. The new models, in addition to two different individually designed etched nickel silver chassis and a major body overhaul, had new tenders offering considerable choice, and one-piece boiler castings were another feature. The model was launched in April 1991 with all the pattern work for the new models coming from Modeltec of Cardiff; the Rice/Neep work prepared for Wills was not used. A key aim of the retooling was to provide daylight under the boiler, and the new chassis and a motor in the firebox driving onto the rear axle allowed this.

The tender attached to the J39/2 was the 4,200 gallon version, but optional parts allowed both straight and flared sided versions to be built. That sounds simple - actually the story of this tender design attached to this class is depressingly complicated. If the issue worries you, then the best you can do is read September 1998 *British Railway Modelling*, page 58.

SEF62/F171 LNER/BR J38 0-6-0

The next two models both used a newly generated model of the smaller 3,500 gallon tender. The only alternative in this case was the buffers, although a number of components included in the kit such as the water scoop were only used with the J39. The small wheeled J38 (4'8" versus 5'2") was very much a Scottish beast. It was this model that received an extensive Modeller review in August. Therein the sheer detail of the new chassis, helped by those smaller wheels, was fully apparent. This revealed that the chassis design was such as to accommodate all the various 4mm gauges and that the chassis could be compensated if desired. Although the J38s were built with a different boiler to the J39, certain engines were fitted with J39 boilers later. SEF went for this option, so modelling a J38 still requires careful choice of prototype.

SEF63/F172 LNER/BR J39/1 0-6-0

The third member of the trio is quite simple - the J39 fitted with the smaller retooled 3,500 gallon tender.

SEF3/F103 LNER/BR K3 2-6-0

The inherited model lasted around four years before replacement in 1992. Under the Wills heading the manifold reasons for a completely new start were made abundantly clear. The old kit was regarded so poorly that despite being in the June 1988 list, the only sales were of old stock.

SEF67/F161 LNER/BR K3 2-6-0

The new kit starts from first principles and has nothing in common with what went before. The 4,200 gallon tender was the recent production from the J39/2 (note the shared adjacent kit references). A finely detailed etched nickel silver chassis and a correct set of valvegear all help to ensure a very satisfactory model. Many variations are possible which were well summarised in a detailed Modeller article in October 1993, appearing a year after the model was released. Four types of etched brass cab are provided allowing the class, from its original GNR inception, into preservation, to be portrayed. The etched chassis, which is available separately, could fit the old kit.

A full one-piece cast boiler, and a motor that is set in the firebox driving the rear axle, ensure daylight under the boiler, without sacrificing a detailed boiler backhead. The valvegear can be assembled in simplified or scale fashion. The credit for much of this innovation must go to Modeltec alias Alistair Rolfe, who Ellis made

(top) South Eastern Finecast LBSCR 0-6-2T locomotives F175 E5 (further) and F176 E6

Photo: Tony Wright, courtesy South Eastern Finecast Collection

(above) South Eastern Finecast F161 K3 2-6-0. A comparison of the cab area against the previously pictured Wills example is worthwhile

Photo: Tony Wright, courtesy South Eastern Finecast Collection

(right) South Eastern Finecast F167 SECR P class 0-6-0T

Photo: Tony Wright, courtesy South Eastern Finecast Collection

**(above) South Eastern Finecast F186 GWR/BR 94xx 0-6-0PT built
with the FC201 chassis which included additional detailing such
as the clearly visible brakegear shown here**

Photo: Tony Wright, courtesy Rob Kinsey

**(below) The vastly improved South Eastern Finecast F146
LSWR/SR/BR M7 0-4-4T built as the long frame push-pull version**

Photo: Tony Wright, courtesy South Eastern Finecast Collection

much use of as kit designer at the time.

One result of the generous provision of alternatives is that a considerable number of spare parts are left over. Some time in the Spring of 1993 a second version of the new K3 was made available (FS161), containing a set of the unduplicated core components enabling, in conjunction with the leftovers of a F161 kit, a second engine to be made economically.

SEF4/F104 LMS/BR Fowler/Hughes Crab 2-6-0

The inherited Crab was another one of the Wills trio of bodyline Moguls. A catalogue announcement by 1993 showed an intention to upgrade to an etched chassis, however this is still awaited. A better Fowler tender has been available with the advent of the 4F kit F179, by which the existing bodyline kit can be improved, and like all the tenders in the range, is available separately. Despite this, the Crab is still packed with the old tender model.

SEF5/F105 SECR/SR/BR Mogul 2-6-0 classes N/N1/U&U1

Specific etched chassis have been generated for the SR Moguls. FC105N for the N and N1 classes came in April 1993. FC105U for the U and U1 classes came in December 1993, and both these used Modeltec's skills. The chassis are used in conjunction with the pre-existing bodyline kit; replacement of that with individual and highly detailed models to the K3 standard is an aspiration with no timeline at present, mainly due to rival product releases.

SEF6/F106 SR/BR Q 0-6-0

The Q is another example of a long serving bodyline kit. As was the case at the end of the Wills era, the etched FC102 chassis can be used.

SEF7/F107 SECR/SR/BR P 0-6-0T

SEF78/F167 SECR/SR/BR P 0-6-0T

I treat these two kits together because their evolution appears to be linked. F107 existed unaltered until October 1994; at this point F167 appears as a reference, but the anticipated release was delayed. Almost two years later, in July 1996, a "new" advert for F167 was followed by an illustrated review in the following month's Modeller, and a more detailed article appeared in the May 1998 Modeller.

Modeltec handled the re-design, and the revision included a new etched chassis which was an absolute work of art! For such a small prototype, the extent of the detail is remarkable, and is exemplified by the treatment of the two inside cylinders. As is typical of recent SEF chassis, the chassis as supplied is rigid, but half etched hornways and optional jointed coupling rods allow the competent to create a sprung or compensated chassis. On top of this, there are actually four possible ways of finishing the coupling rods! The body was totally re-cast because the old cab and windows were not correct. Suffice to say the level of detailing now exhibited far exceeds the old Wills model.

SEF8/F108 LSWR/SR/BR G6 0-6-0T

The G6 had always been a simple bodyline kit whose larger dimensions saved it from the challenges of the class P. From the Wills era it was capable of using the etched FC101 chassis, a situation remaining unaltered today, save that FC101 has been upgraded into FC201; a comment that will apply wherever the FC101 is encountered.

SEF9/F109 LBSCR/SR/BR E2 0-6-0T

The E2 remains largely the Bodyline kit from the Wills era. Instead of using the CK1/FC100 chassis, the upgraded FC200 can now be fitted (see next entry).

SEF10/F110 GWR/BR 94xx 0-6-0PT

SEF82/F186 GWR/BR 94xx 0-6-0PT

For many years the 94xx was the Bodyline kit as inherited from Wills. This changed in 1998 when a purpose-made etched chassis FC201 was incorporated into the kit, and a new reference F186 was created to reflect complete kits with the new chassis. The only alteration to the body has been some upgraded cab detail.

A word on the generic 0-6-0 chassis is relevant here. Wills had passed to SEF three choices, those being CK1/FC100, FC101 and FC102. With the release of FC201, the task of revising these inherited chassis was completed. All the etches have been re-drawn and incorporate brakegear and lamp brackets. The three references have become FC200/201/202 in that respective order. These chassis will be used to thoroughly upgrade engines such as the E2 and G6. Meanwhile, FC201 is compatible with the old bodyline kits.

SEF11/F111 TVR/GWR U1 0-6-2T

The Taff Vale 0-6-2T has undergone absolutely no changes during the SEF years, and continues to use the FC101 chassis.

SEF12/F112 GWR/BR 2251 class 0-6-0

The Collett 0-6-0 is a further kit which so far has not received any revision under SEF. In the 2251's case, since later in the Wills' era, it had used the etched FC102 chassis.

SEF13/F113 GER/LNER/BR Holden Buckjumper 0-6-0T

SEF46/F147 GER/LNER/BR Holden Buckjumper 0-6-0T

By contrast, the first fruits of the SEF approach were seen in the treatment of the Holden tank.

This had launched the Wills loco range and was a fondly regarded model, despite which the inherited model had many shortcomings detailed under the Wills entry. The old model was priced in the initial SEF list and one guesses that this was the residue of stock, because even in the first list another entry indicated that F147 was waiting in the wings. Work on the revision had actually started under the Wills regime.

The new model was designed by Iain Rice who had worked on it since 1986. Rice redesigned the patterns in order to provide a much more flexible kit, providing the key choices of the GER R24 and R24R (LNER J67/69) prototypes. Rod Neep meantime designed a new etched chassis for the model. Thus it was the Wills name that appeared on the chassis components notwithstanding which it was not until August 1988 that the new Buckjumper appeared.

Wealth of alternative components are the key to enabling accurate reproduction of the complicated prototype. The kit now aims at providing most, but not all, of the prototype variants from the original of 1890 to the LNER/BR J67 and J69 classes. After the improved chassis, probably the biggest change is the option for both the high and low cabs. Other choices include two chimneys, two smokebox doors and differing tank profiles. Engines can be finished with condensing equipment if desired. The June 1989 Modeller carried a detailed review.

SEF14/F114 LSWR/SR/BR King Arthur 4-6-0

Wills had themselves upgraded the *King Arthur* kit around 1978, principally by the provision of a dedicated etched chassis. Around 1998 some improvements were effected - hornblock marks were added to the chassis, but it still lacks brakegear. During 1998 work in preparing a new one-piece boiler casting was being undertaken.

SEF15/F115 LMS/BR Stanier 4MT 2-6-4T

F168 LMS/BR Stanier 4MT 2-6-4T

The Stanier 2-6-4T is an elderly model never revised at all under Wills, and always intended to use the now thoroughly aged and obsolete Dublo/Wrenn chassis. The intent of SEF as announced in the catalogue has been to produce a new etched nickel silver chassis (to be referenced FC168) which would improve the body-line kit, and an entirely revamped full kit F168. So far intention has not yet progressed to release of either.

SEF16/F116 LNER/BR Peppercorn A2 4-6-2

SEF60/F160 LNER/BR Peppercorn A2 4-6-2

The A2 is now a revised kit, but the new product appears not to have received the press attention some of its companions have, nor have the alterations been of an entirely radical nature. The

changeover seems to have occurred early in 1991, with Ron Goult of Little Engines undertaking the reworking. The loco body castings were improved, but the major changes effect the tender body and the loco and tender chassis, with the latter being new productions in etched nickel silver. The tender body is now a riveted style correct for the class, unlike Wills' offering. Since both chassis include brakegear, and the loco chassis also includes cylinder blocks and a full set of gear, the changes along with other considerations such as Flushglaze actually do add up, especially when compared against a Wills kit on a *Britannia* chassis.

SEF17/F117 LSWR/SR/BR O2 0-4-4T

SEF52/F153 LSWR/SR/BR O2 0-4-4T

The launch of the revised O2 took place in October 1989, with Ron Goult of Little Engines undertaking the reworking. Wills had provided the Isle of Wight and mainland options; the main alterations on Ron's revamp were the provision of a one-piece boiler and a much improved and fully detailed etched chassis. There was in addition an increased degree of cab detail, although the extent to which the builder can use this depends on motor choice.

SEF18/F118 LSWR/SR/BR M7 0-4-4T

SEF48/F146 LSWR/SR/BR M7 0-4-4T

The revised M7, like the Buckjumper, was promised with the issue of SEF's first list in June 1988, and this model actually took the first new reference issued in the Finecast series by SEF. However, a degree of delay followed and the model, as the reader will realise from the preceding discussion, was not the first fruit of the new regime. The reader will also appreciate that SEF's revisions usually involve two distinct elements - the etched chassis (which can be additionally bought separately as an FC series item) and the cast body. With the M7, the new chassis appeared quickly in August 1988, and it could be used with the old model. The full kit followed in April 1989.

The new chassis was already in existence at the time of the take-over, since Ron Goult of Little Engines had designed it on his own initiative. Once Ellis had taken over from Wills, Goult moved to suggest that they work together, which as you will have seen from various entries, is what actually happened.

The new kit was very different from what went before; the initial release had been limited to the longer 36'3" prototype, but now both frame lengths were possible. Full detail for a push-pull engine was possible for the first time, and there was much more cab detail and a one-piece boiler. Comparison of the two models shows just how different the end products could look. The underframe of the new model appears positively cluttered, particularly when the air reservoir for push-pull working is fitted at the front. Also, the much finer handrail detailing becomes very clear.

SEF19/F119 CR/LMS/BR McIntosh 782 class 0-6-0T

No changes whatsoever have occurred to the Caley tank since the Wills era.

SEF20/F120 LBSCR/SR/BR D1 0-4-2T/E1 0-6-0

SEF58/F155 LBSCR/SR/BR E1 0-6-0T

SEF59/F156 LBSCR/SR/BR D1 0-4-2T

By the early 1990s, the two classes were largely still left to Wills in the 4mm field. The inherited F120 kit was quite a complex beast for its day but was beginning to show its age. A good case for its upgrading existed therefore, and so in early 1991 this took place. Both prototypes were now made into individual kits. The changes principally involved a one-piece boiler casting (ex-F154 E1/R), more cab detail, and individual and improved etched chassis. The original kits had components for Stroudley and rebuilt states, and these choices remained. The new kits seem to have arrived with a minimum of fuss and the redesign once again was by Ron Goult.

SEF21/F121 GWR 1804/1854 class 0-6-0ST

SEF56/F158 GWR 1804/1854 class 0-6-0ST

As was suggested in talking about the Wills version, a model of a GWR 0-6-0ST seems disarmingly simple until the detail of the prototypes is unwrapped. What is a fact, is that SEF launched the revised kit with an illustrated advert in the February 1991 Modeller. Catalogue and advert continue to describe it as an 1854 tank, and both show an engine numbered 907 (Engine 907 is in fact a member of the 1854 class). There are no alternative body components, and the new etched chassis is kept simple. The motor no longer drives the front axle, but is changed to the middle, despite which backhead detail is retained.

As for what you do with your kit, we related under the Wills entry the value of the research into the kit and its prototypes undertaken by the West Mercian EM Group. So fundamental is that, that their review is included with each new SEF kit. In addition, SEF's instructions inform about possible options, showing for instance how by filing the frame profile, Wolverhampton or Swindon built locos result.

SEF22/F122 LMS/BR Fowler 4F 0-6-0

SEF54/F159 MR/LMS/BR Fowler 4F 0-6-0

SEF72/F179 LMS/BR Fowler 4F 0-6-0

Two years into the SEF regime and a new kit for the 4F appeared, but not one that managed to immediately remove the old model. The new F159 reference was advertised in November 1990, its aim being to provide a state-of-the-art Midland Railway built engine. So in addition to the new etched chassis, the body was over-hauled considerably. The old kit had boiler and smokebox in two halves, and these now became one-piece units. The facility to finish the loco for either left or right hand drive was provided. Alternative components such as an MR short chimney or an LMS long one, large and small buffers, tall MR dome, short LMS dome, and Ramsbottom or Ross Pop valves enable the locomotive to be finished during the MR or later periods.

A further scene change for F159 provided an original Midland Railway coal rail tender. These were smaller than the later standard Fowler tender, and had been taken from withdrawn 4-2-2 and 2-4-0 engines. For a while, both F159 and F122 were catalogued; F122, which was a bodyline kit, was able to use the new etched chassis, and whilst stocks remained it was a route for those wishing to use the later tender. In 1993, F122 was finally withdrawn, and a new Fowler tender was produced with an etched chassis, and the beading detail which had never been shown on the old tender despite being quite a prominent feature. This was coupled with the revised F159 loco in order to create the F179 model. It is these two kits which are current and the design of both was by Ron Goult.

The new Fowler 3,500 gallon tender itself is quite a work of art, and was planned so that it could upgrade the former Wills product used additionally with the Crab and Scot. The prototypes showed detail changes over the years, and many of these can now be accommodated - etched coal rails for instance appear as an option. Some parts, such as the bulkheads, were supplied in both cast and etched form allowing an individual modeller to choose precision or strength.

SEF23/F123 GWR/BR original Hall 4-6-0

The Hall model has not been the subject of any changes. It even still retains its individual, but cast chassis, from Wills days.

SEF24/F124 MR/LMS Flatiron 0-6-4T

SEF81/F185 MR/LMS Flatiron 0-6-4T

For a decade the inherited Flatiron bodyline kit was continued. The Wills kit had always been

(above) The revamped South Eastern Finecast LBSCR tanks E1 0-6-0T and D1 0-4-4T, referenced F155 and F156 respectively and dating from 1991

Photo: Tony Wright, courtesy South Eastern Finecast Collection

(below) The South Eastern Finecast LMS/BR Fowler 4F in its F159 guise as a 1990 kit

Photo: Tony Wright, courtesy South Eastern Finecast Collection

(bottom) The Iain Rice redesign of the N7 produced this South Eastern Finecast F165 model, and pictured is Iain's own effort finished as BR 69631. This was originally an N7/1 delivered in 1925 but rebuilt to N7/5 in 1955

Photo: Tony Wright, courtesy Iain Rice

for the rebuilt engines with their extended smokeboxes. The new kit, redesigned by Allan Sibley, is a thorough makeover, albeit the shape of the prototype renders the quest for a one-piece boiler futile. There is now a full set of alternative components enabling both original and rebuilt conditions to be offered. The improved cab detail includes etched components. The detailed chassis is typically in etched nickel silver, but a separate fret of detailing components ranging from the balance weights to the smokebox wrappers are on an etched brass fret. Those wrappers actually offer a choice of three smokeboxes - plain or riveted original, and rebuilt. In 1999 there was still no 4mm competition to model the prototype, and with such a fine new kit now available, SEF are likely to retain their prime spot with the Flatiron.

SEF25/F125 GER/LNER/BR N7 0-6-2T

SEF65/F165 GER/LNER/BR N7/1/4/5 0-6-2T

Like the Flatiron, even in 1999 there is next to no competition for a 4mm model of the N7. Where the Wills Flatiron represented the rebuild of a rather uncommon loco, the Wills N7 represented the original of a GER engine which under the LNER was multiplied into various subclasses to become a stock item. The case therefore for a revision of the N7 to enable more of these further options to be modelled was good, and the result appeared in 1991. In the March advert the model was billed as forthcoming for the Spring, but the hype of a new release actually took place in the November advert.

As would be expected, a fully detailed etched chassis formed the base, and made redundant the rather crude cast Wills rear frame extension in favour of accurate one-piece etches. Above the frames, the body retained fully cast construction and even a two-part boiler barrel. Four core types can be built from the kit - the original GER L77/LNER N7, and its LNER variant N7/1, both with condensing gear option (these were built to 1926), their LNER rebuilds N7/4 and N7/5 being the other choices. Some other detail changes within these classes can be accommodated by varying the cab roof or the safety valves of which there are three choices. Iain Rice was responsible for the redesign.

A major difference between the GER and LNER builds required SEF to produce both Belpaire and round top firebox castings, and therefore reference to prototype pictures is really essential to complete a kit. For instance, all the original GER build did receive round top fireboxes finally, whereas only some received the LNER chimney (the kit has two chimneys). Conversely, the LNER commenced their build with Belpaire fireboxes. Brake fittings are another area to take care - some engines had both Westinghouse and vacuum brakes, and some only one system. What the kit cannot do, because there is no high bunker alternative, is to build the 1927/28 deliveries with larger coal rail-less bunkers.

The locos built after 1927 had pony trucks and not the radial axleboxes of the SEF frames - the sub-classes not modelled by SEF, N7/2 and N7/3, have these pony trucks. It is also clear that the early engines were built with all sorts of minor differences, for instance class L77 were the first two engines of 1915, and one was superheated and one was not. The next ten were classed K85 and were non-superheated, and so the litany continues. The moral quite simply has to be: if having a model built, do a lot of homework!

SEF26/F126 LSWR/SR/BR T9 4-4-0

The T9 is a model which throughout the SEF era has known a variety of competition in 4mm scale. As a result, the model has not been touched, even retaining its separate Wills era cast chassis in 1999.

SEF27/F127 GWR/BR Star 4-6-0

Another Wills bodyline kit not to have been altered is the GWR Star. There has been a catalogue hope that an etched chassis for the kit would be released, but that has not come to fruition by 1999. Instead you still need to find an old Tri-ang Hornby B12.

SEF28/F128 LNER/BR Gresley A1/A3 4-6-2

SEF47/F148 GNR/LNER/BR Gresley A1/A3 4-6-2

Upgrading of the Gresley A1/A3 kit was seen as a priority from the outset of SEF. The old kit was still listed in June 1988, but the December Modeller advert featured the new model. Etched nickel silver provided the engine and tender chassis as well as elephant's ear smoke deflectors and lamp brackets. The previous kit had provided the principal body options for both A1 and A3 classes; now, the tender option for GNR use was added. The old cast nameplates were abandoned and the redesign was by Ron Goult.

SEF29/F129 GWR/BR King 4-6-0

Despite the King class kit remaining in the old Bodyline series, it has received some attention from SEF. The first SEF list promised an etched nickel silver chassis for the loco, and FC129 was advertised from August 1988. In addition, by 1993 the body kit had been revised to incorporate three new one-piece castings, these being for the firebox, boiler and smokebox.

SEF30/F130 GWR/BR 1854 class 0-6-0PT

SEF55/F157 GWR/BR 1854 class 0-6-0PT

Parallels exist, not unnaturally, with the saddle tank version of this engine already encountered at SEF21. It made sense to revise both at the same time since a new etched chassis applicable to both was a major change. Unlike the saddle tank, the pannier's body was worked over by

(above) SEF F149 LNER/BR A4 built with the double chimney option
Photo: Tony Wright, courtesy Tony Wright

(above) SEF F135 GWR County, which in this case is the old Wills era Bodyline design, but built on the new FC177 etched chassis
Photo: Tony Wright, courtesy South Eastern Finecast Collection

(below) SEF F169 SR/BR Schools
Photo: Tony Wright, courtesy South Eastern Finecast Collection

Ron Goult to provide two cab options - closed or open. Some steps around the smokebox were now to be taken from the chassis etch.

SEF31/F131 LMS/BR original Royal Scot 4-6-0

No change has yet taken place to the *Royal Scot* kit. Indeed, the kit has not been available since at least the early 1990s. The intent has been to produce a new etched chassis, and to take advantage of the fine Fowler tender developed in 1993 for the 4F (F179). No date is yet available for the outcome, but a new Scot is a firm intention.

SEF32/F132 LNER/BR A4 4-6-2

SEF49/F149 LNER/BR A4 4-6-2

SEF had three LNER Pacific kits to upgrade, and the middle member of the trio became the A4, released in May 1989. The main new features were the etched loco and tender chassis, although another substantial change was to form the core of the body, from the front through to the rear of the cab, from just two principal castings. SEF achieved this, something which Wills had originally set out to do twenty-odd years before. The old kit had had a chimney choice, but was the choice of round or straight backed driver's seats a novelty new in 1989?

SEF33/F133 GWR/BR Saint 4-6-0

The Saint has survived unchanged for many years at SEF. Catalogue hopes that a specially designed etched chassis to go with the bodyline chassis would be available in 1992 remain unfulfilled. Instead, the former Wills cast design remains current.

SEF34/F134 GWR/BR 61xx 2-6-2T

SEF70/F178 GWR/BR 61xx 2-6-2T

The large Prairie received its makeover early in 1994; the major task being the replacement of the cast Wills chassis with a fine etched design. By 1993, Goult had the intention of retiring, so Paul Vine designed the new chassis for this kit under the Precision Miniature Arts banner. The detailing of this chassis with rivets, full brakegear, optional scale-jointed rods or rigid ones was fitting into the new SEF mould. The work carried out remained somewhat special in that a wide range of body details came from the fret etches. Some of these were duplicated in cast components such as the front steps, and even the cylinder assembly could be either cast or etched. The new front truck was a particularly fine piece of etched construction when finished, although cast components for this were also supplied as an easier option.

Etched numberplates for 6106 were now supplied, and this was significant because 6106 was the preserved example that Wills had originally based their model on, despite which the Wills kit did not have numberplates. Notwithstanding the alterations, the new kit seems to have escaped much press attention.

SEF35/F135 GWR County 4-4-0

The County is one of those few models subject to partial change. The classic Wills era Bodyline kit has survived unaltered into 1999. Like the Prairie, the cast introductions of the early 1970s, at least in respect of their bodies, were much improved over earlier productions. What was not really effectively addressed was the plain cast chassis, increasingly to be perceived as a crude solution. SEF saw merit in replacing this original chassis with an etched version, and this FC177 chassis became available over the Winter of 1992/93, and was designed by Modeltec. For a while, both etched and cast chassis appeared in the lists under FC135 and FC177.

The appearance of the FC177 reference indicates that a fully revised County is intended. Progress with this has reached the point in 1999 that F135 currently has the new chassis, one-piece boiler and other improvements designed by Rolfe, and only a new tender holds back the full F177 release.

SEF36/F136 GWR Metro 2-4-0T

SEF73/F180 GWR Metro 2-4-0T

Not all revisions by SEF have adopted the one-piece boiler barrel philosophy. Both the large Prairie and the Metro tanks which shared a 1993 revision slot retained the two halves to the boiler and smokebox construction. The major effort with the Metro tank was the development of an etched chassis, whilst features such as the alternative open or closed cabs were inherited from Wills. A good piece of etching provided the inside cylinder front covers; all this reworking being completed by Ron Goult. The catalogue furnished the September 1993 revision date, adverts in the Modeller occurred over the following couple of months.

SEF37/F137 SR/BR Schools 4-4-0

SEF79/F169 SR/BR Schools 4-4-0

Despite the relatively recent nature of the Wills kit which was new in 1973, just over 20 years later SEF subjected it to a major overhaul. Release adverts for the new engine appeared in November and December 1994's Modeller. The etched chassis and the one-piece boiler unit were the key innovations, and were the work of Precision Miniature Arts. The prototype choices of the earlier kit with its different cab sides were retained, but what went on beneath the running plate becomes impressively complex. On top of 128 castings, three separate etched frets were involved; additionally a limited number of lost wax brass cast pieces appeared, such as the crossheads.

The sort of choice now provided included etched or cast smoke deflectors, and the etched riveted or plain balance weights individually modelled for the driving and coupled wheels. Despite the Wills' kit having etched gear, this

**(above) South Eastern Finecast F150 SECR/SR/BR Wainwright E class
4-4-0 - the first wholly original kit introduced by SEF**
Photo: Tony Wright, courtesy South Eastern Finecast Collection

**(below) South Eastern Finecast F173 SR/BR Q1 0-6-0, the sole ex-
Little Engines model to be introduced into the SEF range**
Photo: Tony Wright, courtesy South Eastern Finecast Collection

(bottom) South Eastern Finecast F166 LNER rebuilt W1
Photo: Tony Wright, courtesy South Eastern Finecast Collection

was now replaced by a new fret which supplied the scale and simple choices that SEF had made standard and incorporated the mainframes. The reproduction of what went between the frames extended SEF's modelling still further - there was an etched drag box, a cast ashpan, and a detailed construction for the bogie equalising beam.

SEF38/F138 SECR/SR/BR D 4-4-0

SEF50/F150 SECR/SR/BR E 4-4-0

SEF51/F151 SECR/SR/BR D 4-4-0

The D class was subject to change within a year of SEF's ownership despite the original kit only dating from 1974. Modeltec designed the revised kits as the first work they undertook for SEF. I say "kits" because two were spun off the D class upgrade. A class E was a 1905 development of the 1901 class D with a Belpaire boiler and an extended smokebox. The opportunity with upgrading the class D was taken to produce the class E as a separate kit, and this became the first wholly new prototype SEF released. The year 1989 actually saw two kits in this category since the E1/R appeared a little later.

Both D and E classes shared the same tender model, but individual new chassis were created. One-piece castings were used for each of the smokebox, boiler and firebox. Although brakegear was fitted, chassis frame detailing was quite limited. Both engines had two types of chimney, whilst the D was now given two choices of cab front with 2 or 4 windows in the spectacle plate. Each class had a choice of parallel, taper or SR stepped buffers.

SEF39/F139 SECR/SR/BR C 0-6-0

SEF57/F152 SECR/SR/BR C 0-6-0

Exactly when the C class was revised I do not know. Two adverts during 1991 ensure we can be confident that it was around that point. Beyond the expected etched chassis, the main work was a one-piece boiler. Additionally, an entirely new set of cab castings with a separate detailed backhead was generated - the Wills original had been found to be too low. Three sets of buffers covering the life of the prototypes were provided. Modeltec undertook the revisions for SEF.

SEF40/F140 LBSCR/SR/BR I3 4-4-2T

SEF71/F174 LBSCR/SR/BR I3 4-4-2T

It is thought that revising the I3 took place around 1992, but the precise date is unknown. The Wills kit had numerous alternatives including cast or etched steps, and cab detail was improved. Evidently the etched chassis, which was fully detailed including the underhung springs and a finely etched leading bogie, was a key revision. The revision was by Precision Miniature Arts.

SEF41/F141 GNR/LNER/BR C12 4-4-2T

No changes have taken place to the C12. It continues to use chassis FC141 which, whilst etched nickel silver, was a Wills innovation. An upgrade is intended.

SEF42/F142 GWR De Glehn 4-4-2

There have been no changes to this kit.

SEF43/F143 GWR/BR Castle 4-6-0 3,500 gallon tender

SEF44/F144 GWR/BR Castle 4-6-0 4,000 gallon tender

There have been no changes to these kits.

SEF45/F145 SECR/SR/BR H 0-4-4T

SEF75/F182 SECR/SR/BR H 0-4-4T

Evidently the later Wills kits with their own etched chassis were not felt in need of early revision. When we come to the final original Wills kit, the corporate line is changed - five years into the SEF era and the model was revised. The Wills kit had a one-piece boiler, so does the SEF. Both have etched chassis. So what changed? The chassis was redesigned to allow the optional compensation choice which is standard on an SEF etched chassis. Some further body parts are now available from the etched frets. Eleven formerly cast components are now etched; brakegear and lamp brackets being examples.

The New Prototypes

SEF53/F154 SR/BR E1/R 0-6-2T

Late 1989 and only just over a year after the take-over, Ellis was staking out the territory that showed that SEF would produce some totally innovative products. In the preceding text, the model of the class E 4-4-0 has been detailed. In some ways, that kit could be construed as a derivation of another kit. However, just behind it and a kit for the E1/R arrived - this was a totally new kit creation, the evidence of which is in the fact that the revised E1 actually appeared over a year later. By 1999 ten such models had appeared.

For the uninitiated, we had best sort out why the LSBCR E1 0-6-0T and the SR E1/R 0-6-2T are related. Ten E1/Rs were created by Southern in 1927-28. Already elderly Stroudley E1s were taken and subjected to a major rebuild such that their ancestry was almost lost. The result looked quite a modern engine with a voluminous cab and bunker. The main reason for doing this was to provide engines for the North Devon and Cornwall Light which opened in 1925. They lasted until 1959, and away from the Light Railway, examples could often be found around Exeter.

There had never been any sort of commercial model of the class before SEF's, whose launch

(top) South Eastern Finecast F184 LNER W1 "Hush-Hush" 4-6-4
Photo: Tony Wright, courtesy South Eastern Finecast Collection

(above) South Eastern Finecast F181 SECR/SR/BR S class 0-6-0ST
Photo: Tony Wright, courtesy South Eastern Finecast Collection

(below) South Eastern Finecast F164 SR River 2-6-4T
Photo: Tony Wright, courtesy Tony Wright

advert is in the December 1989 Modeller. The standard that would become familiar, of an etched nickel silver chassis with hornblock positions marked in order to allow possible springing, small matters like brass handrail knobs (also largely standard in the revised or new SEF specification), and well detailed castings including a cab interior, create an effective model. The earliest models may not have Flushglaze, an interesting phenomenon which may enable one to identify early production E1/Rs and ex-SECR Es. The Flushglaze was standardised early in 1990, and so all other new arrivals should therefore feature this innovation. The one-piece boiler produced for this model was later used in the D1/E1 revision; it is a particularly complex piece with tank tops cast integrally. Engine 2096 used a Drummond chimney and the kit includes this as an option. Ron Goult was responsible for the design.

SEF64/F173 SR/BR Q1 0-6-0

Little Engines must now enter the account directly. This small manufacturer, alias Ron Goult, had started out around 1986 with cast kits of the NER 4-6-2Ts. Since then, they have continued with a modest range, which are considered to be outside the scope of this particular book. Only one Southern prototype has been manufactured and that is the one model that SEF has bought into their own list.

The engine was Oliver Bulleid's strange Q1, and the release of the kit originally took place in the late Autumn of 1987. Its specification, with a cast body on a detailed etched nickel silver loco and tender chassis, was close to what SEF were standardising upon by that time. The Little Engines model featured in a review of the range in the September 1989 Modeller. As the only Southern engine in a predominantly LNER list, it made sense to let it go to SEF.

The change took place for SEF to place an introductory advert in the August 1991 Modeller. The model certainly needed that etched chassis because the prototype is so bare that whatever detail there is around the frames is clear for all to see. In the event the kit does a very good job at this angle. A rather non-standard and crude element against the usual SEF genre is the use of a slab of casting to reproduce, in one go, the tender axleboxes on each side.

SEF66/F166 LNER W1 rebuilt 4-6-4

SEF76 F184 LNER W1 Hush-Hush 4-6-4

SEF had a good coverage of the LNER Pacifics. In fact, there were some other even larger LNER engines to be modelled. The P2 has been avoided, it had been picked up by the K's/Nu-Cast school. This still left Gresley's W1 experimental one-off 4-6-4 of 1929, which as the 1990s opened had very few models. When built, this was extraordinarily unconventional both visually and technically; it used a Yarrow water tube boiler usually put in ships. The result attracted a lot of attention and became known as the Hush-

Hush engine from the secretive test element. The boiler was not suitable for rail borne use and in 1937 the engine was rebuilt. It reappeared like an A4 with an extra rear wheel and thereafter behaved well in the A4 links until withdrawal in 1959.

SEF offers both versions of the W1 and started with the rebuild, with some of the parameters coming from the revised A4 which had arrived in 1989 - this produced a suitable tender. Since the W1 had a non-corridor tender after 1948, it was necessary to note this and offer some alternative components. The loco body, whilst superficially similar to an A4, is actually quite different and this can be seen in the valances (which are one-piece on the W1 kit and which Thompson took off on the prototype), and in the detail shown on the body side. The main loco chassis is from the A4 (explaining the 1988 revised date on the instructions) but a different pony truck was required. Ron Goult had designed the W1 rebuild, and it was launched in a June 1992 Modeller advert.

February 1994 saw the launch of the original engine, the Hush-Hush, which was featured on SEF's stand at IMREX in 1994. Here the design work was even more radical - the body involved complex shaping from a few large castings, and there were 117 cast components in total. The body design for the Hush-Hush was completed by Ray Rodgers of The Loco Shop, Kenley. The real engine had used two chimneys prior to 1937, and so both single and double options were packed. The corridor tender came from the F166 kit.

SEF74/F181 SECR/SR/BR S 0-6-0ST

Seven of the remaining eight releases have extended SEF's coverage of the home patch with prototypes familiar to the Southern Railway, and which in the main faced no model competition in 1999. The first of these appeared in November 1993's Modeller advert, with examples being available at the Scaleforum exhibition a few weeks prior. The C class was already in the range, and whilst the S class may not apparently relate to it, it was actually a one-off rebuild used for shunting mainly at Bricklayer's Arms in 1917 until being withdrawn in 1951. Precision Miniature Arts designed the new kit, using some work from the C class already in the range. This meant that numerous fittings came from the C class model, although obviously a wholly new cab, running plate (which had been extended), and saddle tank had to be originated. The builder can choose either an etched or a cast tank. The one-piece firebox, boiler and smokebox is new despite being almost identical to the C. Although the mainframes are in many respects similar to the C, there are some important differences such as the extended running plate casting to support the bunker, and as a consequence these etches are new too. A large number of small body details come from the etches, and it is clear that SEF did much more than rebuild their C class kit to create the S! Sadly I have not yet traced any review material for such an interesting release.

(above) South Eastern Finecast F183 USA/SR/BR 0-6-0T

Photo: Tony Wright, courtesy Tony Wright

(below) South Eastern Finecast F188 SECR/SR/BR Kirtley R1 0-4-4T

Photo: Tony Wright, courtesy South Eastern Finecast Collection

(bottom) South Eastern Finecast F192 SECR/SR/BR K1 0-6-0T R1 showing the Wainwright cab (leftmost model) and Stirling cab

Photo: Tony Wright, courtesy South Eastern Finecast Collection

SEF77/F164 SR River 2-6-4T

It is good that the next model did receive some form of review. The River class tank had been anticipated in advertising from back in March 1991. It eventually arrived around March 1994, with an illustrated Modeller advert in the May issue, and a review in the following issue. Tony Wright reviewed the kit in the April and May 1995 issues of *Modelling Railways Illustrated*.

Like the S, the model had practically no competition, but unlike the S class there was more than one full size example. The SECR had built a prototype number 790 in 1917, but it was not until 1925-26 that another nineteen were built. Then the disaster at Sevenoaks in 1927 called their safety into question, and the engines were hurriedly rebuilt to become two cylinder U class Moguls. Therefore, the reluctance to model is apparent - a very limited life and circulation. SEF bit the bullet and produced with Modeltec (not Precision Miniature Arts whose name is on the drawings) a, by now, typically high quality composite kit in which there was no sparing of detail above or below the running plate. It is a kit in which the admiration for the massive one-piece boiler casting is required. An etched wrapper creates the smokebox, and the firebox is another casting. All the nineteen River names are in the kit save the prototype engine which cannot be modelled.

SEF80 F183 USA/SR/BR 0-6-0T

With the USA tank SEF produced yet another fine composite etched and cast model. In this case, the prototypes were rather more familiar albeit with a specialist flavour. A variety of models were already available including a kit in 4mm from Q Kits. The SEF production is clearly a better product being some 14 years newer, and SEF had it on the agenda since at least a listing in the 1993 catalogue. Once again Precision Miniature Arts, but aided by Ray Rogers, did the design work. A comprehensive selection of alternatives enables an engine to be finished in the original USATC condition, or as modified for the fourteen examples that the Southern operated. This is an important choice because a wartime layout could use the USATC engine; additionally some were sold direct into British industrial service. Due to the special design of wheel, these were sourced from Romford and included in the kit. Around 1997, these were changed to Markits' production.

After the kit's appearance in time for the Warley Show in October 1995, it did attract some review attention. There are reviews in the Modeller for February 1996 and in the April 1996 *British Railway Modelling*. An extended article by Tony Wright is in the November 1997 Modeller. To model the prototype's complex bar frames an interesting technique, whereby each frame is etched in mirror image and then folded upon itself, is used. That was one idiosyncrasy of the prototype that the designer had to handle; the lack of a conventional running plate and such a mass of boiler fittings was another challenge.

SEF83/F188 SECR/SR/BR Kirtley R1 0-4-4T

The prototype of the brand new release for 1998 was a class of 15 engines built in 1900 and withdrawn by 1956. Their ancestors were the unmodelled R class of 1891 for the LC&DR (remember this!). Since SEF had in effect challenged Q Kits over their USA tank, it is interesting to note that just the same position applied to the R1. Compared with the couple of kits that have just gone before, this was a straightforward kit but typically finished to the detail now expected. Ray Rogers undertook the design but used the SEF H class boiler and fittings. Like the USA tank and the Hush-Hush, the specification of detail in the 1990s extends to a correct reproduction of the cab floor finish.

SEF84/F192 SECR/SR/BR R1 0-6-0T

SEF85/F193 SER/SECR/SR/BR R 0-6-0T

In 1998 Dave Ellis seemed to have a bee in his bonnet about the nuances of the SECR R and R1 classes because three of four main options were all released. The first, for the R1 0-4-4T has just been described (leaving the R 0-4-4T out). The next two appeared with the minimum of advance fuss that Autumn. These were for the Stirling R and R1 0-6-0T classes. The latter of which, longevity and a Dublo model make familiar. There had been twenty-five R class engines built from 1888 of which thirteen were rebuilt to R1. The key to resolving this conundrum is to remember that when these classes originated back before 1898, the SER and the LC&DR were two rival companies.

Many of the Wills bodyline kits had relied on the Dublo R1 chassis. Along the way they had been upgraded into FC201 (ex-FC101) which forms the base of both these kits, whose prime difference is a lower boiler on the R, and a choice of Wainwright and Stirling cabs on the R1. The first advert for the new kit appeared in the November 1998 Modeller with both cabs illustrated.

SEF86 F189 GER Decapod 0-10-0T

The April 1999 *Railway Modeller* and *Model Rail* magazines both revealed the surprise that a model for the Great Eastern Holden designed Decapod was available. This amazing 1902 creation was very short-lived as an experiment to run Liverpool Street suburban trains. The one example, GER 20, has been the subject of very few models, and about the only mass produced example hitherto being Marklin examples from before World War One which are now as rare as hens' teeth. The SEF model is quite staggering with everything individually designed for it, and that great bulk of a firebox creating an overwhelming impression. Despite its individual nature, the SEF pattern of composite materials with etched frames, and a huge whitemetal boiler is followed. Boiler and firebox each constitute one enormous casting, which only the one-piece running plate rivals.

SEF87 F194 SECR/SR/BR 0-4-0CT

Evidently Ellis thinks that future niches for new products revolve around unusual prototypes. The Decapod was followed by the range's first crane-tank. Rare on the prototype and still rarer in model form, this model was inspired by a SECR prototype, the 1881 prototype of which, as BR 31302, lasted until 1949. The model should appear as this book is in press so few details can be given. Ray Rogers from Kenley, who has done much of the late 1990s patternmaking for Wills, has produced patterns derived from his own 7mm kit.

And there for the moment the account concludes, which doubtless will be a temporary state of affairs.

(above) SEF F193 SER/SECR/SR/BR R class 0-6-0T. Note that the chimney, smokebox wing plates and boiler height are all different from the rebuilt locomotive shown on page 130 (bottom rightmost)

Photo: Tony Wright, courtesy South Eastern Finecast Collection

(below) The unusual GER Decapod 0-10-0T, modelled as SEF F189

Photo: Dave Wheatstone, courtesy Dave Wheatstone Collection

South Eastern Finecast Locomotives Table

Text Reference	SEF Reference	Description	New Date	Withdrawal Date	Notes
SEF1	F101	LBSCR/SR/BR E5 0-6-2T	6/1988	for 12/1992	
SEF2	F102	LNER/BR J39 0-6-0	6/1988	for 4/1991	
SEF3	F103	LNER/BR K3 2-6-0	6/1988	for 10/1992	
SEF4	F104	LMS/BR Crab 2-6-0	6/1988		
SEF5	F105	SECR/SR/BR Mogul 2-6-0 classes N/N1/U&U1	6/1988		
SEF6	F106	SR/BR Q 0-6-0	6/1988		
SEF7	F107	SECR/SR/BR P 0-6-0T	6/1988	for 10/1994	
SEF8	F108	LSWR/SR/BR G6 0-6-0T	6/1988		
SEF9	F109	LBSCR/SR/BR E2 0-6-0T	6/1988		
SEF10	F110	GWR/BR 94xx 0-6-0PT	6/1988	for 3/1998	
SEF11	F111	TVR/GWR U1 0-6-2T	6/1988		
SEF12	F112	GWR/BR 2251 class 0-6-0	6/1988		
SEF13	F113	GER/LNER/BR Holden Buckjumper 0-6-0T	6/1988	for 8/1988	
SEF14	F114	LSWR/SR/BR *King Arthur* 4-6-0	6/1988		
SEF15	F115	LMS/BR Stanier 4MT 2-6-4T	6/1988		
SEF16	F116	LNER/BR Peppercorn A2 4-6-2	6/1988	for 3/1991	
SEF17	F117	LSWR/SR/BR O2 0-4-4T	6/1988	for 10/1989	
SEF18	F118	LSWR/SR/BR M7 0-4-4T	6/1988	for 4/1989	
SEF19	F119	CR/LMS/BR McIntosh 782 class 0-6-0T	6/1988		
SEF20	F120	LBSCR/SR/BR D1 0-4-2T/E1 0-6-0	6/1988	for 2/1991	
SEF21	F121	GWR 1804/1854 0-6-0ST	6/1988	for 2/1991	
SEF22	F122	LMS/BR Fowler 4F 0-6-0	6/1988	for 7/1993	
SEF23	F123	GWR/BR original Hall 4-6-0	6/1988		
SEF24	F124	MR/LMS Flatiron 0-6-4T	6/1988	for 3/1998	
SEF25	F125	GER/LNER/BR N7 0-6-2T	6/1988	for 11/1991	
SEF26	F126	LSWR/SR/BR T9 4-4-0	6/1988		
SEF27	F127	GWR/BR Star 4-6-0	6/1988		
SEF28	F128	LNER/BR Gresley A1/A3 4-6-2	6/1988	12/1988	

Text Reference	SEF Reference	Description	New Date	Withdrawal Date	Notes
SEF29	F129	GWR/BR King 4-6-0	6/1988		
SEF30	F130	GWR/BR 1854 0-6-0PT	6/1988	2/1991	
SEF31	F131	LMS/BR original *Royal Scot* 4-6-0	6/1988	by 1993	
SEF32	F132	LNER/BR A4 4-6-2	6/1988	for 5/1989	
SEF33	F133	GWR/BR Saint 4-6-0	6/1988		
SEF34	F134	GWR/BR 61xx 2-6-2T	6/1988	for 4/1993	
SEF35	F135	GWR County 4-4-0	6/1988		
SEF36	F136	GWR Metro Tank 2-4-0T	6/1988	for 9/1993	
SEF37	F137	SR/BR Schools 4-4-0	6/1988	for 10/1994	
SEF38	F138	SECR/SR/BR D 4-4-0	6/1988	for 9/1989	
SEF39	F139	SECR/SR/BR C 0-6-0	6/1988	by 3/1991	
SEF40	F140	LBSCR/SR/BR I3 4-4-2T	6/1988	c.1992	
SEF41	F141	GNR/LNER/BR C12 4-4-2T	6/1988		
SEF42	F142	GWR De Glehn 4-4-2	6/1988		
SEF43	F143	GWR Castle 4-6-0	6/1988		3,500 gallon tender
SEF44	F144	GWR/BR Castle 4-6-0	6/1988		4,000 gallon tender
SEF45	F145	SECR/SR/BR H 0-4-4T	6/1988	for 2/1994	
SEF46	F147	GER/LNER/BR Holden Buckjumper 0-6-0T	8/1988		From here models are SEF revised or wholly new
SEF47	F148	GNR/LNER/BR Gresley A1/A3 4-6-2	12/1988		
SEF48	F146	LSWR/SR/BR M7 0-4-4T	3/1989		
SEF49	F149	LNER/BR A4 4-6-2	5/1989		
SEF50	F150	SECR/SR/BR E 4-4-0	9/1989		The first wholly new SEF prototype to be issued.
SEF51	F151	SECR/SR/BR D 4-4-0	c.10/1989		
SEF52	F153	LSWR/SR/BR O2 0-4-4T	10/1989		
SEF53	F154	SR/BR E1/R 0-6-2T	12/1989		New to SEF
SEF54	F159	MR/LMS/BR Fowler 4F 0-6-0	11/1990		
SEF55	F157	GWR/BR 1854 0-6-0PT	2/1991		
SEF56	F158	GWR 1854 0-6-0ST	2/1991		

Text Reference	SEF Reference	Description	New Date	Withdrawal Date	Notes
SEF57	F152	SECR/SR/BR C 0-6-0	by 3/1991		
SEF58	F155	LBSCR/SR/BR E1 0-6-0T	by 3/1991		
SEF59	F156	LBSCR/SR/BR D1 0-4-2T	by 3/1991		
SEF60	F160	LNER/BR Peppercorn A2 4-6-2	by 3/1991		
SEF61	F162	LNER/BR J39/2 0-6-0	4/1991		
SEF62	F171	LNER/BR J38 0-6-0	4/1991		
SEF63	F172	LNER/BR J39/1 0-6-0	4/1991		
SEF64	F173	SR/BR Q1 0-6-0	8/1991		Ex-Little Engines
SEF65	F165	GER/LNER/BR N7/1/4/5 0-6-2T	11/1991		
SEF66	F166	LNER W1 4-6-4	6/1992		New to SEF
SEF67	F161	LNER/BR K3 2-6-0	10/1992		
(na)	FS161	LNER/BR K3 2-6-0	6/1993		Short kit version of above
SEF68	F175	LBSCR/SR/BR E5 0-6-2T	12/1992		
SEF69	F176	LBSCR/SR/BR E6 0-6-2T	12/1992		New to SEF
SEF70	F178	GWR/BR 61xx 2-6-2T	4/1993		
SEF71	F174	LBSCR/SR/BR I3 4-4-2T	by 8/1993		
SEF72	F179	LMS/BR Fowler 4F 0-6-0	7/1993		
SEF73	F180	GWR Metro 2-4-0T	9/1993		
SEF74	F181	SECR/SR/BR S 0-6-0ST	11/1993		New to SEF
SEF75	F182	SECR/SR/BR H 0-4-4T	11/1993		
SEF76	F184	LNER W1 Hush-Hush 4-6-4	2/1994		New to SEF
SEF77	F164	SR River 2-6-4T	3/1994		New to SEF
SEF78	F167	SECR/SR/BR P 0-6-0T	11/1994		
SEF79	F169	SR/BR Schools 4-4-0	10/1994		
SEF80	F183	USA/SR/BR 0-6-0T	10/1995		New to SEF
SEF81	F185	MR/LMS Flatiron 0-6-4T	3/1998		
SEF82	F186	GWR/BR 94xx 0-6-0T	3/1998		
SEF83	F188	SECR/SR/BR Kirtley R1 0-4-4T	4/1998		New to SEF

Text Reference	SEF Reference	Description	New Date	Withdrawal Date	Notes
SEF84	F192	SECR/SR/BR R1 0-6-0T	9/1998		New to SEF
SEF85	F193	SER/SECR/SR/BR R 0-6-0T	10/1998		New to SEF
SEF86	F189	GER Decapod 0-10-0T	2/1999		New to SEF
SEF87	F194	SECR/SR/BR 0-4-0CT	10/999		New to SEF
(na)	F163	SR/BR U 2-6-0	Not yet known		
(na)	F168	LMS/BR Stanier 4MT 2-6-4T	Not yet known		
(na)	F170	LMS/BR original *Royal Scot* 4-6-0	Not yet known		
(na)	F177	GWR County 4-4-0	Not yet known		

South Eastern Finecast Catalogues Table

Date	Cover	Price	Notes
3/1992	(unknown cover)	£2	RM 3.92 p55a advert
8/1993	Gresley A4 + MG A in brown	not known	Says Second Edition 8/1993
10/1994	Gresley A4 + MG A in brown	£3	Says Second Edition 8/1994
7/1996	Gresley A4 + MG A in blue	£3	Says Second Edition 8/1994 but preface page is different.

Further Notes
The catalogue is always referenced FP002. FP001 is a Car and Traction Engine-only catalogue. As can be seen, the catalogues are not simple to date, although an indicator is the pricelist which is separate and enclosed.

Further Acknowledgements

This chapter has been assembled with the generous help of Dave Ellis.

(below) Following on in the vein of unusual prototypes, the SECR/SR/BR 0-4-0CT modelled as South Eastern Finecast F194

Photo: Tony Wright, courtesy South Eastern Finecast Collection